The Conservative Party

AN ILLUSTRATED HISTORY

Anthony Seldon & Peter Snowdon

Foreword by Michael Howard

SUTTON PUBLISHING

First published in 2004 by
Sutton Publishing Limited · Phoenix Mill
Thrupp · Stroud · Gloucestershire · GL5 2BU

British Library Cataloguing in Publication Data
A catalogue record for this book is available from the British Library

ISBN 0 7509 3535 9

This book is dedicated to John Barnes and to Stuart Ball, two of the finest thinkers and writers on the Conservative Party of the last fifty years

Typeset in 10½/16½pt Galliard.
Typesetting and origination by
Sutton Publishing Limited.
Printed and bound in England by
J.H. Haynes & Co. Ltd, Sparkford.

CONTENTS

FOREWORD

Anyone who becomes leader of the Conservative Party is deeply conscious of its long and remarkable history. There is the roll-call of famous names: William Pitt the Younger, the Duke of Wellington, Sir Robert Peel, Benjamin Disraeli, Lord Salisbury, Winston Churchill and Margaret Thatcher. There is also the long list of great events – milestones in our island story – for which the Conservative Party has been responsible. The list includes the repeal of the Corn Laws, which laid the basis for late-Victorian prosperity (though the short-term interests of the Party itself were gravely damaged by the political consequences); the rapid expansion of Britain's largely beneficent empire; the growth of the electorate by giving the vote to urban working men in 1867 and to younger women in 1928; the huge widening of educational opportunities through Rab Butler's 1944 Act, a Tory-inspired measure passed by the wartime coalition; and, most recently, the 'Thatcherite revolution', which will inspire much historical writing in the years ahead.

Conservatism itself does not spring from the works of any single philosopher. It embodies a long historical tradition which has adapted itself with immense skill to changing circumstances over the centuries. As one of the many influential publications produced by the party itself after 1945, *The Conservative Faith in a Modern Age*, put it: 'On Conservatism there are many books. But the only textbook of Conservatism is the history of the British people, their institutions, their traditions, their accumulated wisdom and their character.' While recognising the substantial contributions that other political parties have made to the development of Britain, Conservatives are deeply aware of the extent to which their history is also the history of their country.

How far back do the Conservative Party and its unique traditions go? There are some who argue that they stem from the era of parliamentary reform in the 1830s. The name 'Conservative Party' first appeared in the political vocabulary in 1830 itself. But I have always taken the view that our political bloodline goes back to the Exclusion Crisis of 1680 when the Gaelic word 'Tory', meaning thief or brigand, was first applied to a group of British politicians. The occasion was the likely succession to the throne of the Catholic Duke of York, later King James II. Other politicians, to whom the word 'Whig' was applied, meaning sour milk, formed a second political party with the aim of altering the line of hereditary succession to exclude the Duke from the throne. The Tories, of course, won the immediate political argument! Recent historical research tends to support the long political antecedents of the modern Conservative Party. Certainly, the Duke of Wellington and Sir Robert Peel – the leaders of the Party in the 1830s – did not regard themselves as the creators of a new party but as the heirs of distinctive Tory political force which had existed throughout most of the eighteenth century.

What has been the Conservative Party's secret of success, and the source of its political longevity? The answer to that question is quite simple: it has never set its face against change or sought to become a reactionary force like some right-wing continental parties in the past. Disraeli gave eloquent expression to the point in a famous speech in Edinburgh in 1867:

> In a progressive country change is a constant; and the question is not whether you should resist change which is inevitable, but whether that change should be carried out in deference to the manners, the customs, the laws, and the traditions of a people, or whether it should be carried out in deference to abstract principles, and arbitrary and general doctrines.

Throughout its long history the Conservative Party has rejected 'abstract principles and arbitrary and general doctrines' in favour of policies that respect the unique history and character of the British people. In the nineteenth century the Party turned itself from being the spokesman of the narrow views of the landed interest into the representative of all types and conditions of men with an organisation after 1867 which linked the Party in the constituencies to the leaders at Westminster. Time and again it showed its clear understanding of peoples' real wishes and needs. As long ago as 1926 a Tory councillor in Leeds defiantly told his Labour opponents 'it is a good thing for people to buy their homes' at a time when most lived in rented property. History was on his side, as the remarkable success of Margaret Thatcher's 'right to buy' policy was to show in the 1980s.

Like all bodies and institutions that span the centuries, the Conservative Party has had its share of reverses. But on each occasion it set to work to restore its fortunes, re-examining both the structure of its organisation and the fundamentals of its policies in the tradition that Disraeli had provided for it.

This book depicts the achievements of the oldest political party in the democratic world, and shows how it recovered from its setbacks.

Michael Howard

July 2004

THE ARGUMENT

Many histories of the Conservative Party have been written, although not an illustrated one since Sheila Moore's twenty-five years ago. The authors believe illustrated histories have a unique role to play in gaining a full and rounded understanding of the past. The photographs, posters, paintings, cartoons and caricatures in the following pages convey a sense of the party's past that words alone can never fully capture.

This is not a freshly researched history, although it has tried to convey recent trends in research and interpretation. For academic history, one should turn above all to the work of John Ramsden, who has taken over from Robert Blake as the leading historian of the party, and whose work is listed, with others, in the bibliography.

The argument in this book is that the Conservative Party is a far less settled body than popularly believed: indeed, its very fluidity and adaptability has allowed it to survive for so long and through such seismic changes in the political landscape. The party swiftly and regularly adapted itself to each new political system as it emerged. A more rigid, rule-defined party might not have survived (the party did not adopt a formal constitution until 1998). Core beliefs do exist – defence of property, importance of the nation, a belief in organic, not sudden change – but this is not saying much. Many left-of-centre parties hold such beliefs. Much more remarkable have been the many changes, indeed, often complete reversals in what the party has stood for. The party thus championed the aristocracy, the empire and a universal welfare state, then moved away from them when they were no longer in tune with the electorate. The party organisation has provided some continuity, but much less than might appear at first sight. The party organisation, as the book reveals, has invented and reinvented itself: at times an elite, a mass membership, a voluntary and a professional, a parliamentary and an extra-parliamentary organisation. Not even the name of the party has been constant: Tory, Conservative, Unionist, National are labels that have been used to describe the party at different times.

The party's extraordinary electoral success has come from its ability to align itself with the powerful interests in the nation – which have themselves evolved over two hundred years – and by its finding a succession of leaders, nine in number, who have personified and defined the party, given it its particular policies, appeal, style and structure, to suit different ages. These leaders – William Pitt 'the Younger', Lord Liverpool, Robert Peel, Benjamin Disraeli, Lord Salisbury, Stanley Baldwin, Winston Churchill, Harold Macmillan and Margaret Thatcher – have so dominated the party that it makes sense, as the book does, to call the party after them – for example, 'Pitt's Party', which was utterly different to 'Thatcher's Party'.

There was, however, no 'Derby Party', 'Bonar Law Party' nor 'Heath Party'. The challenge is for Michael Howard to define the party. He has, at last, ended the Thatcher Party, which lasted a full thirteen years after her fall. He now has to provide the policies fit for the twenty-first century, devise a modern organisation, and ensure the message reaches a broad enough section of the nation to inspire them to vote for the party. The challenge is heightened because New Labour has, since 1994, stolen the Conservative Party's two secret weapons, its non-doctrinaire adaptability, and its hunger for office. In Tony Blair, Michael Howard faces the party's most formidable opponent since Palmerston in the mid-nineteenth century, a figure, like Blair, whose policies gave him the appeal of a Tory and who parked his Liberal Party solidly in the middle ground of politics, fortified by a strong economy and by the support of the middle classes. Blair is the first Labour leader in the party's history to emulate the winning Tory formula: that is his genius.

Time will tell whether Howard will be the tenth Conservative leader to define the party and lead it back to power. What is certain is that without such a historic figure, any recovery would be short-lived, not epoch-making.

O N E

EARLY BEGINNINGS TO THE PARTY OF PEEL: 1640–1867

There has never been one Conservative Party. Rather, throughout the last three and a half centuries, under a variety of names and with different purposes and fluctuating beliefs, there has been a grouping that has formed and reformed itself, but which is recognisably the same entity. Its nature at any given moment has been defined largely by the character and views of the dominant leader of the day, by the political system in which it operated and by the nature of the Opposition that it confronted. Generations of historians have argued over exactly when the party was born. While the earliest roots lie with the Royalist cause in the English Civil War, contemporary historians such as John Barnes refer to the 140 years between the beheading of Charles I in 1649 and that of Louis XVI in 1789 as the party's 'pre-history'. Pitt the Younger's eighteen and a half years in office is often cited as the party's true starting point, while others insist Peel's leadership in the 1830s marked the birth of the modern party. Ultimately, looking for evidence of a coherent Conservative Party through the centuries is a mistake. It is better to see each of the phases in the party's existence since the Civil War in terms of a family tree with each generation less and less like its ancestors. Michael Howard might look at Edward Hyde in the 1640s and see some similarities, but the grouping they head is radically different.

TORY ANCESTORS: 1640–1714

In his seminal work *The History of the Tory Party 1640–1714* (1924), the historian Keith Feiling traces the origins of the Conservative Party to the Royalists who backed Charles I in the civil wars of the 1640s. The Royalists sought to maintain the authority of the Crown in the face of the puritan challenge that led ultimately to the beheading of Charles I in January 1649. More subtly, the origins of Toryism can be traced to the moderate royalists like Sir Edward Hyde and Lord Falkland, who tried to find a 'middle way' between the intransigence of the monarchy and the increasing radicalism of the parliamentary and extra-parliamentary forces ranged against it.

No middle way could be found and the Royalists went into exile or underground until the monarchy was restored in 1660. The financial situation in which the restored monarch, Charles II, found himself meant that he could not do without Parliament. He had to look to his ministers, principally Hyde (now Earl of Clarendon) and subsequently the Earl of Danby to organise a 'Court' party, which would back him in the House of Commons. Part of the difficulty in tracing the ancestry of the Tory party springs from the fact that as long as the Crown was an active player in the political game, groups that supported the royal prerogative found it hard to distinguish themselves as entities in their own right. The next phase in party development came when the legitimacy of the monarch was called into question during the Exclusion Crisis of 1679–81. As Charles

The execution in London's Whitehall of Charles I in 1649 by Weesop *(Bridgeman)*

had no children, his brother James, the Duke of York, was next in line for the throne. Yet because James was a Catholic, a group of parliamentarians, known as the 'Whigs', tried to pass a law barring him from the succession. Those who stood against the Whigs and supported the Crown were dubbed 'Tories', initially a gibe which implied Catholic brigands from Ireland, but soon, as a result of Royalist propaganda, a label worn with pride. While the Tories disliked Catholicism just as much as the Whigs, they viewed the attempt to interfere in the succession as unconstitutional and thought it threatened England with a return to the horrors of the 1640s.

With the Tories on side, Charles II saw off the Whig challenge and James II came to the throne in 1685. But many of those who had supported the Crown were soon alienated by the way in which James advanced Catholics and sought to recast the monarchy along the absolutist model of his French contemporary, Louis XIV. Torn between their support for the Crown and their deep attachment to the Church of England, which they saw to be threatened by James II, many Tories chose the latter and secretly invited William of Orange to intervene. The Glorious Revolution, though largely bloodless, still remained of considerable embarrassment to the Tories, who although pleased that James had fled the country, remained instinctively hostile to William assuming the title of king. The emergence of a dual monarchy, James's daughter Mary sharing the throne with her husband William, did much to reconcile them to what had happened, but they felt considerably happier once William was dead and James's younger daughter Anne succeeded to the throne in 1702.

Initially, however, Anne's accession did not bring about the boon in influence that many Tories had hoped for. While the Queen's principal allies, Godolphin and Marlborough, were Tory in sympathy, they were determined to maintain a cross-party administration. Yet as the character of the administration began to tilt towards the Whigs, Anne, a staunch Anglican, grew increasingly resentful. In the end she turned to Harley and a predominantly Tory administration, and Harley's younger ally, the mercurial Lord Bolingbroke, worked to deliver the Tories a monopoly of power.

Queen Anne's death in 1714 changed everything. Her successor, George of Hanover, Anne's second cousin once removed, had been selected by Parliament over James II's Catholic descendants on the grounds that he was Protestant. Feiling argues that the 'first' Tory party came to an end with Queen Anne's death. It would be more correct to say that the Tory administration was bitterly divided between the supporters of the incoming Hanoverian monarch, and a significant minority who looked to a King 'over the water', James II's son, as the rightful heir. The Whigs exploited the frustrations of this minority, claiming that the Tories had tried to engineer the succession of a Catholic to the throne. An abortive invasion by the 'Old Pretender' (James II's son) in 1715 served to confirm that the threat was real. In the next twenty-five years, the Whig Robert Walpole was to make good use of the 'Jacobite taint' to keep the Tories out of power.

OUT IN THE COLD: 1714–83

Few anticipated the swiftness of the Tory party's decline. A critical mistake was the refusal of the entire 'Hanoverian' faction, Nottingham apart, to take office, but they had no reason to anticipate the disastrous defeat the party suffered in the January 1715 election. By then the Whigs had conducted a ferocious purge of the royal household, lord lieutenancies, revenue departments, military posts, legal offices and magistracies. The votes cast for the two parties were roughly equal, but Whig success in edging home in the smaller boroughs gave them a crucial victory, 341 Whigs being returned against 217 Tories. In September, Scottish Tories joined in the unsuccessful 'Jacobite' uprising against the new King, which further reinforced the identity of purpose between King George and his Whig ministers.

Despite long years in the cold, the Tory grouping did not lose its cohesion, and successive splits in the governing Whigs seemed to afford them a chance to return to office. On every occasion, however, temporary allies betrayed them. Their strength diminished: in 1715 they still commanded almost a third of MPs, but by 1742 that proportion had fallen to a quarter. Yet support also fell for Walpole. A key contributing factor was the return of Bolingbroke from exile and his co-founding of *The Craftsman* with the most brilliant of the Whig dissidents, Pulteney. The journal lambasted Walpole's corrupt practices and, more constructively, preached the virtues of a national administration that would bury forever the names of Whig and Tory. Later generations of Tories have looked back to Bolingbroke for eternal truths about Toryism, but his purpose was more pragmatic and short term. He and Pulteney wanted Walpole out. Although it took time for the dissident Whigs to join in a broad-bottomed opposition to Walpole, the Tories already enjoyed their co-operation at constituency level. The 1741 election destroyed Walpole's majority and brought about his fall within months, but the Tories gained little because the Whig Duke of Newcastle engineered a pact with Pulteney that ensured that the new administration remained almost entirely Whig.

The Tories now placed their hopes in the future, or more precisely, in the next king, George II's grandson. Under the tutelage of Lord Bute, the future George III became

George III, portrait after Allan Ramsay
(*Bridgeman*)

convinced that, when he came to the throne, he should appoint politicians on their personal strengths, not their party affiliation: the Whig hegemony looked set to end. Sure enough, when George III succeeded his grandfather in 1760, he brought Tories back to court and installed Bute as a Secretary of State. The Tories supported Bute in his desire for peace with France, which came to fruition with the Treaty of Paris in 1763. Bute then stood down and Grenville emerged as his successor, heading what William Pitt immediately dubbed 'a Tory administration'. Considered an insult at that time, Pitt's claim was that the new ministry supported 'royal' government along pre-1688 lines. Yet this was only partially true. Many of Grenville's ministers were Whigs and while a majority of Tories were ready to give their support to the King, the party was now split and a considerable number sided with the Opposition.

Gradually, a new party alignment began to take shape as George III manoeuvred to secure a ministry more to his liking. Although at one on policy, Grenville and the King were at odds on patronage and the continued influence of Bute, and in 1765, George dismissed him as Prime Minister. His replacement, the Marquess of Rockingham, adopted a conciliatory tone towards the increasingly rebellious American colonies. He even succeeded in repealing Grenville's Stamp Act, which had placed new duties on the American colonialists, despite vociferous opposition from within his administration, most notably from the self-styled 'King's Friends', backed by the monarch. In 1766, the divided government finally collapsed and the King charged Pitt with forming a new ministry. By now the Tory party was hopelessly divided, one group working closely with the King's Friends, while those who had followed Rockingham or Grenville into opposition remained loyal to their new leaders.

Under Pitt's ministry from 1766, the King's Friends became increasingly prominent. The press and opposition parties branded the government as 'Tory', to the fury of Pitt's supporters. After just two years, mounting protests from the American colonies about duties on trade and Pitt's increasingly poor health precipitated his departure, making way for the Duke of Grafton. Grafton too found his time dominated by the American colonies and proved no more able than Pitt to hold a government together. In 1770, he resigned. His successor, Lord North, described himself as a Whig, but came from a Tory family that had come to terms with the Whig ascendancy. His command of parliamentary debate and his skill at managing the country's finances were the major reasons for his twelve-year tenure of power. A successful minister while peace lasted, North's reputation was destroyed by the loss of the American colonies and his refusal to embrace calls for government reform. The Crown's defeat at Yorktown in November 1781 left North in no doubt that he must make peace with the colonialists. George III would not let him do so but neither would he let North resign. When defeat became inevitable, the King finally let him go and turned to the Opposition.

There followed considerable government instability, with three different prime ministers serving between 1782 and 1783, until in December 1873, George asked the 24-year-old William Pitt ('the Younger') to form a ministry. Pitt could count on the support from the Court and Treasury element in the Commons and also had the support of avowed King's men. But what mattered more was his public reputation as the champion of reform and retrenchment. That brought him support from the independents, who had brought down North in 1782. Consequently, even before the election in 1784, Pitt was well on the way to achieving a majority in the Commons.

THE PITT PARTY: 1783–1806

There followed a 23-year period of Tory dominance. Except it was not really a period of 'Tory' hegemony at all, with Pitt terming himself an 'independent Whig', and 'Tory' remaining a term of abuse. Not until the early nineteenth century did MPs generally describe themselves as 'Tories', while the label 'Tory', applying to newspapers and journals, the principal media forms of the day, was not in general use until after 1820. More confusingly still, Pitt (like his father, William Pitt 'the Elder') was identified originally not with Anglicanism, one of the Tories' core beliefs, but with the Dissenters. Nor could one say that Pitt was 'right-wing' in contrast to the 'left-wing' Whigs, as the terms right-wing and left-wing did not exist before they were coined based on the seating plan of the pro- and anti-reform groupings in the French Assembly in 1789.

Opposite: Pitt straddles the Speaker's Chair in the House of Commons, crushing the Opposition with one foot, while the other is propped up by his supporters. This famous cartoon shows Pitt rising to the height of his power, with an eye on the globe and his pockets bursting with money to pay for the war with France *(National Portrait Gallery)*

Js Gill.: invt. et fect   Pubd Jan 21 1797. by H. Humphrey New Bond Street

The GIANT-FACTOTUM amusing himself.

In what sense, then, can one label the period from 1783 to 1806 (under Pitt until 1801, then Addington until 1804 and under Pitt again until 1806) one of *Tory* hegemony? Until 1788–9, it made no real sense to label Pitt's administration 'Tory'. He saw his primary duty more as providing stable and efficient government than following any particular set of principles. But Pitt's own independence and position was greatly enhanced following George's first period of incapacity through mental illness from 1788, which accelerated the long-term shift in power from the monarchy to government ministers. Some historians have seen George's madness as the moment when a 'Tory' government came into existence (in place of the 'King's government'). A further boost to the Tory cause came from the French Revolution in 1789. Although the events were welcomed in some quarters as a just fate for Louis XVI as head of England's old enemy, it soon became alarmingly clear that if not only the monarchy but also landed interests were to be terminated in France, they could be in Britain also. After war was begun in 1793 against Revolutionary France, the status quo in Britain bound ever more tightly together in a common cause against the republicans and radicals across the English Channel. The following year, the Whigs split, and a faction led by Rockingham came over to join Pitt's government, establishing an alliance between monarchists and the landed interests, and leaving just a small rump of the more radical Whigs on the outside. The identification of a common enemy produced a popular upsurge of Toryism, spawning across the country 'King' and 'Constitution' clubs, 'Pitt' clubs and 'Constitutional Associations'.

One of the Whigs to join Pitt in 1794 was Edmund Burke, regarded as the profoundest thinker on the evolution of Conservatism in Britain. Burke's fundamental insight was that

The Duke of Portland, Tory Prime Minister in 1808, with Castlereagh and Canning, both of whom were to feature prominently in Tory politics in the years ahead, dreaming of victory over Napoleon in this Gillray cartoon *(Bridgeman)*

Edmund Burke, portrait by James Barry. Burke laid important foundations of modern Conservatism, not least in his *Reflections on the Revolution in France* (1790) *(National Portrait Gallery)*

society is organic, and that change must be evolutionary, not revolutionary, and in line with social and national traditions. Authority, hallowed over the ages, had an automatic entitlement to be respected, but change was inevitable and desirable; as he wrote, a 'state without the means of some change is without the means of its conservation'. This thinking explained and justified the conservative preference for gradual reform as opposed to reactionary obstruction of change at all costs, which ran the risk of a build-up of pressure to the point that it became unmanageable. But lest one overestimate Burke's significance for the Conservative Party, it is worth remembering that his key positions, including support for the landed interest, property, the hereditary principle, the Church of England, order and moderate reform, and constitutional rather than radical change, had been part of the conservative tradition long before Burke joined its ranks. One must thus treat with some scepticism assertions by those like John Gray who see Burke as 'the founder of British Conservatism'. British Conservatism has always been much more about what British conservatives have done and thought than what philosophers have written.

THE LIVERPOOL PARTY: 1812–27

The general election in 1807, which followed Pitt's death in 1806, saw the Whigs again branding government supporters 'Tories'. The dividing line between both groups began to become clearer, although the number of independent MPs in the Commons remained high. Events in France continued to polarise opinion in Britain between supporters of the King and Church of England, the Tories, and those who favoured reform, the Whigs. Supporters of the Tory leader Lord Liverpool were also united in their belief in strict law and order, a rejection of anything that smacked of radicalism, and their dislike of the Foxite Whigs. The distinct identity of the emerging Tories under Liverpool was given a boost by their unbroken period of domination of government, under the Duke of Portland until 1809, then under Spencer Percival until his assassination in May 1812, and then under Liverpool himself until 1827. During these years, far more than under Pitt, a recognisably

'Tory' government could be said to be in power, even though Liverpool and his ministerial colleagues saw themselves as Pitt's successors, and barely thought of themselves as a distinctive 'party' at all. Developments were occurring, however, which encouraged the emergence of a more clear-cut Tory party. Prime Minister Liverpool did a great deal to boost collective responsibility among his ministers. Whips in the House of Commons began to advise MPs on how to vote (although this advice stopped short of coercion), the number of 'independent' MPs began to fall, and the fashionable St James's clubs, Brook's and White's, emerged as the social settings for rival parliamentary teams. Party organisation at Westminster may still have been only skeletal, and in the country non-existent, but it was a start. It would be wrong, however, to see the labels 'Whig' and 'Tory' as relating to much more than a series of social networks and to a type or temperament. We are not yet speaking of a defined or disciplined group of politicians, although the Foxite Whigs, who were in permanent opposition after 1807, exhibited some traits of what later came to be understood as a political party.

Liverpool has not always been regarded kindly by posterity. Disraeli later dismissed him as an 'arch mediocrity'. The historian Norman Gash, however, sees Liverpool as 'the first great Conservative Prime Minister'. He had a difficult hand to play. Abroad, the Napoleonic war was still raging, which he brought to a successful conclusion in 1814–15. At home, he had to face industrial unrest, including Luddism, as a response to rapid industrialisation, disagreements with George IV (who finally succeeded George III in 1820) over his wish to divorce Queen Caroline, and struggles with Parliament to find the money to pay off war debts. As the 1820s wore on, Liverpool's problems eased, and a new era of 'Liberal Toryism' was popularly seen as beginning in 1822, following a repressive period of 'High Toryism' during the unstable war and immediate postwar years. Historians now generally deny that Liverpool's premiership saw such a conscious shift in emphasis in 1822, and stress instead the eased economic position which allowed Liverpool to adopt

Lord Liverpool, the second-longest serving Tory Prime Minister (1812–27). Portrait by Sir Thomas Lawrence *(National Portrait Gallery)*

a more liberal regime. An influx of talented new ministers (notably Canning at the Foreign Office, 'Prosperity' Robinson at the Treasury, William Huskisson – one of the first fatalities of the new steam locomotives – at the Board of Trade and Robert Peel at the Home Office) also provided the government with new life. By 1827, when Liverpool retired after a stroke, he had achieved a record many later prime ministers would have been pleased to emulate, including a reduction of tax, stimulating commerce and achieving peace at home and abroad.

Two great issues of the day, however, had not been tackled. The first, the status of Catholics in Ireland, was deliberately avoided by Liverpool, who knew that it would generate great tensions within the party. Pitt had negotiated the Act of Union with Ireland in 1801 to ward off the risk of a French invasion using that country as a base. Pitt's promise was that civil discrimination against Irish Catholics would be terminated in return for the Irish Parliament agreeing to the Act. But George III refused to agree, which presented a dilemma for the Tories: the desire to preserve the Union with Ireland

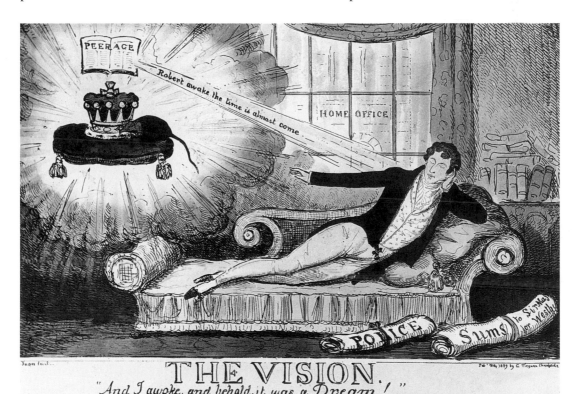

THE VISION.
"And I awoke, and behold, it was a Dream !"

Sir Robert Peel reclines on a chaise-longue in the Home Office in 1829, dreaming of an elevation to the peerage. As a pioneering Home Secretary in the Liverpool and Canning governments, Peel soon set his sights on greater things. He remained, however, in the House of Commons and within five years he was to become party leader and Prime Minister *(Hulton/Getty)*

A satirical cartoon from 1831 depicting Peel and Wellington desperately trying to defend the status quo against the clamour for electoral reform which flowered in the 1832 Reform Act *(Bridgeman)*

suggested giving Catholics their civil rights rather than attempting to govern Ireland through an unrepresentative Protestant elite; but granting them civil rights went against their visceral support for the King and Church of England. In 1812 the issue was temporarily put on ice by agreement to the 'neutrality principle' on Catholic Emancipation, though Liverpool realised that such procrastination was only storing up problems for the future. The other issue dodged by Liverpool was parliamentary reform. The need to address 'rotten boroughs' – districts that elected MPs but which lacked voters – and to reallocate parliamentary seats to the new industrial towns had been clear since the late eighteenth century. Pitt, indeed, had proposed a modest Reform Bill to address the manifest unfairness of the old electoral system, but it had been defeated in Parliament. When the issue came onto the agenda again after the Napoleonic wars, the Tories were adamant about retaining the status quo – unsurprisingly: they benefited greatly from it. Liverpool recognised the blatant unfairness of the current system of parliamentary representation, but he also saw that there was no great support in Parliament for reform, and he was strongly opposed to any plan for strengthening the influence of the urban electorate, with all the fears of radical reform that it might produce. The most trenchant opposition among Liverpool's supporters on both Irish and electoral reform issues came from the High Tories – or 'Ultras' – who in today's terms would be labelled the 'far right'.

Neither Canning nor Goderich, Liverpool's immediate successors during 1827–8, was willing to address either problem. Their successor, Wellington, however, resolved to enter the minefield. A High Tory, he presided not only over the repeal of the Test and Corporation Acts, which restored civil rights to Protestant Nonconformists, but also oversaw, on a free vote in May 1829, Catholic emancipation in Ireland, which resulted in a restoration of full civil rights to Catholics. The Ultras were incandescent with Wellington, and responded by campaigning hard against him. Wellington hoped to win back their support by staunch opposition to parliamentary reform, but his plan went awry when, in June 1830, George IV's death led to the succession of his brother William IV. The new king was much more open not only to dealing with Whigs and their leader, Lord Grey, but also to the question of parliamentary reform.

In this new environment, Wellington failed to win back the Ultras, while his opposition to reform alienated totally the Whigs. Unsurprisingly, Wellington was defeated in a vote in the Commons in November 1830, which led to William IV summoning Grey and asking him to form a mainly Whig ministry. This invitation marked not only the end of the long period in the party's history which had been dominated by Liverpool but also broke up the old Tory party. Canningites, Goderich and even old Ultras joined Grey's government with a view to producing a final settlement on parliamentary reform. A new age for the party was about to begin.

The Duke of Wellington, Prime Minister (1828–30). Portrait by John Lucas *(Palace of Westminster Collection)*

WHAT'S IN A NAME?

It is a symptom of the party's perennial quest for power that different names have either been adopted or seriously considered as a way of capturing the electorate's attention. Here are some of the names that survived, which came and went, and some which never saw the light of day:

TORY

The oldest attributable name for the party, 'Tory', has survived over three centuries of political and constitutional change. Despite being used interchangeably with the party's modern (and official) name, 'Conservative', its origins and meaning are quite distinct. Originally coined as a term of abuse for Irish cattle thieves, the word 'Tory' can be traced back to the political struggles in the reign of Charles II. The Tories, branded as such by their Whig opponents, supported Charles's Catholic son, James, as the legitimate heir to the throne. As long as the succession to the throne remained a political issue, the labels 'Tory' and 'Whig' were used pejoratively by rival factions in Parliament. Pitt the Younger never referred to himself as a 'Tory', and it was not until the first two decades of the nineteenth century, when party politics began to take shape, that the term was used unashamedly by leading figures like Canning.

CONSERVATIVE

In the early years of the nineteenth century, Burke's concept of 'conservation' had become increasingly attractive to politicians on the right, so much so that by 1827 the Duke of Wellington declared himself leader of the parti des conservateurs. Like so many other terms in political debate during this time, the words Conservative and Liberal were exported from post-Revolutionary France. It was the reform crisis of 1830–2 which brought about a new name for the party. 'We now are, as we have always been, decidedly and conscientiously attached to what is called the Tory, and which might with more propriety be called the Conservative Party', wrote the lawyer John Miller in Quarterly Review in January 1830. Now firmly in the public domain, the label came to symbolise a more forward-looking approach than that of the old Tory Party, which had been vanquished over the struggle for electoral reform in 1832. Two years later, Sir Robert Peel sought to give substance to the party's new name in his Tamworth Manifesto. Following the split over the Corn Laws in 1846, the Conservative Party temporarily lost its identity, amid the factional warfare between the 'Peelites' and the 'Protectionists', but it was the latter who within only a few years reclaimed the 'Conservative' title. Ever since, the party has retained the name.

UNIONIST

Unionism (referring to the union of Scotland, Ireland and Wales with England) has been a thread that has run through the party's history since the nineteenth century, when the issue of Irish Home Rule split Gladstone's Liberal Party. Although Liberal Unionists and Conservatives had formed an alliance in 1886, it was not until 1912, when the two parties formally merged, that the Conservative Party changed its name to the 'Conservative and Unionist Party'. During the Edwardian period it looked as if 'Unionist' might be adopted as the party's main title, with increasing numbers of Conservative candidates using the label. It remained in common use in England and Wales until the Second World War. Until 1972 Ulster Unionist MPs took the Conservative Whip. However, during the next three years, the Ulster Unionists severed all formal links with the party following disagreements over devolution in the Province. The name proved particularly popular in Scotland until the 1970s, with maintenance of the union a key plank of policy as opposed to the Scots seeking independence or extreme devolution. The party in Scotland continues to campaign as the 'Scottish Conservative and Unionist Party', despite calls after the 1997 defeat to drop the word Conservative from its title (because of its 'English' connotations).

WHAT MIGHT HAVE BEEN . . .

The party considered dropping the word 'Conservative', particularly after heavy defeats. During the 1945 election, many candidates, including Churchill himself, preferred to campaign with the name 'National' (reviving the appeal of the 1930s), rather than Conservative — an indication that the latter had become a vote-loser. In the aftermath of the defeat, both Churchill and the new party chairman, Lord Woolton, favoured 'the Union Party' as a replacement for Conservative. The suggestion fell on deaf ears, particularly among the backbench 1922 Committee and the party conference, who feared that a name change would compromise the party's integrity. It was thought to be too similar to the Unionist label, which had already lost some of its resonance in England. Following the landslide defeat in 1997, there was discussion, albeit not at such a high level, that a different name would signal a fresh start for the party — as happened to the Conservative Party in Canada after its near-annihilation in 1993. 'Progressive' or 'Reform' Conservatives have been suggested as possible alternatives. But amid all the soul-searching in opposition, there seems to be little appetite for jettisoning the official title.

THE PEEL PARTY: 1832–46

The 1832 Reform Act was to prove a vital turning point in the evolution of the Conservative Party. The Act had the potential significantly to damage the party as it had been so much the beneficiary, especially in Scotland, of the unreformed electoral system. Its very dominance since 1783 had indeed depended much upon it. Yet the party emerged from the episode much the stronger.

The Ultras and others who wanted to resist change at all costs eventually yielded to the moderates, realising that some accommodation with the pressure for reform was inevitable. Even Wellington realised that, once the Reform Act was passed, resistance was futile, and his duty dictated he accept the status quo. As John Ramsden notes, the party was thus spared the fate of many contemporary aristocratic parties in Europe, which became merely reactionary. It was at this time that the party rejected the outdated term 'Tory' and became known as the 'Conservative Party'. The passage of the Reform Act schooled the party into becoming a loyal opposition and also weaned it off its umbilical connection with the monarchy, as William IV endorsed the need for reform. The title of being 'His Majesty's Loyal Opposition' thus became established for the non-government party which existed independently of the monarch.

The 1832 Reform Act did not turn out to be the radical, still less revolutionary, reform that its opponents had feared. The powers of the monarchy were unaffected, as were the powers of the House of Lords, which became a bastion of both reaction and conservatism until the 1911 Parliament Act whittled down its powers. The aristocracy was still dominant within government and the country, and the position of the landed interest was in fact strengthened rather than weakened by the 1832 Act. It did, however, establish the principle that it would be success in general elections, rather than the will of the monarch, that would in future result in changes in government. This development gave both parties a powerful spur to organise themselves better as forces to win elections, and then to retain power and fight off challenges to it.

The Conservatives reached a low point in the first post-Reform Act general election of December 1832, when they were reduced to some 175 MPs ranged against some 480 'Reformers' in a House of Commons with 658 members. Pessimists feared that the Whigs were set to extinguish Toryism altogether by, for example, moving policy against protectionism, thus crippling the landed interest. Yet within eight years of the demoralised and depleted Conservatives convening in Parliament in January 1833, virtually leaderless, they were back in power. The recovery was remarkable, although their prolonged period out of office after 1846 suggested that the party's problems were not yet entirely over.

Conservative revival was facilitated by the chance falling-out among the Whigs in November 1834, which led to William IV asking the Tories to form a government in their place. Wellington gratefully accepted the King's offer, but recognised that in the post-1832 Reform Act era a leader in the Commons was needed, and one less associated with opposition to the 1832 Act. He duly recommended to the King that Robert Peel become Prime Minister in his place, and undertook to act as caretaker while his younger colleague returned from a sojourn in Italy.

Peel was to be in office for just three months. However, he realised the huge gain to the party's cohesion and credibility that would be achieved from showing it could govern in the new post-reform political era. Fighting the January 1835 general election as the government party, and with the support of the monarch, helped the Conservatives. The party gained ninety-four more MPs from the low point of 1832, which established it as a credible political force rather than a demoralised rump. Peel was still a long way short of a majority, and clung on to power for a while, until, after inevitable defeats in the Commons the Whigs under Melbourne returned to office. William's death in 1837 necessitated another general election, in which the Conservatives gained thirty-four more seats, giving them a majority in England. Four years later, in mid-1841, a further general election saw the Tories gain another fifty-nine seats, giving them an overall majority and putting Peel back in office, this time with far higher prospects of being able to achieve stability and some longevity in power.

Peel's own leadership was one of several key factors that explain the Conservative recovery after 1832. He had established a record as a pragmatic reformer at the Home Office under Liverpool (most famously his initiation of the 'peelers', the Metropolitan Police Force). His brief premiership in 1834–5 showed that the Conservatives accepted the 1832 Act and would not repeal it, and he proved himself willing to embrace further reforms. In his 'Tamworth Manifesto' of December 1834, he laid out many of the key themes of Conservatism. In the days before the party published a national manifesto or the leader campaigned nationally, the leader used the document he released in his own constituency to represent the common ideals around which the party could cohere. In essence, Peel's manifesto to his constituents in Tamworth restated Conservatives' thinking on the 'middle way' between the rejectionism of the reactionary Ultras and the dramatic, even revolutionary, change sought by the radicals. Peel, rather, argued for organic or evolutionary change.

The House of Commons in 1833, a year after the passage of the Great Reform Act and two years before its destruction by fire. The Conservatives are on the Speaker's left. Peel has his legs crossed and is wearing a yellow

waistcoat. Wellington is in the bottom right, facing forwards, with a red ribbon around his neck. Painting by Sir George Hayter *(National Portrait Gallery)*

Sir Robert Peel, portrait by William B. Essex
(Palace of Westminster Collection)

The Tamworth Manifesto, as Bruce Coleman observes, was also designed by Peel to blur the distinctions between Toryism and moderate Whigism, and to woo disillusioned Reformers like the followers of Edward Stanley, the future Lord Derby, into the Tory ranks. The capturing of moderate Whigs was thus another factor in the Conservative recovery. After the 1837 election, the Stanley group of some twenty MPs were treated as Conservatives, and three were to join Peel's Cabinet in 1841. A further forty Whig MPs defected to the Conservatives between 1835 and 1841, leaving the Whig leadership increasingly dependent upon the support of radical Whig and Irish MPs, which further detracted from the party's appeal. The arrival of the fleeing Whigs in the Conservatives' ranks meanwhile reduced Peel's dependence upon his own radicals, the Ultras. He cleverly encouraged his party to support Whig measures when he deemed them sensible, thus enhancing the perception of his leading a responsible opposition party.

Improved party organisation further facilitated Conservative recovery. The Carlton Club flourished in its new premises in Pall Mall from 1835, not only as the social but also the organisational centre of the party. F.R. Bonham, the party organiser paid for by new fund, proved an inspired appointment, and by 1841 party organisations in some form, often extensions of local dining clubs, were in evidence in many constituencies. There is no way of knowing the electoral importance of these early gropings towards some form of structure at the centre and in the localities, but it was clearly significant, not least in allowing party managers to find suitable candidates to stand and in the party's growing self-confidence and sense of purpose.

Enhanced organisation within Parliament also helped boost the party's recovery. Critical here was Peel's selection of Thomas Freemantle as the party's Chief Whip from 1837. Devices such as a weekly 'Whip's letter' to MPs and regular meetings of members helped instil a sense of identity and common cause. Party unity in divisions was one of the fruits of this new emphasis on organisation, although traditions of independence among backbench MPs, not least that of the country party, still remained strong.

Peel's leadership, at least until 1845, has received high praise down the years. He helped rebuild the Conservative Party and gave it shape, yet had the handicap of taking office at a time of economic depression and political unrest. Where the Whig administrations that preceded it were seen as failing, Peel's economic and financial policies were credited with restoring prosperity and business confidence. With the recovery came the ability for Peel to increase spending on the armed forces, especially the Navy, thus showing that he was safeguarding national security. Some modest social legislation, on factories, public health and the poor law, showed that Conservatives were not deaf to the need to reform, albeit falling far short of what the radicals demanded. For all the acclaim, little about Peel's second Ministry of 1841–6 was new. He continued in the broad Pittite and Liverpool traditions of upholding social order and property interest, staunch defence of the Crown and Church of England, and support for the Constitution.

On two main issues, however, Peel fell out with his party. On Ireland, some in his party still regarded him with suspicion for his role in Catholic Emancipation in 1829, and his policy merely fuelled mistrust from his own right wing while proving insufficient to disarm opposition from the Irish. But far deeper division followed his decision, promoted by the failure of the potato crop in Ireland in 1845, to repeal the Corn Laws, which taxed the import of foreign food that was now needed urgently to prevent starvation. Bar three ministers, his Cabinet did not agree with him, with Stanley emerging as the leading critic of his policy. They believed that support for the Corn Laws was a core item of faith and reason why

This sketch from the *Illustrated London News* shows Peel being followed by fellow MPs shortly after his resignation as Prime Minister in June 1846, following open revolt with the party on the repeal of the Corn Laws

the party had been elected in 1841, and to abandon protectionism in favour of a policy of free trade, as demanded by the industrial and middle-class interest, would be to jettison the party's traditional support of agriculture and the landed interest. Stanley also offered those who disagreed with Peel a respected and moderate leader, and one who exemplified a different view of party from the one Peel espoused as Prime Minister. For all his partisan work building up the Conservative Party since becoming its leader in 1834, as premier, Peel saw himself as serving the country as a whole, and prepared to put national interest above party. A crisis in December 1845 saw Pitt yield to Russell, who tried and

THE THREE GREAT SPLITS

Since 1832 there have been three great splits causing the party to fall from office, lose its way in opposition and even threaten its survival. The policy disputes that have rent the party asunder – repeal of the Corn Laws, Tarrif Reform and European integration – have arisen from two interlocking concerns for the Conservatives: providing a prosperous economy and maintaining Britain's standing in the world. On each occasion, the party was split with powerful economic interests on both sides of the dispute and it also became deeply divided about how to maintain Britain's position in the world. Coming to terms with, and managing, the country's decline from a great imperial power in the mid-nineteenth century to being a member of an expanding European Union in the early twenty-first century was bound to be a painful process for the party. It was this mix of domestic and international policy and interest that led to the difficulties, as we shall see in the following chapters.

REPEAL OF THE CORN LAWS

1846 saw the party divided over whether or not to abandon the Corn Laws, taxes on the import of foreign food. Peel, supported by three Cabinet ministers, forced a repeal of the laws, arguing that cheap food imports were needed to prevent starvation following the failure of the potato crop in 1845. But other Conservatives, led by Lord Stanley, were firmly against free trade. They insisted that preserving the Corn Laws was an article of faith for the party, crucial to retaining the support of agriculture and landed interests. As the party split in two, Peel was forced to resign as Prime Minister in 1846 and the party failed to win another decisive election victory until 1874.

failed to form a Whig government. Only Stanley refused to serve in a renewed Peel administration, which spluttered on for the first six months of 1846 until Peel's eventual resignation at the end of June.

Benjamin Disraeli was one of Peel's most trenchant critics, but it was Lord George Bentinck, younger son of the Duke of Portland, who had the credibility and standing to organise resistance to Peel's policy among Conservative MPs. The leader retained the active support of only one third of his party's MPs, with the party split between the landed interest on Bentinck's and Stanley's side and the commercial and industrial

TARIFF REFORM

In 1903, largely due to an initiative by Joseph Chamberlain, the party split once again over the issue of free trade. Through Tariff Reform, Chamberlain aimed to transform the British Empire into a unified trading block, and impose hefty duties on non-Empire goods. Chamberlain campaigned on this issue up and down the country, urging the deselection of pro-free trade Conservative candidates. The deeply divided party lost the 1906 election to the Liberals, who favoured free trade and who won by a landslide. It was not until 1924 that the party again won a convincing general election victory.

EUROPE

Most recently, the party has torn itself apart over Britain's future in Europe. These differ-
ences, apparent from the end of the 1950s, when Macmillan first contemplated Britain's entry into the European Economic Community, were fuelled by the growing Euro-scepticism of Margaret Thatcher, many others in the Tory party and in the Tory press in the 1980s. Although in favour of Europe as a free trade area, Mrs Thatcher grew deeply suspicious of moves to accelerate European integration and abrogate British sovereignty. Many Conservative MPs followed her lead and spoke out against Europe with increasing vehemence, particularly during John Major's premiership, when open warfare broke out between the 'Europhiles' and the 'Euro-phobes', especially over the party's policy on membership of the single European currency. The resulting disunity played a key part in the devastating 1997 election defeat and continued to hamper the party in opposition until after the 2001 general election and beyond.

interests on Peel's. The combination of Peel's remaining supporters and the Whigs was sufficient, however, for the repeal of the Corn Laws to pass through Parliament in June, the month of Peel's own fall and of Russell forming a minority Whig government. In July, Stanley accepted the leadership of the 'protectionists', that is, the anti-Peelite supporters of the Corn Laws, and in the 1847 election they had some 230 MPs returned in contrast to only 100 Peelites. The following year, Stanley insisted that the protectionists were the true Conservatives and thus deserved to adopt the party name. In July 1850, amid widespread national mourning, Peel died. It was to be another twenty-four years before the party won a decisive election victory.

THE WILDERNESS YEARS: 1850–74

Numerous attempts were made after 1846 to bind the two factions back together again. Peel's death removed the most obvious stumbling block to a rapprochement, but his supporters were fired up by an even greater conviction after he died that he had been unjustly brought down in 1846 and that they were guardians of his flame. They became even closer to the Whigs in the 1850s before joining them formally in the 1859 Parliament, the time traditionally seen as the official formation of the Liberal Party.

The schism went all the way from Westminster down to constituencies. Embryonic local organisations split or otherwise just petered out. At the centre, meanwhile, the chief organiser Bonham took off, taking with him the party records and files. Organisation within the parliamentary party, another achievement of the 1830s, was similarly rent asunder as Bentinck proved an ineffectual leader, and Beresford an even less successful Chief Whip in succession to Freemantle.

Revival in the party's fortunes owed almost everything to one man, Disraeli. Initially, however, the party had to learn to trust a man they regarded as an opportunist, a writer of novels and an urban tradesman rather than a landed aristocrat. Even the fact that he had converted to the Church of England at an early age did little to placate those who regarded his Jewish background as a fatal handicap. After Bentinck's death, a triumvirate was set up with Disraeli leading the party in the Commons harnessed to two less able men. Eventually Stanley realised that there was no alternative to Disraeli, and he became sole leader in the Commons. To make himself more acceptable to the party, Disraeli took advantage of a bequest from the Bentinck family and bought Hughenden Manor in Buckinghamshire. He had become a landowner.

Disraeli was still hampered by the continued presence of Stanley, who became known

Lord Stanley lead the protectionist Conservatives in opposition after the split of 1846. Portrait by Frederick Richard Say *(National Portrait Gallery)*

as 'Derby' in 1851 when he inherited the earldom. While Derby's impeccable aristocratic credentials provided some ballast to Disraeli, he presided over two lacklustre Conservative administrations in 1852 and 1858. Shortage of talent was a major handicap. Economic prosperity further produced a general mood of contentment in the 1850s and early 1860s, which played to the Whigs' benefit and their free trade policy. A contented population is also not given to dangerous radicalism, and hence for twenty years after the fading of Chartism – the often violent movement that campaigned for parliamentary reform to further the demands of the working class – there were no popular movements to alarm the nation and make it want to find succour in Conservatism. In the constituencies, only two-fifths of seats were contested in general elections, leaving the Tories achieving between 281 and 307 seats in successive elections, but never able to win a majority. Above all these factors, the huge figure of Lord Palmerston bestrode the Liberal Party. As long as he was there, many voters who might have been inclined to support the Conservatives gave him their vote.

Palmerston's death in 1865 thus provided Disraeli with just the opportunity he needed. Palmerston's successor, Earl Russell, with Gladstone as Leader in the Commons, immediately promised the advent of a more domestically active Liberal administration. The downturn in the economy rekindled pressure for reform and attendant fears of rampant working-class demands. The Conservative Party organisation began to recover, with first William Joliffe then Edward Taylor taking over as Chief Whip from the feeble Beresford, and restoring the office as the linchpin between the leadership, the MPs and the party in the country. The solicitors Spofforth and Rose became the party's chief fund-raisers and organisers, taking over the task that had hitherto been performed within the Carlton Club, while leaving it with its key grooming and social role.

REFORM

THE POLITICAL EGG-DANCE.

Clamour began to be heard more loudly for another long overdue, extension of the franchise. This time, the Conservatives were determined that they would be in control of it. Guided by Disraeli's brilliant command of parliamentary tactics, Conservative MPs taunted the divided government of Russell and Gladstone, who fell from office in June 1866. Queen Victoria asked Derby to form his third administration, established with the principal objective of passing a reform bill and taking the credit themselves from an action almost all shades of opinion deemed inevitable. The Act that finally emerged was more radical than any Liberal proposal, and passed the Commons helped by support from radicals in the Liberal Party as well as from the House of Lords on Derby's personal authority. Once enacted, Derby's mission had been accomplished and he bowed out suffering from ill health and the effects of old age. Together with Queen Victoria, he conspired against some Conservatives (who were partly motivated by anti-Semitism) to install Disraeli as party leader and Prime Minister. In the Disraeli era, the Conservative Party would at last come of age.

T W O

THE PARTIES OF DISRAELI AND SALISBURY: 1868–1915

These were see-saw years for the Conservative Party, during which it was led by two of the giants of its history, Benjamin Disraeli and the third Marquess of Salisbury. Having pulled off a brilliant coup with the Second Reform Act, Disraeli had reached the top of the 'greasy pole' in February 1868 to realise his ambition as Prime Minister. His days leading a minority government were, however, numbered, and it would take another six years of tireless opposition to regain power. The 1874 election was a major breakthrough, providing the party with its first parliamentary majority in over thirty years. What followed was one of the most dominant periods of Tory government in the party's history. When Salisbury bowed out as leader in 1902, there had been some fifteen years of Conservative hegemony and Liberal disarray. The tables were, however, soon to turn, for within another four years, the party would experience one of its worst election defeats. Events outside Britain would help bring to an end this 'crisis of Edwardian Conservatism'. In 1915, the Conservatives would return to office as part of Asquith's wartime coalition after ten years in the wilderness.

THE DISRAELI PARTY

The events of 1866–7 had shown that the Conservatives had re-established their credentials as an alternative government. By successfully sabotaging the Liberals' Reform Bill and taking the initiative, both Lord Derby and Disraeli proved that the party, as Lord Blake put it, could 'move with the times'. But power also brought Disraeli problems. Derby bequeathed him a minority in the House of Commons, and Gladstone, enraged by his adversary's tactics over the Reform Bill, was ready to strike. Disraeli suffered from being unable to command Derby's respect in Cabinet: he had yet to acquire the social authority among his peers for which he so desperately yearned.

Gladstone chose the Irish Church as an instrument with which to galvanise the Liberal Party and taunt the government, and launched a powerful campaign in support of the

Church's disestablishment in the summer of 1868. He knew that Disraeli's party stood on shaky ground on the issue, the Cabinet being divided between those who sought compromise, like Lord Stanley (Derby's son), and devout Anglicans, like Gathorne-Hardy, who ardently opposed any change to the status quo. In siding with the latter, Disraeli pinned his hopes on stirring up popular anti-Catholic sentiment with the use of some rather fiery rhetoric. His strategy badly misfired; the Liberals reunited around a theme which their leader believed to be of real moral importance, while the Conservative defence of the Anglican establishment in Ireland proved unpopular in Ireland and won little support from the wider electorate in England. Disraeli's party was derided by *The Times* as offering 'many promises to resist the policies of others, but no signs of any policy for the

Disraeli reaches the top of the 'greasy pole' of politics, becoming Prime Minister at last in February 1868 (*Corbis*)

great Conservative Party itself'. Wrong-footed himself now by his opponent, Disraeli had badly misjudged the public mood.

The first election held under the new (post-1867 Reform Act) franchise produced a blow for the Conservative Party. Gladstone's Liberals won a decisive mandate – a majority of over 100 – for reform in Ireland. Disraeli set a precedent as the first Prime Minister to resign office at the behest of the electorate rather than of Parliament or the monarch. The party had failed to prepare adequately for the new enlarged electorate which it had itself brought into existence only one year earlier. The National Union of Conservative Associations, which had been formed in 1867 to coordinate the party's organisation in the country, had got off to an unpropitious start and received little support from the party leadership. In contrast to the Liberal Party machine, the Conservatives remained stuck in a pre-1867 electioneering groove. There were, nevertheless, some signs of encouragement in the 1868 election results. Spectacular advances were made in Lancashire and Cheshire, where Protestant feeling ran high, and in London and Middlesex, where the party won a string of seats from the Liberal Party, including Westminster, in which the political philosopher John Stuart Mill was defeated by the newspaper wholesaler, W.H. Smith. These results gave hope that the growing conurbations of England and the middle classes were turning to the party.

The first years back in opposition were unsettling. Disraeli, by now 65 years old, looked increasingly insecure as leader: he appeared tired, and many of his senior colleagues were doubtful of his ability to survive a full parliamentary session on the Opposition benches. With Derby's death in October 1869 he lost an important counsellor. Disraeli became distracted with his wife's failing health (she died in 1872) and by the resumption of his literary career. But, in the absence of a credible alternative for the leadership, and determined to hang on, Disraeli survived any threat of challenge. His declared intention that the Conservatives should exude 'the utmost reserve and quietness' after the 1868 defeat soon yielded to a more determined plan of attack on the Liberal government. Within two years, Gladstone's reforming administration was running into trouble over its plans for education, the civil service and the army.

It was Gladstone's decision to take on the brewing industry, however, which provided Disraeli with an opportunity to reinvigorate his party. By attempting to introduce tight licensing laws, Gladstone alienated the liquor trade, prompting many brewers to switch allegiance to the Conservatives. This was to have a major impact on the party's finances and electioneering, seen in the winning of the East Surrey by-election in 1871. The brewers would become one of the party's best friends for years to come.

Disraeli returns to Opposition, tired and dejected by the party's defeat in 1868. Cartoon by Carlo Peligrini (*Palace of Westminster Collection*)

The year 1872 was a significant turning point for the party's fortunes. The leadership launched a vigorous attack on the Liberal government and its 'restless' urge to legislate in as many areas of public life as possible. Disraeli accused his opponents of spending too much time on 'the pains and penalties of the Ballot Act', which introduced the secret ballot, to the neglect of improving living – particularly sanitary – conditions for ordinary voters. Disraeli was not alone in advancing a Tory concern for social policy. A new generation of Conservative MPs, elected mainly from the urban boroughs, joined forces with party activists to form the 'New Social Alliance'. Mindful of working-class discontent, which had been heightened by the news from France of the Paris Commune in 1871, they pressed the leadership to respond to the plight of working people by producing positive policies. Despite opposition from some in the party, Disraeli stole the initiative in 1872 with two of the most celebrated speeches of his career.

Speaking for three hours to a crowd of 6,000 at the Free Trade Hall in Manchester, Disraeli launched a scathing attack on Gladstone's 'exhausted volcanoes', while at Crystal Palace three months later he proudly declared that only the Conservatives could be entrusted 'to maintain institutions, to uphold empire and to elevate the condition of the people'. The speeches were enthusiastically received in the press and in the country. Disraeli thus repositioned the party as both the standard-bearer of social reform and the champion of national unity and empire. As Lord Morley, a close adviser of Gladstone and later his biographer, commented, Disraeli had accurately read the 'characteristics of the time [with] . . . a rare faculty of wide and sweeping forecast'. With a further string of by-election successes, the party was set on a course of seemingly unstoppable progress. Despite a last-minute attempt by Gladstone to regain public support with a pledge to abolish income tax, it was Disraeli who had his finger more on the pulse of the nation.

Disraeli led the party to triumph in the general election of February 1874. A 7 per cent swing from the Liberals to Conservatives produced the first Tory overall majority (of fifty) in the Commons since 1841. The party made gains throughout urban England and achieved almost a clean sweep of the rural counties. Progress also occurred in Scotland, where the party took a third of the seats. Disraeli's bid to win working-class support had paid off, and these new voters joined the forces of property and middle-class support which had become disillusioned with Gladstone's Liberals.

The Tory party's new electoral machine also passed muster, and it was further fortified by the creation of Conservative Central Office in 1870 and an improved organisation in the country. Under the supervision of John Gorst, Disraeli's Principal Agent, the combined forces of the new party headquarters and a National Union beginning to find its stride, the party had mounted a formidable challenge across the land. The party's effort had been aided by a new sophistication in management of the press, improved propaganda and a systematic attempt, through party handbooks such as *Hints for Candidates*, to persuade the party to campaign on a united front.

Disraeli raised high expectations for what his new government and its ministers might achieve. He sought to appease Lord Salisbury, with whom he had barely been on speaking terms after his resignation over the Reform Bill and who had accused him of being a 'mere political gamester' in the aftermath of the 1868 defeat, by appointing him Secretary of State for India. As Ramsden observed, 'this was a vital moment in Conservative history, for it returned a future leader to the inside track, and even chastened him a little in the process.' The Prime Minister also brought fresh blood into the Cabinet: Richard Cross, a middle-class Lancastrian, was offered the Home Office; while

Disraeli and senior Cabinet Ministers in 1876. Left to right, Earl Derby, Lord Cairns, Stafford Northcote, Benjamin Disraeli, Gathorne-Hardy, and the Marquess of Salisbury (*Hulton/Getty*)

CHAMPIONING THE EMPIRE

One of Disraeli's main legacies to the party was reclaiming its position as the patriotic 'party of empire', reviving the glory days of Pitt and Wellington. Until his death in 1865, Palmerston had ensured that that patriotic mantle rested firmly in the Liberal tradition: his gunboat diplomacy and success over the Crimean War (1854–6) deprived the Conservatives of an important source of strength. But Disraeli, who had at one time described the colonies as 'millstones round our neck', saw an opportunity after Palmerston's death to champion the Empire and bolster Britain's prestige, and he squeezed every last drop out of the opportunity – more than his record merited. Gladstone in fact added far more territory to the British Empire than Disraeli and it was Salisbury who made the Empire central to Conservative Party's thinking and policy.

Early success came for Disraeli in 1868 with the Napier expedition to Abyssinia. He then carefully read the shifting balance of power in Europe. Conscious of the rising power of the newly unified nations of Germany and Italy, as well as of the United States, he wanted Britain's own standing and prestige in the world to be raised. 'England is no longer a mere European power . . . she has duties devolving upon her upon a much larger scale', he declared grandly. Sensing a growing public demand for patriotism, Disraeli used his speeches at Manchester and Crystal Palace in 1872 to mark out a bold imperial vision for his party.

Disraeli's commitment to the Empire continued in office after 1874. The following year, he took the audacious step of purchasing nearly half of the Suez Canal Company shares. Overriding the objections of Derby, his cautious Foreign Secretary, and of most of the Cabinet, Disraeli's coup, which was financed by a loan of £4 million from Rothschilds Bank, opened the door for a major expansion of Britain's trading links with India and the Far East, and helped ensure her naval supremacy. In 1876, Disraeli cemented his warm relationship with Victoria, his 'Faerie Queen', by bestowing on her the title 'Empress of India'. Gladstone denounced the gesture as distinctly 'un-English', but it instantaneously raised the status of the monarchy and India became the 'jewel in the crown' of the Empire.

In the last four years of his premiership (1876–80), Disraeli devoted much of his time and energy to international diplomacy. Confronted with a serious dispute involving Russia's imperial ambitions on Turkey in 1877, which came to be known as the Eastern Question, Disraeli and his energetic new Foreign Secretary, Lord Salisbury, rode to the rescue. In 1878 both went to the Congress of Berlin with the specific intention of resolving the crisis and negotiating a more advantageous position of influence for Britain and her empire. By restricting Russia's advances and persuading Turkey to surrender Cyprus to the British, they achieved their objectives. It was arguably Disraeli's finest hour on the world

Punch cartoon showing an obsequious Disraeli offering his adored Queen the crown of India in 1876 (*Hulton/Getty*)

stage. Proclaiming 'peace with honour', the Prime Minister and his Foreign Secretary were greeted with heroes' welcomes when they arrived back at London's Charing Cross Station to garlands of flowers. Conservatives at Westminster and across the country would come to eulogise Disraeli as the standard-bearer of the party's new-found imperial pride. Events elsewhere, however, were to soil his achievements. British expeditions in Zululand and Afghanistan in 1879 were military disasters, cleverly exploited by Gladstone, contributing to the Conservative Party's defeat the following year.

Richard Cross, Home Secretary 1874–80, the architect of many of Disraeli's social reforms *(Mary Evans)*

Stafford Northcote, a rising star in the 1867–8 administration, was made Chancellor of the Exchequer. Northcote provided a steady hand at the Treasury, seeing off Gladstone's countless attacks, while Cross immediately set to work turning the Disraelian vision of social reform into some form of reality. It was Cross (opposite) who emerged as the architect of the largest tranche of social legislation to be passed by a nineteenth-century government.

In the first two years of the government, Cross drove through a programme of domestic legislation designed to 'elevate the condition of the people'. From public health bills to factory acts and a series of educational reforms, Disraeli's government won praise from trade unionists (which it legitimised) and from the working classes. By modern-day standards, the measures were quite limited in nature, but their significance as measures of support for the needy and underprivileged could not be overstated. The radical Liberal mayor of Birmingham, Joseph Chamberlain, remarked that the 1875 Artisan's Dwelling Act, which was a major step towards slum clearance and town planning, had 'done more for the town of Birmingham than had been done in twenty preceding years of Liberal legislation'.

Disraeli left much of the detailed work to his ministers, and increasingly so as the years in office began to take their toll on his stocks of energy. The administration's initial impetus slowed down after 1876, and Disraeli gave serious consideration to standing down as premier, offering his Cabinet the choice between his retirement from public life altogether and his elevation to the more sedate surroundings of the House of Lords. The Queen, who was extremely fond of her ageing Prime Minister, pleaded with him successfully to take the latter course, creating him Earl of Beaconsfield. The Disraelian agenda for domestic reform was largely complete and settled. Further afield, however, matters were very different, as discussed on the preceding two pages.

The final years of Disraeli's leadership of the Conservative Party had been an exhausting experience. Faced with a resurgent Liberal opposition under Gladstone, who had sharpened his attacks during his celebrated Midlothian campaigns, Disraeli's party was battered and bruised by difficulties abroad and by industrial and agricultural depression at home. Neither party had an answer to the economy, though Gladstone managed to lay blame on 'Beaconsfieldism'. Disraeli had always believed that 'hard times' would be his downfall and so it proved in 1880, when his party fell to a crushing defeat at the hands of the Liberals. The party won just 238 seats, compared with 354 Liberals and 60 Irish Home Rulers. Losses were particularly heavy outside England.

The party eschewed the main issues of the day in the election, including the depression, social reform and foreign wars, and concentrated on defending the union with Ireland. Unlike in 1874, there was virtually no positive platform or promise to relieve those bearing the brunt of the economic downturn. He was stoical in defeat. His last hurrah was to publish his novel, *Endymion*, before he died in office as party leader in April 1881. He had bequeathed to the party a powerful inheritance. Generations of future Conservatives were to find inspiration in Disraeli as the creator of 'One Nation Conservatism', a tag which owed in truth more to his speeches and pronouncements than to his record in government. The very term 'one nation', which was later championed by progressive Tories after 1945, appeared first in one of his novels. Some would argue that Disraeli's importance lay less in his active record of social reform, which some historians have downplayed, than in convincing the party that he had given it such a profile. That said, however, he was more committed to social reform than many in his party and he left the party with a sense of self-belief in its ability to govern the interests of a broad swathe of the nation rather than the interests of a few. It was a massive achievement.

THE SALISBURY PARTY

The passing of Disraeli left a power vacuum in the party. Senior Conservatives turned on each other and dissent spread in the lower ranks. Northcote proved to be an uninspiring leader of the Commons (a post he had held since Disraeli's elevation to the Lords in 1876) and his joint leadership, with Salisbury in the Lords, provoked the tiny ginger group called the 'Fourth Party', with Lord Randolph Churchill a leading light, to attack the leadership. Northcote opted for the traditional strategy in politics and tried to win over moderate Liberals unhappy with Gladstone's missionary zeal as Prime Minister after 1880.

Sir Stafford Northcote, an impressive Chancellor of the Exchequer in Disraeli's 1874–80 administration, but an uninspiring leader of the Commons in opposition after 1880. (*Hulton/Getty*)

'Spy' cartoon of the 'Fourth Party' in the Commons (left to right): Lord Randolph Churchill, A.J. Balfour, Sir Henry Drummond Wolff and John Gorst (*Mary Evans*)

The years 1881–5 saw a struggle for the identity of the party, with Churchill and the 'Tory Democrats' trying to champion a somewhat spurious Disraelian legacy, in part as a shield to allow Churchill to wrest leadership in the Commons from Northcote. But, after Churchill's failed attempt to seize control of the National Union, his challenge faded for a time and Salisbury gained the control he had had in all but name since before Disraeli's death. In 1885, Akers-Douglas took over as Chief Whip, a most significant step in the leadership's regaining of control of the party. Organisational changes helped the party to regain the initiative, with the National Union being managed well by Captain R.W.E. Middleton, Principal Agent from 1885, at the head of a strong network of area agents. The Primrose League, founded in November 1883 and named after what was allegedly Disraeli's favourite flower, proved a powerful stimulus to the growth of active Toryism in the country. It also helped to persuade new voters, and women, to support the party and to become volunteers, who were vital to service its growing activities.

The Conservatives duly launched a campaign of resistance to Home Rule, which proved the ideal rallying cry for discontented Liberals, leading to an eventual realignment in which Whigs and disillusioned Liberals joined the Tories, a move which had been in the air for many years. The 1885 general election, the first to be fought on the new post-1884 Reform Act franchise, produced a mixed result for the Conservatives – 250 MPs, just twelve more than in 1880, but relief that the broader social franchise had not resulted in a turning away from the party. There followed an unsettled and complex time, with power changing hands several times. In March 1886, Joseph Chamberlain resigned

The Marquess of Salisbury in 1884 plans his next manoeuvre. Drawing from the *Illustrated London News (Bridgeman)*

from Gladstone's government in protest at his Home Rule policy, and in the election that year the Conservative Party was triumphant, benefitting from a pact with the Liberal Unionists. Salisbury was to dominate the Conservative Party for the next sixteen years, an achievement he never imagined possible and with which he was never entirely sure what to do. He had accepted the extensions to the franchise in 1867 and 1884 only reluctantly, retained a deep distrust of unfettered democracy, and had fought a trenchant battle with the Liberals over the 1885 Redistribution Act. He saw the House of Lords and the Conservative Party as the best guarantees of maintaining the status quo, which was his primary concern, and he proved himself to be a brilliant tactician, ensuring that the Conservative Party would achieve his objectives. This skill was never better seen than in the period 1886–92, when he ruthlessly exploited the Liberal split over Irish Home Rule and constructed a political realignment with prominent Whigs and Liberal Unionists, above all Chamberlain himself. This realignment, albeit aided by Gladstone's remaining as Liberal leader, was by no means a foregone conclusion.

The Marquess of Salisbury by George Frederic Watts, 1882 *(National Portrait Gallery)*

To ensure that the Liberals were kept divided, and to ward off any prospects of their imminent revival, he brought the Liberal Unionists into government as minority partners in 1895. Chamberlain himself was appointed to his favoured job of Colonial Secretary. Gladstone's continuing obsession with Home Rule for Ireland had alienated wide sections of the country and, without this windfall, the Conservatives would not have won the elections of 1886 or 1895. It is significant that a decline in the importance of the Irish issue played a key part in the revival of the Liberal Party, albeit briefly, in the early twentieth century. The Irish issue was therefore key, but it was not the only factor that accounted for the dominance of the party under Salisbury.

A London suburb at the turn of the century, where Salisbury's 'Villa Toryism' was firmly to take root *(Memories Picture Library)*

The positive appeal of patriotic imperialism and Protestantism also played their parts.

Although Salisbury was to become less reactionary in his later days in politics, he never believed in the efficacy of government intervention to solve economic and social problems. He was thus a less progressive figure than Disraeli; but he was also the leader for his time. It was, therefore, not surprising that his 1886–92 government was light on reform. Such drive as there was in this direction came from his own Tory lieutenants, like Churchill until his eventual resignation (which proved a damp squib) in December 1886 and C.T. Ritchie, as well as from Chamberlain who, unlike the majority of Liberal Unionists, positively favoured social reform. The desire to outmanoeuvre the Liberals for the new working-class electorate provided another motive for the legislation that was introduced. The 1884 Reform Act had enfranchised agricultural labourers and many other adult males, which benefited the Liberals and forced the Tories, despite Salisbury's distaste for middle-class politics, to deepen their appeal to the suburban voter. This became the so-called 'Villa Toryism'. Another motive for government action was the need to respond to those suffering from the prolonged depression of 1873–96. A variety of measures to assist smallholders, the creation of the first County Councils in 1888 and some mild social reforms such as the Housing of the Working Classes Act of 1890 (a personal interest of Salisbury's) had all been introduced by the election of 1892. It was a limited domestic record after six years. The principal political achievement for the Tories of the 1886–92 government was the tactical one of retaining the alliance with the Liberal Unionists, with whom they again fought the 1892 general election in partnership.

The 1892 election saw the Liberals under Gladstone snatch a narrow victory. Overall, 274 Liberal MPs were returned as against 268 Conservatives (down by 48) and 47 Liberal Unionists (down by 32). But the Liberals were dependent upon the support of the large cohort of 81 Irish Nationalist MPs at Westminster. The Liberal government under

Gladstone from 1892 to 1894, and Lord Rosebery from 1894 to 1895, failed to impress even its own supporters. Continued attachment to Home Rule, internal divisions over policy direction and lack of legislative success all help explain the Tories victory in 1895. The 1892–95 Liberal government was one of the least glorious in the party's history.

Hopes from younger Tories and some Liberal Unionists that Salisbury's government after 1895 would see greater legislative activism were dashed by their leader's entrenched reluctance to give priority to such issues, especially as it would entail increasing taxes and redistributing wealth, both of which were anathema to the old man. Chamberlain's own focus too in his new Colonial Office post perhaps inevitably shifted away from social reform towards the Empire. The Workmen's Compensation Act of 1897, however, did owe much to Chamberlain and was the principal legislative achievement of the 1895–1900 government. It compelled employers to insure their workers against injury but, significantly, at little cost to the Treasury. An ambitious scheme for old-age pensions was discussed but shelved for reasons of financial conservatism, with some damage to the party's appeal. The modest domestic record of the 1895–1900 government was above all due to the lack of agreement within the party about what it stood for domestically – merely resistance to change, or a positive programme of economic and social policy.

Salisbury's latter years, like Disraeli's, were dominated by foreign and imperial issues. Here, at least, there was a policy of sorts. Unusually for a prime minister, he also served as Foreign Secretary (until 1900), and regarded himself as *the* authority in the government on the subject. His awareness of Britain's weakness as a military power in Europe and as a naval power further afield, was his dominant outlook. His prime objective was to remain free from overseas alliances while maintaining British interests through fostering cooperation with Germany and the Triple Alliance (also including Austria-Hungary and Italy), as well as by limiting the costs of Empire. Salisbury memorably defined British policy in laconic style as 'to float lazily downstream, occasionally putting out a diplomatic boat hook to avoid collisions'. But events in the world from the late 1880s, and Bismarck's fall from power in 1890 which led to a deterioration in Britain's relations with Germany, called for a more active stance than merely meandering downstream. When Salisbury finally relinquished the Foreign Secretaryship, after prolonged pressure from his Cabinet, it is significant that his successor Lord Lansdowne had within two years negotiated an alliance with Japan. Britain's Entente with France followed in 1904. Salisbury's policy of 'isolationism' was seen to be no longer appropriate or wise in the new century.

The Tories benefited greatly from the upsurge of imperial pride in the nation, as seen

A 'Joe Chamberlain' gun in action, named after the Colonial Secretary in Salisbury's 1895–1902 administration. It was used to great effect by British artillery in the Boer War *(Imperial War Museum)*

in Queen Victoria's Golden Jubilee in 1887 and Diamond Jubilee in 1897, both of which provided opportunities for great imperial pageants with representatives of the colonies proudly parading through the streets of London for all to behold. The Boer War, which broke out in 1899, saw patriotism reaching its height in the early months. In the 'khaki election' of 1900, the popular mood helped carry the Tories to victory, with over 50 per cent of the popular vote and 402 MPs. The Liberals were divided over the war and failed to put up candidates in a quarter of the constituencies. Salisbury's shrewd timing of the election also played to the Conservatives' advantage. But, his greatest electoral victory comfortably secured the storm clouds soon began to gather around him. His own performance as premier was deteriorating, but he stayed on until the new king, Edward VII, was settled in following Victoria's death in 1901, and the long-protracted Boer War was successfully concluded in 1902.

THE SHATTERING OF TORY CONFIDENCE, 1902–15

The new Prime Minister was Salisbury's nephew, A.J. Balfour (which gave rise to the popular expression 'Bob's your uncle', Robert being Salisbury's first name). The 'Hotel Cecil' was the term coined to describe the dominance of the Cecil (Salisbury) family on Conservative politics. To many, it reeked of the aristocratic 'old' (i.e. nineteenth) century. Balfour was intellectually brilliant and wrote a learned book, *In Defence of Philosophical Doubt*, but he had few of the skills required to lead a party, especially one for which the tide was running out. Almost every decision the government took after 1900 aroused dissent from some quarter or other. The Education Act, steered through Parliament by Balfour in 1902 shortly before he became Prime Minister, helped change the face of state education by entrusting local authorities with the provision of schools. But it alienated nonconformists, whose schools were excluded from the Act, and terminated their further drift to the Conservatives, which had been a feature of the previous decade.

The working classes, vital to the party's electoral success, also became upset with the government. The Taff Vale legal judgment of 1901 had severely limited the ability of trade unions to take part in strikes. Pleas to Balfour to legislate to restore trade union rights were rebuffed. In a variety of other ways, including the continued failure to introduce old-age pensions, the government showed itself to be insensitive to working-class aspirations, and drove unions into the newly formed Labour Party. The Hotel Cecil characteristic of the government was highlighted when in 1903 Salisbury's son joined the Cabinet, which already contained four other family members. The powerful brewing industry, as well as the anti-drink lobby, were incensed by the Licensing Act of 1904. But it was the Tariff Reform issue which did the greatest damage to the party. The policy was launched by Chamberlain in May 1903. It had a brilliant simplicity to it: to bind the Empire closer together to allow it to compete against powerful economic nations, including Germany and the United States. To achieve this end, Chamberlain sought to impose a higher tariff on the import into Britain of non-Empire goods, thus favouring merchandise from within the Empire. Monies raised from tariffs would then be directed to social reforms, thus avoiding the need to raise taxes to finance them, which had proved such an obstacle for orthodox Tories in the past. But Chamberlain's deceptively

Joseph Chamberlain delivering his speech on the tariff
question at Bingley Hall in Birmingham on 4 November 1903.
He holds up two loaves of bread to demonstrate his point.
(Hulton/Getty)

persuasive master-plan had disastrous practical implications and was to divide the party as deeply as the repeal of the Corn Laws had done sixty years before.

Although some Conservative free-traders like Winston Churchill chose to defect on the issue to the Liberals, Chamberlain won many converts to the policy within Parliament. Tory voters in the country were less impressed. Their principal concern, ruthlessly exploited by a resurgent Liberal Party, was that Tarrif Reform would mean dearer food, particularly bread. More than anything else, the issue reunited the Liberals after the traumas of Home Rule. With his party split from top to bottom, Balfour tried to steer a middle course, alienating zealots on both wings (not unlike Major in the 1990s). Balfour was haunted by the spectre of Peel splitting the party: he would wander around saying 'I will not be another Sir Robert Peel'. In late 1905, he decided on the gambit of resigning, leaving the Liberals to form a ministry, hoping that their divisions over Home Rule would resurface and that they would be seen as a failed force incapable of meriting the nation's trust. But Henry Campbell-Bannerman, Liberal leader since 1898, seized the initiative and ensured that it was *his* party that appeared the united one and the Conservatives the split and indecisive force. The Liberals also benefited from the Lib-Lab electoral pact of 1903, which gave the newly formed Labour Party a free hand in some fifty seats in return for Labour agreeing not to run candidates against Liberals in the remaining constituencies in England and Wales. This arrangement ensured that the Conservatives were unable to capitalise on the possibility that their two main opposition parties would split the anti-Tory vote. At the general election which the Liberals called in January–February 1906, the Conservative result was worse even than in 1832. The party won just 157 seats (132 Conservatives and 25 Liberal Unionists), and was even outvoted in London and the South-East. Even Balfour lost his seat. It was to take eighteen years for the party to recover fully from the massacre.

The party's organisation had also taken a severe hammering. Chamberlain had succeeded by 1905 in taking hold over the National Union in his bid to impose Tarrif Reform, a move which engendered great bitterness. After Middleton's retirement in 1903, Central Office went into decline. Alexander Acland-Hood, appointed Chief Whip in 1902, proved to be one of the least successful incumbents of the office in its history. Following the 1906 defeat, Balfour realised that the party organisation needed reform, and this culminated in 1911 in the establishment of a new post of Chairman of the Party Organisation, whose task included running Central Office, while the role of Chief Whip was scaled down to overseeing just the parliamentary party. But the party's policy remained confused.

A Budget Protest League poster in 1909.
Conservatives bitterly resisted tax-raising
measures in Lloyd George's budget that year
(Bodleian Library)

Balfour, for all his tactical brilliance, proved little more successful as Leader of the Opposition than he had as Prime Minister. Fearful of the rise of militant trade unionism in Britain, and of communism abroad, as seen in the unsuccessful 1905 Revolution in Russia, Balfour adopted his uncle's policy of setting the party firmly against redistribution and social reform. The party thus moved away from attempts to placate or win over working-class voters, and set itself against the reforming Liberal government, which introduced old-age pensions in 1908 and which became even more activist after H.H. Asquith succeeded Campbell-Bannerman that year. Chamberlain's severe stroke in 1906 removed him altogether from the political fray, but Balfour had already decided, nevertheless, that the party should endorse the policy of Tarrif Reform, albeit shorn of its social policy dimension. Yet even this did not satisfy the 'whole-hogger' protectionists, who were determined to eliminate free-traders in the constituencies.

The Conservative Party recovered much of the support lost in 1906 in the two inconclusive general elections in 1910. But, with 272 MPs elected in both contests, it could not unseat the Liberals from power, who now ruled by virtue of their Labour partners and on sufferance of the Irish MPs. A bitter fight came in 1911 over the Parliament Act, which reduced the power of the House of Lords after its fight over Lloyd George's 1909 budget (known as the 'people versus the peers' struggle). When Balfour eventually decided to stand down as leader in 1911, Andrew Bonar Law was chosen by the parliamentary party as the candidate most likely to heal its continuing divisions.

A crowd of several thousand listen to Bonar Law addressing the Unionist Rally at Blenheim Palace in 1912 *(Hulton/Getty)*

Rather than seize the moment to adopt a positive platform of his own, Bonar Law opted to continue with a policy of all-out attack on the Liberals as the best strategy for unifying the party. Liberal policy on Home Rule for Ireland, the Welsh Church, social reform and taxation were all castigated. When the Home Rule issue re-emerged at Westminster it was to prompt the formal merging of the Conservative and Liberal Unionist parties in 1912. In that year the third Irish Home Rule Bill passed the House of Commons. It was defeated, unsurprisingly, by the Conservative majority in the House of Lords. But, under the terms of the 1911 Parliament Act, the Lords could now only delay a Bill that had passed through the Commons for a maximum of two years. Home Rule was thus due to become law in 1914, and all Ireland would become independent. The prospect frightened and deeply antagonised many Conservatives. Bonar Law, who himself came from an Ulster family, told a Conservative Party rally in July 1912, 'I can imagine no length of resistance to which Ulster will go, which I will not be ready to support.' Here was the Conservative leader apparently endorsing the use of force by a

Bonar Law with Edward Carson, leader of the Irish Unionists in Parliament in August 1915. Bonar Law had deep sympathy for the Unionist cause *(Hulton/Getty)*

section of the community to frustrate the will of Parliament. It was a stance without precedent in the party's history. New research by Jeremy Smith, however, shows that Bonar Law's stance was mainly bluster and brinkmanship. The Home Rule Bill passed the Commons for the required third time in May 1914. But, with the threat of civil war in Ireland looming, the Liberal government decided to suspend the Act's implementation until after the war.

Although Bonar Law failed to delineate a distinctive platform for the Conservative Party, the evidence from by-elections since 1910 was that the mood was swinging back towards the party. He dropped Tarrif Reform in 1913 to improve Conservative appeal in the coming election. Had a general election been held in 1914 or 1915, aided by a transformation in the party organisation after 1911 under Arthur Steel-Maitland as the first party chairman, the Conservatives may have won it. In the event, there was to be no general election for another four years, and war was declared against Germany on 4 August 1914.

THREE

THE BALDWIN PARTY: 1915–45

During the thirty years covered by this chapter, the Conservative Party was the dominant force in British politics. It recovered the momentum it had lost in the split over Tarrif Reform at the beginning of the twentieth century and found, in the figure of Stanley Baldwin, the perfect, reassuring leader around whom it could regroup to meet the serious challenges that emerged in the post-First World War world, the rise to power of Labour, militant trade unionism culminating in a general strike, the decline of Britain's staple export industries and the challenge from the dictators abroad.

RECOVERY 1915–23

The war came to the rescue of a still-confused and divided Tory party. It manoeuvred its way into office in May 1915 as junior partner in the Coalition under the Liberal Prime Minister H.H. Asquith, avoiding a general election neither party wanted. Its leader, Andrew Bonar Law, became Colonial Secretary, while fellow Conservatives also gained jobs, Lord Curzon as Lord Privy Seal, Austen Chamberlain India Secretary, and Arthur Balfour First Lord of the Admiralty. The four principal posts in the Coalition Government – Prime Minister, Chancellor of the Exchequer, Foreign Secretary and Home Secretary – were, however, all held by the Liberals who dominated the Coalition, while several

Members of Lloyd George's Coalition. Lloyd George sits with grey jacked on the left of the table. Churchill faces forward in the middle of the table, Balfour stands in black above him to the right, and Bonar Law on the far right, facing out. Painting by Sir James Guthrie *(National Portrait Gallery)*

Conservative MPs refused to support it. Bonar Law, alienated by Asquith and the conduct of the war, increasingly sided with his Liberal ally David Lloyd George.

In December 1916 the Asquith government broke up, the Liberal Party split, and a new Coalition Government under Lloyd George came to power. With the loss of many leading Liberals into opposition with Asquith, senior positions were now filled by Conservatives, with Bonar Law becoming the Chancellor of the Exchequer and Leader of the Commons and Balfour Foreign Secretary. For the first time in eleven years, Conservatives again were able to shape government policy. Recovery was helped by the continuing split between the followers of Lloyd George and Asquith, and by the war continuing to pose difficult questions for the Liberal Party, including conscription and other coercive measures demanded by this new brand of 'total' war, which conflicted with the Liberals' traditional support for the liberty of the individual. War posed no such difficulties for the Conservatives, however, as they were traditionally the party of patriotism and strong defence. The party made much of its 'good' pre-war record, including the negotiation of the Anglo-Japanese Alliance in 1902, the Anglo-French Entente of 1904, and the active defence policy followed by the Balfour government until it resigned in December 1905. In opposition after that date, moreover, the Conservatives could claim with some justice that they had consistently pressed for increased expenditure on defence and a strong line in the face of German militarism.

The first full year of the Lloyd George Coalition, 1917, saw continued failure to make progress on the western front, with the third battle of Ypres (culminating in the battle of Passchendaele) achieving no more of a breakthrough than had the battle of the Somme the year before. But 1917 also saw the entry of the United States into the war. After the failure of the German spring offensive which began in March 1918, it was these American forces, now beginning to arrive in number, and the British blockades that tipped the balance in favour of the Allies, and led to the German retreat. The Armistice on 11 November 1918 was followed immediately by a general election in December.

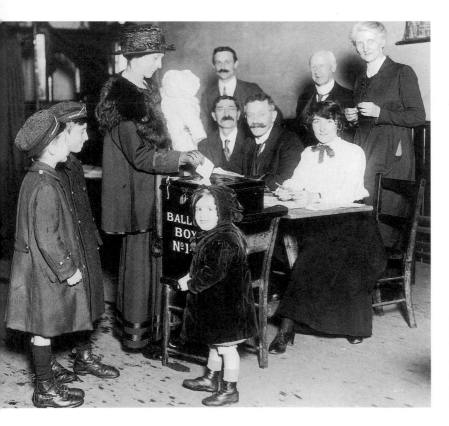

A young mother brings her family with her into the polling station in the 'coupon election' of 1918. Women over 30 were given the vote for the first time in the 1918 Reform Act – the party made strenuous efforts to win them over (Hulton/Getty)

The Conservative leadership decided to remain within the Lloyd George Coalition, not wishing as yet to break off on their own. In the election itself a pact was made in which Lloyd George and Bonar Law signed a joint letter endorsing Coalition candidates in what was known as the 'coupon election'. The Coalition carried all before it; 523 of its parliamentary supporters were elected, of whom 382 were Conservatives. The party would almost certainly have won an outright victory if it had fought on its own in 1918: the anti-Conservative vote was split, with the 1903 Lib-Lab electoral pact no longer holding as Labour was determined to fight alone. Yet Bonar Law was fearful of the prospect of unbridled adult suffrage (unleashed for the first time by the Reform Act of 1918) and of the prospect of trade union unrest rearing its head again after the war, given added heart by the success of the Bolshevik Revolution in Russia in 1917. The Tory leader was also fearful of the growing challenge of the still-young Labour Party, which was to win fourteen by-elections in the years 1918 to 1922. These were demanding years for any government, with a postwar boom and sudden slump, major international issues to be resolved on the future of the postwar world, and a very different electorate with demanding expectations to manage.

Bonar Law, like Balfour, was not to be one of the Tory leaders who defined his age or his party. He was essentially a cautious figure, a negative one even, concerned to ward off threats to Conservatism and to preserve the party but without offering it a positive platform of its own or even presenting it with a model of leadership around which the party could confidently amass. His tactical skills, which allowed the party to emerge from the First World War in such a strong parliamentary position, should not be under-estimated, nor should his work as Chancellor. But he was never going to become a great war leader in his own right, and was eclipsed utterly on that front by Lloyd George. Nor would he become the figure to lead the party to new levels in the postwar world.

The Conservatives remained within the Lloyd George Coalition for four years until October 1922. The break-up of the Coalition was due to a growing revulsion among Tory MPs against Lloyd George, an anger that was widely shared by the party in the country. Lloyd George's presidential style of leadership, his perceived corruption, lapses of taste and immorality, and the dislike by some of the 1921 Treaty, which gave self-government to southern Ireland, and of the 'free-trade' policy, all played their part in increasing numbers of Tories wishing to quit the Coalition. The Conservative leadership failed to engage sufficiently in creative thinking of its own which would have helped prepare the party for power: the two principal reforms of the government, H.A.L. Fisher's Education Act of 1918 and Christopher Addison's Housing Act 1919 were both

THE PARTY IN THE FIRST WORLD WAR

The Conservatives traditionally prided themselves on being the party that supported the military and the national interest. They had taken the party into the Boer War in 1899 and had won the 'khaki election' in 1900 partly on the strength of it. The early years of the twentieth century had seen invasion scares reach new heights, epitomised by Erskine Childers' The Riddle of the Sands. The Edwardian era saw a wave of anti-German feeling and zealous patriotism sweep across Britain. In power up to 1905, the party staunchly supported the army and the navy, and subsequently pressed hard for greater expenditure on both, including on the new class of battleship, the Dreadnought. Tories even criticised Asquith's government for its neglect of the emerging air service. Once war began in August 1914, and it became clear that it would not be 'over by Christmas', the Conservatives pressed hard for all-out war, including conscription.

When the crisis erupted in May 1915 over the inadequate supply of shells for the army, the

A scene of devastation from the battle of Pozières Ridge, during the disastrous Somme offensive whose failure helped bring about Lloyd George's premiership (July–November 1916). (Imperial War Museum)

Balfour, the former Tory leader inspects a garrison of troops in York in 1916. He was Foreign Secretary in Lloyd George's wartime coalition *(Hulton/Getty)*

desire to avoid an election provided the Tories with the opportunity to re-enter the government, and the party gained some direct say in the conduct of the war. But the prosecution of the war was to prove no more successful, with a series of military setbacks in 1915 epitomised by Gallipoli, followed by the disaster of the Somme in 1916. The indecisive naval battle of Jutland also failed to show that the Royal Navy had mastered the German Navy had and its submarines.

The failure of the Somme offensive, which petered out in November 1916, played its part in the ousting of Asquith in December and his replacement by Lloyd George. Bonar Law

refused the premiership himself but had decided that support for Lloyd George's government with full Conservative backing offered the best prospect for a successful conclusion to the war. Three of the figures in Lloyd George's five-man War Cabinet were Tories, and, while the Liberal split between the Lloyd George and Asquith factions continued, the Tories' self-confidence and influence grew. Tory support for the key decisions of the First World War from December 1916 to November 1918 ensured that they gained some credit for the victory. The war had indeed always been more in tune with the Conservatives' thinking than with that of the Liberals.

Bonar Law in conversation with Lloyd George at Cannes a few weeks before the Chanak crisis which precipitated the collapse of Lloyd George's Coalition Government in October 1922 (Hulton/Getty)

the work of Liberal ministers. The contrast with the creative work that occurred in the party during and after the Second World War is stark. The post-1918 Tory outlook was characterised by the brooding presence of the retrenchment-minded Chancellor of the Exchequer, Austen Chamberlain, who had succeeded an ailing Bonar Law as Chancellor in January 1919. The party was going nowhere under Bonar Law; or, at least, nowhere in a forward direction.

Nor was it going to go anywhere in particular under Austen Chamberlain, who then succeeded Bonar Law as party leader in March 1921. Chamberlain, indicatively, was in favour of the Tories continuing in the Lloyd George Coalition, which illustrated a lack of ambition on his part for the party. The reputation of his father as a wrecker was partly responsible for Austen's extreme caution. The growing pressure against remaining in the Coalition came to the surface at the celebrated meeting at the Carlton Club on 19 October 1922, instigated by Chamberlain to pre-empt trouble at the party conference. Chamberlain himself tried and failed to persuade Tory MPs of the virtues of anti-socialist forces remaining joined together in the face of the challenge of Labour. The two most persuasive speeches at the meeting were made by Stanley Baldwin, who castigated Lloyd George's dynamism as a 'very terrible thing', and by a partially rejuvenated Bonar Law, who argued passionately for the importance of the maintenance of party unity. Bonar Law's speech indicated to MPs his willingness to lay his ill health to one side and to return, if required, as party leader as Chamberlain was too wedded to the Coalition for him to lead the party outside it. Conservative MPs voted by a margin of more than two to one (187:86) to leave. Even without the Carlton Club meeting, however, the Coalition would probably not have survived much longer, as increasing numbers of Conservative MPs were already deciding

Austen Chamberlain, Conservative leader for a year and a half after March 1921, at a dinner in Birmingham in May 1922 *(Hulton/Getty)*

to stand as independents at the following general election rather than remain under the Coalition banner.

Austen Chamberlain duly resigned as leader of the party, and Lloyd George as Prime Minister, immediately after the fateful Carlton Club vote. Bonar Law promptly became Prime Minister and called an election the following month. In the November 1922 election, 344 Tory MPs were elected, and for the first time in the party's history it won over five million votes. It secured an outright majority of eighty-eight over all other parties, its first clear victory since 1900. The departure of the Irish Nationalist MPs to their own newly independent country was a windfall of the 1918–22 years for the Tories, as immediately some eighty MPs who had collaborated with the Conservatives' opponents were lost to British politics.

Bonar Law and J.C.C. Davidson (the future party chairman) to his left leave the Carlton Club on 19 October 1922 following the parliamentary party's momentous decision to withdraw support from Lloyd George's Coalition (*Hulton/Getty*)

Bonar Law now had a final opportunity to show that he could offer the Conservative Party a positive platform. He failed to take that opportunity. By playing the 'red-scare' card in the election, persuading voters worried about socialism to support the Tory party, he helped the party win. The split vote between Liberals and Labour helped far more. But he had no clear strategy for office, and his failure himself to engage in or to instigate any serious policy work during the war and postwar years now came back to haunt him. He was further handicapped by being unable to call upon the pro-Coalitionists, who included some of the most senior figures in the party, notably Austen Chamberlain and F.E. Smith (dubbed 'the slice off the top'). This meant he had to draw heavily on peers and on the party's Tarrif Reform wing. His failing health proved a final handicap and prevented him being a more energetic and robust figure. On 20 May 1923, he tendered his resignation as Prime Minister to King George V, thus ending his political career, and he died six months later. He refused to offer the King official advice as to his successor and the contest became a two-horse race between Baldwin, now Chancellor of the Exchequer, and Lord Curzon, Foreign Secretary. Baldwin, a commoner, was the King's perhaps inevitable choice. He was immediately faced with the job of repairing a party still divided with the pro-Coalitionists outside, and with little agreement over what postwar Tory government should be all about. From this unpropitious start, Baldwin was to go on to become the defining Tory figure of the interwar years.

THE BALDWIN PARTY

Baldwin did not at first appear to be promising material to lead the party back into a place in the sun it had not known since the Marquess of Salisbury had been leader. Baldwin's family had made their money in iron. After an unremarkable record at Harrow and Cambridge, he had worked in the family firm and owned a country estate in Worcestershire. He acquired a deep love of the countryside and a certain knowledge of handling employees. But he had acquired little feel for policy, or how or where to lead a political party. When he entered Parliament in 1908 he was a Tarrif Reformer as opposed to a free-trader. He spoke little in his first nine years in Parliament, and became a junior minister only in 1917, though he was promoted rapidly thereafter. Once he became leader, he fell on protection as the best way to combat rising unemployment as well as of coaxing Conservative ex-Coalitionists back into the

1923 general election poster attacking Lloyd George's 'free trade' policy (Bodleian Library)

fold. In October 1923, therefore, he decided to adopt protection as official policy. But, as this policy entailed the abandonment of a specific pledge not to introduce a general tariff that Bonar Law had given during the 1922 general election, Baldwin felt obliged to call a general election to seek a mandate for the policy – a decision with which many disagreed: Walter Elliot, a junior Scottish minister, said, 'the best way to lose a general election is to hold one'. Baldwin duly announced at the party conference at Plymouth that, if challenged on the policy, he would call an election, which duly took place two months later in December 1923.

Baldwin's first major decision as party leader united the party but was not his most successful electorally, and led some to question his ability. Although the Conservatives' popular vote fell only half a per cent to 30 per cent, the number of MPs collapsed from 344 to 258. The Conservatives remained the largest single party, but Labour moved into second place with 191 seats, while the Liberals came third with 158. Baldwin had the option of combining with the Liberals to recreate an anti-Labour coalition but rejected the idea, thereby affording Labour its first opportunity of power. Baldwin used the subsequent period in opposition to create the first official shadow Cabinet and set up groups to examine policy. Labour formed its government in January 1924 under Ramsay MacDonald, amid widespread fear in Tory Britain of what evils a socialist government might inflict on the nation. In the event, the 'red scare' fears proved absurdly alarmist. After a fairly docile nine months in power, the Labour government had fallen, and a general election called.

The election in October 1924 provided Baldwin with just the success he needed. The Conservatives' popular vote rose to just under eight million, which translated into 412 MPs, in contrast to Labour's 151 and the Liberals' mere 40. The scale of the victory shocked many, not least the Conservatives. It owed more to the state of Labour and the Liberals than to the new positive platform offered by the Conservatives. In June 1924 they had published a policy statement, *Aims and Principles*, and Baldwin himself had given a series of speeches in which he discussed his ideas of a 'new Conservatism'. These initiatives chimed with the aspirations of some younger Tory MPs who had been arguing before, during and after the war for a positive Tory social and economic policy but whose ideas had not been taken up by the leadership. In contrast, the right wanted to bolster the House of Lords and restrict union rights. Baldwin was presented with a choice of whether to adopt the Peelite/Salisbury formula of an alliance between property and order to contain the clamour for reform while dispersing piecemeal, limited morsels, or whether to adopt the Disraelian response of appealing to the working class directly with a

Stanley Baldwin with his wife Lucy at Chequers in November 1924, a month after leading the party to victory at the polls. Their 'no airs' demeanour chimed with interwar voters *(Hulton/Getty)*

programme of policies to gain their loyalty. Baldwin's solution was to blend both approaches but to veer sharply towards the latter; and in so doing he defined what the interwar Conservative Party was about.

The 1924–9 Conservative government was to prove to be one of the most important reforming administrations of the century. The Widows, Orphans and Old-Age Pensions Act of 1925, one of its principal social reforms, was a compulsory contribution scheme paid by both workers and employers. By enshrining the principle of individual contributions, it helped delineate the future shape of the welfare state in Britain. The government devoted much energy to slum clearance and to housing, and Britain began to move firmly in the direction of owner-occupation. The term 'property-owning democracy' was coined in 1924 (although it did not become a commonly used phrase to describe party policy for another twenty-five years). Many towns and cities in Britain retain the distinctive interwar housing erected under Baldwin's leadership. In handling militant unionism, Baldwin displayed sensitivity and moderation. The long-brewing crisis came to a head in the general strike of 1926; some on both left and right saw it as the

600,000 more at work than in 1924

BRITISH INDUSTRY

CONSERVATIVES ARE INCREASING EMPLOYMENT

The party attempted to make as much capital out of its economic record as its programme of social reform after 1924, as this 1929 election poster shows *(Bodleian Library)*

beginning of a working-class, trade union-led revolution. A more abrasive response than Baldwin's might have provoked considerable backlash. In the event, the strike lasted less than two weeks, and in the ensuing Trades Dispute Act of 1927 the government confined itself to outlawing sympathetic strike action. It was a firm response but would have been harsher still under a less enlightened premier.

The Equal Franchise Act of 1928 brought women's voting age down from 30 to the men's age of 21, giving women voting equality with men. On the economic front, government measures included the rationalisation of the coal and cotton industries, the creation of the Central Electricity Board, which set up the national grid, and the establishment of the British Broadcasting Corporation (BBC) as a public corporation in 1926. The government's greatest economic error was arguably the decision to return to the gold standard in 1925 at a rate of £1 to $4.86, which overpriced British exports and thus exacerbated domestic unemployment. Unemployment stood at one million in 1929, though numbers in work rose between 1924 and 1929, partly in response to government action (see poster above).

The gold standard decision aside, which was taken by Churchill (who had returned to the Tory fold in 1924) as Chancellor of the Exchequer, the government's achievement overall was remarkable. Its work was helped by the return of the ex-Coalitionists, with Austen Chamberlain becoming Foreign Secretary and Lord Birkenhead (F.E. Smith) being given the India Office. In an unusually talented administration, the most impressive minister was Neville Chamberlain, half-brother to Austen and second son of Joseph Chamberlain. He served as Minister of Health throughout the government and was the powerhouse behind much of its social reform. But chief credit is due to Baldwin,

Mounted police protect a lorry bearing key supplies in south London during the General Strike in May 1926 *(Hulton/Getty)*

Neville Chamberlain, the dynamic Health Minister in Baldwin's 1924–9 government, attends the opening of the pharmacological laboratories of the Pharmaceutical Society at Bloomsbury Square in London *(Hulton/Getty)*

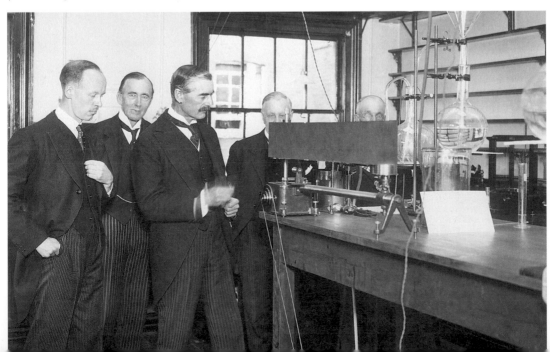

LET *The* LIGHTHOUSE OF CONSERVATISM

SAVE "S.S.BRITAIN"

FROM THE ROCKS OF SOCIALISM

Left: 'Red Scare'! 1929 general election. One of the more striking posters raising the spectre of socialism as a continuing threat *(Bodleian Library)*

Right: A memorable slogan, but not one which could help the party in 1929 *(Bodleian Library)*

who had succeeded in reuniting the party and overseeing a series of fresh policies to present to the electorate as the face of modern Conservatism.

The record of the government did not translate, however, into payback at the polls. At the general election in May 1929, the party's seats fell in number from 412 to 260, and for the first time Labour emerged as the largest single party, with 288 seats, albeit still short of an overall majority. The Liberals, despite a tremendous effort and a very positive policy platform, secured just 59 MPs. They had fielded candidates in 513 constituencies, which resulted in votes being taken from Tories. It was to be Lloyd George's last serious bid for power as leader. A second Labour government was duly formed and Ramsay MacDonald again became Prime Minister.

Labour's great misfortune was to come to office in the year of the Wall Street crash and at the start of the Great Depression. Had Baldwin won in 1929, he would have faced similar difficulties: it was a very good election for the party to have lost. MacDonald was no more socialist-minded than he had been in 1924: he opted, not for interventionist policies financed by high taxes, but for prudence, presided over by the ultra-orthodox Chancellor of the Exchequer, Philip Snowden. The Cabinet then tore itself apart over cuts necessitated by the economic crisis, and in August 1931 MacDonald tendered the government's resignation, establishing in its place the first National Government. Most of the Parliamentary Labour Party thought his actions treacherous, and refused to serve under him. The government's ranks were thus made up of a handful of 'National' Labour MPs, the majority of the Liberals and all of the Conservative MPs, who now found themselves the overwhelming majority.

The period 1929–31 had not been any happier for Baldwin than for MacDonald. The Tory leader suffered personal attacks from right-wingers like Churchill, who opposed his support for gradual steps towards Indian self-government. He was attacked further for failing to espouse empire free-trade as a response to rising unemployment (protection of British industry became official government policy in 1932). The press, especially two proprietors, Lords Beaverbrook and Rothermere, were notably hostile. The onslaught reached a peak in 1930. Feelings were still raw at the by-election in Westminster St George's in March 1931, when Baldwin roundly denounced the power of the 'press lords', saying that they had 'power without responsibility'. Had the right wing of the party in fact been united against his leadership, Baldwin might not have survived. But its forces, to his relief, were disjointed. The main positive development for the party during

The three 'National' party leaders, Stanley Baldwin, Ramsay MacDonald and John Simon (mid picture) inspect daylight cinema vans outside the House of Commons, ahead of the general election in 1935 (Hulton/Getty)

The Cabinet of the National Government in August 1931. Bandwin is on MacDonald's right side, and Herbert Samuel, the Liberal leader, on his left. Philip Snowden is on Baldwin's right *(Hulton/Getty)*

1929–31 was the establishment of the Conservative Research Department, which became the party's principal think-tank for the next forty-five years.

Neville Chamberlain in particular argued that supporting the National Government was a way of entrenching the division of Labour. This strategy was triumphantly vindicated at the October 1931 general election at which 'independent' Labour secured just 52 MPs, while only 13 Labour MPs, including MacDonald, won seats who supported the National Government. The Conservatives, who won 470 seats, achieved their highest total of the twentieth century.

The National Government of 1931–5 became increasingly a Conservative government in all but name, though historians highlight the Labour and Liberal influences within it. It was presided over by a triumvirate of Ramsay MacDonald as Prime Minister, Baldwin as Lord President, and Neville Chamberlain as Chancellor of the Exchequer and the most forceful of the three. MacDonald became progressively less effective and become increasingly unwell. While Chamberlain continued to see the National Government as the most effective way of keeping Labour divided, Baldwin was also pleased that it kept one of his enemies, Lloyd George, out of power, as well as providing the means to outflank the party's right wing which had stung him so badly between 1929 and 1931. Baldwin was also happy that the requirement for a broad base of support, on which the National Government was predicated, demanded a continuation of the progressive

WILL KEEP THOSE
STACKS OF WORK GOING

A poster from the 1935 general election arguing that the National Government would best protect jobs (*Bodleian Library*)

reforms of 1924–9 and a moderate 'one nation' hue to party policy. Baldwin thus saw the National Government as the ideal way of seeing his own brand of moderate Conservatism triumph, while piloting a delicate path between the extremes of right and left which seemed to be engulfing the rest of the industrialised world.

The National Government went on to win a further victory in the election of November 1935, which came five months after Baldwin had succeeded MacDonald as Prime Minister. Argument earlier over government policy on India, and failure to do more to reduce unemployment, convinced some that the National Government's majority would be dramatically cut. In the event, it won its second-biggest victory, some 54 per cent of the national vote and 432 MPs (including National Liberals) out of 615 MPs in total. The policies of the National government were more interventionist and less laissez-faire than have been traditionally credited. Measures such as the Depressed Areas Act of 1934 sought to tackle regional unemployment by encouraging firms to move to areas of high unemployment, while measures to rationalise and streamline industry extended to the creation of London Transport in 1933 and, later, to airlines with Imperial Airways. The Education Act of 1936 raised the school-leaving age to 15, slum clearance and house building were resumed with a vengeance after the Depression, and subsidies were introduced to help agriculture and industry. Cheap money from 1932 and debt conversion probably did more than anything to stimulate recovery.

Policy under Baldwin can perhaps best be understood as a response to the advent of the mass franchise, the rise of Labour and the leftward shift of the electorate. Limited though the reforms may have been, they were the most activist the party had introduced since the Disraeli government of 1874–80. Baldwin's personal role was to provide

Baldwin filmed in the garden of 10 Downing Street for a newsreel in 1928. Notice his enjoyment *(Hulton/Getty)*

reassurance as leader, an image which he exploited brilliantly in newsreels and radio. He was indeed the first party leader to become well known to the electorate at large. His pipe became one of his trademark characteristics, a formula later to be repeated with less success by Harold Wilson from 1963 to 1976. As leader during 1923–37, Baldwin exuded trust and decency. His calm, pragmatic stance on many issues reassured an electorate weary of war, civil unrest and demagoguery. He was a shrewd judge of character, made good appointments and knew whom to trust. His command of language and knowledge of literature shamed many other Tory Prime Ministers. His achievement at holding together a party deeply torn between left and right over issues such as India, free trade, the Empire and rearmament was no less great than Bonar Law's had earlier been. Baldwin brilliantly exploited his own and the party's national image in an uncertain world at home and abroad. John Barnes believes 'his greatest role was to brand Labour as the creation of the unions (i.e. sectional) inspired by a foreign creed (i.e. socialism)'. Even his theme of 'safety first' used in the 1929 election chimed with many voters who did not want to see their government offering anything deemed radical.

Baldwin was also a shrewd manager of the party. He was fortunate to find, in J.C.C. Davidson after 1926, a dynamic new party chairman, who oversaw a radical regeneration of the party both at the centre and in the constituencies. Party finances were transformed, which allowed Central Office to be galvanised and re-established on a more ambitious footing. Throughout the interwar years the party was able to field a candidate in almost

Baldwin bows out, with Lucy by his side. Neville Chamberlain presents Baldwin with a volume containing tributes from Conservative Associations at a meeting of the party's Central Council in June 1937. Such a presentation to a retiring leader had never been made before in the party's history. Notice again Baldwin's easy aplomb before the camera *(Topfoto)*

every constituency and to employ full-time agents in almost all its safe and marginal seats. Membership rose, and women in particular were utilised to canvass, organise events and raise money. Aided by the 1928 Reform Act giving women voting equality (at 21) with men, the Conservative Party came to be seen even more as friendly and open to women. Over 50 per cent of women may have voted Conservative in the interwar years. A majority of the working class also voted Tory in this period, despite the rise of Labour and the continued, if dwindling, appeal of the Liberals. Baldwin's achievement was to make the party look leftward, attracting the working-class vote while not alienating the party's lower middle-class and upper middle-class supporters. The 1930s saw, after the Depression, a big consumer boom aided by cheap land and cheap money, which meant that consumer goods such as cars, telephones and radios began to be common even in less affluent homes. As in the 1950s and 1980s, the party was fortunate to be in power at a time of prosperity. Labour remained a broken force, as were the Liberals. Had a peacetime election been held in 1940, the Conservatives would have won it.

THE END OF THE BALDWIN ERA

Not everything went the Tories' way. The persistence of high unemployment in certain regions was just one of the storm clouds that refused to clear. The rise of fascism was another, as seen in the Olympia rally in 1934 and at the Cable Street riot in London in

1936. Oswald Mosley's British Union of Fascists (BUF) proved a more vocal threat to order in the 1930s than communist-inspired agitation, but the attractions of Marxism to young intellectuals and to some in trade unions remained strong. The crisis over the monarchy in 1936, resulting in Edward VIII's abdication and the succession of his tongue-tied brother, George VI, was handled well by Baldwin, although recently released Cabinet records reveal how close Baldwin came to misjudging the crisis. Chamberlain's succession in May 1937 resulted in little immediate change in domestic policy, although he proved a more inept prime minister than many had anticipated. Foreign affairs loomed much larger, however, due to ever bolder ambitions of Hitler and Mussolini, which were beyond his control. His preference for 'appeasing' the dictators, popular in the country, was at variance with a vocal minority in the party, notably Churchill. For the time being they could be dismissed as mavericks and malcontents. But with Hitler's invasion of Poland in September 1939 and the fall of France in May 1940, it was clear that Chamberlain's policy had been a total failure. Churchill's succession in May 1940 ushered in a new era for the party.

Chamberlain shakes hands with Nazi Foreign Minister Joachim Von Ribbentrop at Munich Aerodrome on 3 October 1938. Alec Douglas-Home (Chamberlain's Parliamentary Private Secretary and future party leader) stands between them. Appeasement was to cast a long shadow over the party's postwar history *(Hulton/Getty)*

THE PARTY IN THE SECOND WORLD WAR

Whereas the Conservatives could claim to have been better prepared for war than the Liberals or Labour, and more united in meeting its demands in 1914, the advent of the Second World War on 3 September 1939 and the disastrous first nine months shattered that image of military competence completely. Some party unity was restored by the offer of posts in September 1939 in Chamberlain's government to Churchill and Eden, but the tensions during the 'phoney war' period were always present. Chamberlain, who remained reluctant to commit the British economy to total war, clashed with the firebrands who wanted a far more dynamic approach. Britain's failure to avert the invasions of Poland and Finland heightened tensions within the party. It was testament to Churchill's genius that responsibility for military defeat in Norway, which was primarily his, was laid not at his door but

at Chamberlain's. The Prime Minister could not, however, survive the invasion of France and Belgium. Labour's refusal to serve under Chamberlain, with his long history of hatred for their party, made his fall inevitable. Lord Halifax was an obvious successor with a solid pedigree in the Conservative Party, but he was too closely identified with appeasement and had the handicap of being in the House of Lords. Labour would also not serve under him. It was thus Churchill who succeeded to office on 10 May 1940.

Churchill's pugnacious leadership over the next five years was devoted wholly to winning the war, to the detriment of thinking about the postwar world for which the British soldiers were fighting. Rather than giving ministerial jobs to party stalwarts, he appointed cronies and individuals with talent to key posts in running the war. Thus the press proprietors,

Winston Churchill inspects the House of Commons Home Guard at a sandbag-protected Parliament in May 1942 (Hulton/Getty)

Lord Buckhurst, the Conservative candidate for Bethnal Green, campaigning in a bombsite during the 1945 general election. The masses keep their distance, a stance replicated in their voting *(Hulton/Getty)*

Beaverbrook and Bracken, were given posts, as were Anthony Eden, Leo Amery and Harold Macmillan, all of whom had been critical of Chamberlain's policy. Figures from outside politics like Andrew Duncan, James Grigg and Oliver Lyttelton were brought in, while industrialists like Lord Woolton and former civil servants like Sir John Anderson also retained in important portfolios.

Tellingly, it was Labour ministers who were given the principal posts concerned with the home front. Clement Attlee, the Labour leader, was given responsibility after 1943 for coordinating domestic policy, while Herbert Morrison and Ernest Bevin were given the Home Office and Ministry of Labour respectively.

Considerable thinking was, however, taking place among Tories on the shape of the postwar world, seemingly without Churchill's knowledge or interest, especially early on. He deliberately stood aside from the partisan post of Conservative leader, imagining he could pick up the banner again once the war was over. In 1941, a seminal Conservative body, the Post-War Problems Central Committee (PWPCC), was set up under the chairmanship of R.A. Butler with David Maxwell-Fyfe as his deputy. This body published a wide range of reports and surveys and conducted a thorough review of all party policy. Butler himself produced the Education Act 1944, which powerfully shaped postwar state education. Yet, because of Churchill's neglect of the PWPCC's work, little of its analysis found its way into the party's 1945 manifesto. In contrast, Labour, which remained closely identified with economic and social policy throughout the war, had the credibility and public recognition when it came to presenting its policies to the electorate. The Conservatives, under Churchill, may have been primarily responsible for winning the war: but it was Labour that won the peace.

F O U R

THE CHURCHILL AND MACMILLAN
PARTIES: 1945–75

Winston Churchill, as we have seen, barely acknowledged his role as Conservative Party leader in the war, and, indeed, Neville Chamberlain retained the title until his death in October 1940, five months after Churchill succeeded to the premiership. But, when the wartime Coalition Government broke up in May 1945, Churchill's gloves were off. His last ten years in power, as Opposition Leader until 1951 and then as Prime Minister, have been judged harshly by historians. He has been derided for being an anachronism, 'ga-ga' or even drunk much of the time. He was none of these, although the publication of the diaries of his doctor, Lord Moran, shortly after his death in 1965 made many believe he was. Churchill's peacetime leadership, we argue, is the most underrated of all Tory leaderships in the century. Churchill provided the perfect figure around which the party could adjust to the demands of the postwar world: no one else in the party could have performed this role.

If Churchill held the party together and personified it during this transitional phase, Harold Macmillan, Prime Minister in 1957–63, articulated a new vision of the party as one which could outdo Labour on welfare provision, which calmly oversaw the end of the empire and the spreading of ownership of property, if not yet of shares, and promoted the possession of consumer durables among lower-middle-class and working-class families.

None of the other leaders of these years, Anthony Eden (1955–7), Alec Douglas-Home (1963–5) or Edward Heath (1965–75), ever defined the party. That was their problem. Under them, the party lost five general elections and won only two, under Eden in May 1955 before his deficiencies as Prime Minister had had a chance to be displayed, and one by Heath in June 1970, just. Only at the end of this period did the party find another figure, capable of defining the party and taking it forward, and it was to be one of the most surprising leaders in the history of the party, neither an establishment figure, nor a conservative, nor a man.

THE CHURCHILL PARTY

Churchill's abrogation of the job as party leader during the war meant that, when the European war concluded, the party lacked a policy on which to fight an election, a unified team of ministers, or an organisation in the country. Churchill returned to the political fray with a vengeance once the Coalition government broke up and normal party politics recommenced in May 1945. He castigated Labour for abandoning the Coalition before the war with Japan was complete, and cautioned against voting for Labour, which, he argued, would divide Britain along ideological lines. He alone could lead the country in the national interest. Churchill believed that gratitude to him as war leader would carry the day, and he decided to call an early election for 5 July, a full month before the atomic bombs in Japan ended the war in the Far East, to capitalise on this belief.

The party, however, failed to convince the middle classes in particular of the merits of its case. Memories of the party's failure in the 1930s to stand up to the dictators, Churchill's overblown rhetoric in the campaign (with talk of the socialists introducing a 'Gestapo' into Britain) and the steady domestic record of Labour ministers in the Coalition made Labour appear the more credible force. Although the Tory party managed to gain just under 40 per cent of the

The 1945 election campaign invested much in Churchill's wartime reputation. The ploy, however, failed *(Bodleian Library)*

vote, the strength of the Labour challenge meant that Labour had almost a clean run, winning 393 MPs. The figure for the Tories eventually rose to just 213 once various independent and 'National' MPs opted to accept the Tory Whip. It was a shattering defeat, comparable in the twentieth century only to 1906 and 1997. The swing against the Tories during the war had gone so far that no campaign in 1945, however brilliant, could recover the ground.

Churchill's leadership was denigrated not least by the ambitious figure of R.A. Butler, who in a variety of forums for reasons of self-aggrandisement made out that the real work in opposition was overseen by him at the head of the Conservative Research Department, not by Eden or Macmillan or anyone else, while Churchill was preoccupied with foreign affairs (such as his 'iron curtain' speech at Fulton, Missouri in 1946) and with writing his

Churchill addressing a crowd of 8,000 voters in High Wycombe during the 1945 general election *(Corbis)*

Front cover of the Industrial Charter, the party's most important postwar
policy document, published in 1947 *(Bodleian Library)*

**THE
INDUSTRIAL
CHARTER**

*A Statement of
Conservative
Industrial
Policy*

One Shilling
CONSERVATIVE AND UNIONIST
CENTRAL OFFICE

six volumes of self-justificatory War Memoirs. Butler and
his like further argued that Churchill's leadership of the
party consisted of little more than hosting irregular lunches
for the shadow Cabinet at London's Savoy Hotel. Many of
these same shadow ministers wanted him to quit, not least
for leading the party so badly to a shattering general
election defeat. They also wanted someone who would
listen to them more – even be able to boss. For a year after
1945, exhausted and depressed, Churchill dithered, but
from 1946 he was adamant that he would stay. Attempts
by senior Tories to manoeuvre him out were a constant
theme of the years 1947–55, but he eventually departed of
his own accord. In refusing to be shifted by his lieutenants,
he proved himself a shrewder judge and a better servant of
the Tory party interest than those who tried to depose him. Much to the chagrin of his
detractors, he became an increasingly loved and admired figure in the party after 1945, a
sentiment that reached a high point in the extraordinary public acclaim on his 80th
birthday on 30 November 1954.

For much of this period until 1950, Churchill remained above the fray. He was a
benign presence around which the party could regroup and the shadow Cabinet find a
cohesion it had lacked since 1940. He fought to keep the Conservatives in the centre
ground of politics, a continuation of the tone of his leadership of the Coalition
government. He even sought to change the name 'Conservative' to another, such as
'Union Party', to highlight its broad appeal, and he tried to unite the party with the
Liberals in an anti-socialist alliance. His shadow ministers resisted such a move fiercely,
though he did succeed in merging the Conservative and National Liberal parties in 1947.

Even though he played no active part in it, Churchill's centrist beliefs were echoed in
the work on policy reformulation overseen by Butler. The work of the Post-War
Problems Central Committee since 1941 had paved the way. At first, Churchill had not
wanted such work to continue after 1945, as he preferred to wait for Labour to destroy
itself; he did not want policy work undertaken that could be seen as divisive or alienate
potential voters or MPs from other parties taking the Tory Whip. But he bowed under
pressure from the party. The Industrial Policy Committee was thus set up under Butler in

1946. Its work has been praised by Ramsden as 'one of the key moments of Conservative Party history', akin to Peel's drafting of the *Tamworth Manifesto* in 1834. Peel had accepted the reforms of 1830–4 but said 'no more': so too did the *Industrial Charter* accept the Attlee government's establishment of the National Health Service and the nationalisation of rail, coal, gas, and so forth, but it refused to let it go any further and abandon the 'mixed economy', which blended public with private ownership. The party's right wing fought to defeat the new approach, but was seen off at the party conference in Brighton in October 1947. The battle for the heart of the party had been won, bar a few right-wingers, most of whom were extinct volcanoes. Many of the key figures of the *Industrial Charter* – Butler himself, Harold Macmillan, Derick Heathcoat Amory, Reginald Maudling and Iain Macleod – were to play major roles in implementing these centrist, consensual policies over the following fifteen years.

Butler's leadership was vital in ensuring that the work of the Conservative Research Department (revived in 1946) received more recognition than earlier bodies, such as the Unionist Social Reform Committee, overlooked by Bonar Law, which had pressed for

The postwar team – from left to right (back row): Harold Macmillan, Captain H.F. Crookshank, Sir David Maxwell-Fyfe and (at front) Lord Salisbury, Lord Woolton, Anthony Eden and R.A. Butler meeting in Central Office in January 1950 *(Hulton/Getty)*

fresh, positive policies during 1911–14. Macmillan too was becoming an increasingly central figure. He had published an important if little-noticed book, *The Middle Way*, in 1938, arguing for a halfway position between outright capitalism and socialism (a stance which at the time placed him on the left of the party). In his later *Memoirs* he summed up the achievement after 1945: 'We had to convince the great postwar electorate that we accepted the need for full employment in the welfare state: we accepted equally the need for central planning and even, in times of scarcity, physical control. We had to devise and publicise a position between the old Liberalism and the new Socialism.' Macmillan perfectly encapsulated the position the Tory party held for thirty years after 1945. In his final sentence, change the words 'Liberalism' to 'Labour' and 'Socialism' to 'Right' and one also has the rationale behind, and explanation for, Labour's unique electoral success after 1997. Macmillan, not Blair, first championed the 'third way'.

The Conservative thinking bore fruit in the policy statement, *The Right Road for Britain*, in 1949 and in the manifesto for the 1950 general election, *This is the Road*. Thanks to an overhaul in party organisation, the party was much better equipped to fight this election than it had been in 1945. Call-up of agents and party workers had been partly responsible for the damage to organisation during the war, but matters began to improve dramatically when the retailer, Lord Woolton (who had been Minister for Food in the war), was appointed party chairman in July 1946, building on the underrated work of his predecessor, Ralph Assheton. By 1948, Central Office was fully operational again, and constituency and regional personnel and structures were reviving. A drive was made for new members, and by 1951 a figure approaching an extraordinary 2.8 million had been reached, with the Young Conservatives, set up in July 1946, a flourishing arm. Churchill's popularity provided a major reason for the increase in membership – another and under-recognised indicator of his importance as party head. After his departure, party membership indicatively began to fall.

Modernisation of candidate selection was overseen by David Maxwell-Fyfe, the future Home Secretary, who oversaw a report published in 1949 arguing that those of moderate means should not be debarred from becoming parliamentary candidates. This partly fulfilled Baldwin's dream in his 'new Conservatism' of 1924 of broadening the social base of the parliamentary party – although it was to be another twenty and more years before the party's social base showed clear signs of being genuinely widened. Political education was given a higher profile too after 1945, with the Conservative Political Centre (CPC) running courses and producing literature for the party membership to debate and disseminate. Quintin Hogg (Lord Hailsham) was commissioned to write the influential

'Penguin Special' book *The Case for Conservatism*. It was all part of a move to win intellectuals back to the party. The party's finances were revitalised too under Woolton, and its propaganda and media arms revolutionised. He began a fund for a new home for party headquarters, eventually to be opened in Smith Square, Westminster, in 1958.

The work of Butler and Woolton played its part, as did new constituency boundaries and postal voting, in the major Conservative recovery in the February 1950 general election. Although their share of the popular vote rose by less than 4 per cent, the Tories won back eighty-four seats, slashing Labour's overall majority from 146 to six. Churchill, sensing victory in his nostrils, became more active over the eighteen months of the second Attlee government. He tried unsuccessfully to convince the party of the value of a Con-Lib Pact. In the October 1951 election, the Liberals, without a pact and short of money to fight another general election so soon after 1950, would field only 109 candidates, of whom just six were successful with only 2.5 per cent of the popular vote, the Liberals' twentieth-century nadir. The absence of a Liberal candidate in so many constituencies (in contrast to 1950) meant anti-socialist voters often backed the Tory

candidate, helping to explain why a further twenty-eight seats were gained, giving the Tories a majority of seventeen. Ironically, the October 1951 general election saw Labour obtain 200,000 more votes than the Conservatives, and 48.8 per cent of the popular vote, the highest degree of public support in its history.

Churchill, once again in Downing Street, had a final opportunity to stamp his mark on his party and country. His appointments showed what the character of his government would be. He appointed Butler as Chancellor of the Exchequer rather than the more red-

Party workers prepare the eye-catching posters for the 1950 general election campaign. The messages are driven home unashamedly (*Bodleian Library*)

The 1951 general election. The scoreboard at the election night reception held by Lord Camrose, the owner of the *Daily Telegraph*, at the Savoy Hotel on election night, 25 October 1951. One of the results shows a certain Margaret Roberts failing to win the Kent seat of Dartford *(Hulton/Getty)*

blooded capitalist, Oliver Lyttelton, and the emollient Walter Monckton as Minister of Labour rather than David Maxwell-Fyfe, who had alarmed the trade unions with talk about their financial links to Labour. Right-wingers, such as former party chairman Ralph Assheton, Richard Law (son of Bonar Law) and Charles Waterhouse, were kept on the backbenches, while elder statesmen like Harry Crookshank and Lord Swinton were denied the ear of the leader they sought.

In area after area, Churchill, albeit with some wobbles, embedded a moderate, progressive Conservatism, which defined the party for a generation. In economic policy, the government was committed to maintaining full employment, in both rhetoric and practice – and unemployment never rose above half a million. Norman Macrae of *The Economist* coined the phrase 'Mr Butskell' to indicate the similarity of policies between the Labour Chancellor Hugh Gaitskell (1950–1) and Butler. Historians like Harriet

R.A. Butler arrives at Downing Street in 1953, pleased as Punch to be chairing Cabinet during Churchill's absence with a stroke (Hulton/Getty)

Jones have since questioned the extent of continuity of policy after 1951, and indeed the whole notion of a Labour-Conservative broad 'consensus' on policy between 1945 and 1975 pointing out how radical Labour was in power after 1945, and moves like the Tories' failed plan to make sterling convertible in 1952. But the fact is that, if one looks at the policies that governments of both parties pursued in power (as opposed to what they said in opposition), then continuity rather than abrupt reversal is what one sees across broad swathes of policy.

In industrial relations, the *Industrial Charter* complimented the trade unions on their 'great and vital part to play in industry'. The record of the unions in the Second World War, when they had loyally served the war effort, had been decisive in changing Tory thinking. After 1951 Monckton, with Churchill's warm encouragement, ensured that industrial harmony reigned: fewer days were lost in strikes each year under Churchill's premiership than under Attlee's. (Monckton became known as the 'oil can' for his easing of disputes.) The right grumbled about 'union appeasement', and later praised Thatcher's tough stance. But the task after 1951 was to show that the Conservatives, with the memories of the 1920s and 1930s still fresh, could work with the unions, especially as Labour before 1951 had predicted industrial anarchy if the Conservatives were to be elected to power.

After 1951, Churchill's only 'denationalisation' (as privatisation was then called) was two of the industries nationalised by Labour: iron and steel, and road haulage. The Tories argued that neither was a natural monopoly; in contrast, the other industries nationalised by Labour had suffered from years of under-investment, were ripe for a new national organisation, and were not viable standing on their own in a free market. In broadcasting, however, Churchill refused to back Attlee's move in 1950 to renew the BBC's monopoly, and under his leadership independent television first went on air in 1954.

Acceptance of the Attlee government's social policy was more problematic for the Conservatives. Despite the party's record of introducing social policy in the 1920s and 1930s, the *Industrial Charter* and other policy statements in opposition after 1945 had not produced a clear party line on welfare. The dominant view up to 1951 was in favour of selectivity and means testing. But, once in office, and boosted by the money flowing into the Exchequer in the affluent 1950s, the Tories were happy to finance a free and universal welfare state out of general taxation even at the cost of some mild inflation. Tough choices did not have to be made. Again, their acceptance of the welfare state owed much to Churchill. In housing, he even went beyond Labour. Appointing Macmillan in 1951 with an active brief as Minister of Housing, by 1953 the government had met its target of building 300,000 new houses a year. In the period up to 1964, the proportion of families owning their own houses doubled to almost half the population. The housing boom was facilitated by a relaxation of controls on building which was in tune with the Conservatives' wish to abandon Labour's unnecessary restrictions, summed up in the Tories' 1951 election slogan 'Set the People Free'.

Minister for Housing, Harold Macmillan, at the opening ceremony of a house in Barnet, Hertfordshire, the final one of the 300,000 new houses built in 1953. Macmillan had yet to cultivate his easy style in front of cameras: his rigid, uneasy manner is mirrored by his audience *(Hulton/Getty)*

In foreign policy, Churchill was the dominant force. Eden had disliked his staunchly anti-Soviet Union and pro-US line after 1945, but the deepening of the Cold War meant that Eden had to bow to Churchill's line. Churchill's warm espousal of a 'United States of Europe' proved to amount to little in policy terms after 1951, and Britain stood apart from plans to unite Europe in defence and economic federations. On the Empire, Churchill's unhappiness with India's independence in 1947 was echoed by his backing after 1951 for quelling insurgents fighting for independence in Malaya and Kenya. But he did not prove the reactionary leader resisting moves to self-government across the Empire that Labour had predicted. Most tellingly, he eventually backed, at a key meeting of the 1922 Committee, Eden's policy on pulling troops out of Egypt including, fatefully, the Suez zone. By siding with Eden rather than the pro-imperial right-wing caucus, Churchill had shown that, even on the policy most dear to his heart, he would move with the times. Even the cause of the 'Empire free trade', the last gasp of Joseph Chamberlain's 1903 policy, was killed off under his premiership, despite protests from Leo Amery and the old guard at successive party conferences.

In his response to Stalin's death in March 1953, Churchill also laid another ghost to rest, namely, that he would be a belligerent Prime Minister (the *Daily Mirror*, the Labour-supporting news-paper, had deployed the scare tactic on election day in 1951 with a headline 'Whose Finger on the Trigger?', imply-ing that Churchill would lead the country back into war, possibly even a nuclear one). Yet Churchill saw Stalin's death as conferring a unique historic opportunity, as the last survivor of the wartime Big Three (Roosevelt, Stalin and himself), to bring about a new understanding between the two sides in the Cold War. Although unsuccessful,

Succession at last: Churchill makes way for Eden in April 1955. Churchill doubted his ability to succeed – with justification (Hulton/Getty)

A 1955 election poster reminding voters of the austerity measures introduced by Labour after the war. An early example of negative advertising *(Bodleian Library)*

queues, controls, rationing

don't risk it again!

VOTE CONSERVATIVE

largely because he was thwarted by America's Eisenhower administration, he nevertheless anticipated the thaw of the late 1950s and the detente policy of the 1970s. Here again, Churchill was ahead of his time.

But time was one commodity Churchill did not have himself. He suffered a serious stroke in mid-1953, after minor strokes in 1949 and 1952. He kept giving Anthony Eden, his nominated successor since 1942, dates for his retirement: Queen Elizabeth's coronation in June 1953, his 80th birthday in November 1954. But he ultimately left in April 1955 at a moment of his choosing.

Tony Blair later had doubts about whether Gordon Brown, his long-serving heir apparent, was really up to the job. In Churchill's case, his doubts proved fully justified. At first, however, all looked well for Eden. He called an election in May 1955, weeks after his succession. Boosted by the aura of success at home and abroad, the Conservatives reached a postwar record in terms of the proportion of votes, with 49.7 per cent voting for the party, which translated into a very satisfactory majority of fifty-five. Eden was elated to have won his own mandate. But very soon his premiership came under attack, most vehemently from Churchill's son, Randolph, as well as from the *Daily Telegraph*, which famously bemoaned the absence of 'the smack of firm government' under his leadership. A deteriorating economy and a botched second budget in October 1955 did not help him. He became gloomy and defensive, exacerbated by what historians have since found out to be severe ill-health, requiring high levels of medication. He appeared neither knowledgeable nor comfortable with domestic policy. But it was his speciality, foreign policy, that was to be his undoing, as discussed in the box on the next two pages.

EDEN AND SUEZ 1956

Anthony Eden had first come to public prominence as the debonair, handsome and young Foreign Secretary appointed in December 1935 in the National Government. He resigned nominally over appeasement in February 1938, to be succeeded by Halifax, though vanity had as much to do with his decision as policy disagreement. He returned as Foreign Secretary in December 1940, but remained overshadowed by Churchill. As Churchill's designated successor, he effectively led the party for much of the 1945–51 period, and was an impressive Foreign Secretary from 1951 to 1955, with a particularly notable year in 1954 when he helped oversee a settlement at Geneva of the crisis in Vietnam, which held for a few years.

It is ironic, given his expertise, that that it was a foreign crisis that would break his premiership and his reputation, though recent biographers, notably Richard Thorpe, have tried to rehabilitate him. In July 1956 Abdul Nasser, the Egyptian leader, nationalised the Suez Canal. Since Disraeli's purchase, Britain had retained a substantial share in the international company based in Paris which owned the Canal. The legality of Nasser's action in international law was unclear, denying Eden an easy way out. The United Nations proved unhelpful in offering him an acceptable solution avoiding the need for war.

Eden was in a dilemma. Do nothing, and he would be hounded, possibly from office, by the party's right wing, who had not forgiven him for withdrawing from Egypt in 1954. But if he went for a military response, without UN backing, and without even any guarantee of American support, he risked isolation on the world stage. His conjuring up of images of Nasser as the new Hitler or Mussolini carried little weight abroad, but more at home above all in the Conservative Party, which at its annual conference in October 1956 bayed for a military success. Eden had already let himself

The handsome face of Anthony Eden, emblazoned on this 1955 election poster, had huge appeal – especially with women voters. Eden wanted, ironically, to sell himself as a 'man of peace' *(Bodleian Library)*

become embroiled in a secret plan in association with France and Israel: an Israeli attack on Egypt was to be halted by an Anglo-French invasion to keep the warring parties apart. The plan was as flawed as it was naive, but it was Eden's lying to his Cabinet about any such 'collusion' with Israel that so damaged his good name.

America did not come to Britain's defence when hostilities began, as Eden had hoped. Rather, Eisenhower, in the midst of his re-election in early November, effectively pulled the plug on the operation by withdrawing American support for sterling, and ensured that Britain and France retreated in humiliation to make way for a UN force. Eden, his health having crumbled, resigned in January 1957. He died almost exactly twenty years later to the day, carrying to his grave the conviction that he was right on Suez.

British troops in the sands of Egypt in 1956 *(PA)*

THE MACMILLAN PARTY

Macmillan had been one of the strongest advocates of a military response to Nasser in 1956. His confident line, in contrast to Butler's vacillating, was one factor that led the Cabinet to back him, not Butler, for the succession. He took over a divided and demoralised party, and a government widely expected to fall after a few weeks following what remains Britain's greatest humiliation of the last one hundred years. Yet he went on to revive the party, to lead it to one of the greatest victories of the century, and to become the leader who personified a whole period of Tory rule.

Macmillan proved the perfect leader for the age, as Baldwin and Churchill had done before him. His Etonian and Grenadier Guards background and marriage to the daughter of the Duke of Devonshire connected him backwards to the aristocratic tradition of the Salisburys and Churchills, while his family's humble origins in a Scottish

Harold Macmillan boards a train during the 1959 election campaign. He had good reason to be cheerful, with so much going his way *(Hulton/Getty)*

croft pointed forward to the meritocratic background of Heath, Thatcher and Major. With his languid, Edwardian style, he epitomised a bygone age, yet he was the first British Prime Minister to master television (as effectively as Baldwin had earlier mastered the radio and newsreel), he championed British power on the world stage, yet realised Britain had to relinquish its empire, seek its place in the European Community, and would have to depend on the United States for its nuclear technology; and he inflated the economy to pay for the burgeoning welfare state, yet also realised that government, industry and the social services (though not the unions) had to modernise and become more efficient.

His formative experiences as an officer in the trenches in the First World War (one shared with Churchill and Eden, but with no later Tory leader) inclined him towards a paternalistic attitude to those in his care, while his experience after 1924 as MP for the economically deprived Stockton-on-Tees constituency led him to see at first hand the suffering caused by depression and unemployment. Such experience informed his book *The Middle Way*, and, once in Number 10, he resolved that he would not let Treasury conservatism dampen the economy and cause unemployment, even at the risk of causing some inflation – 'a little inflation never hurt anyone', he used to say. He thus stood up to Peter Thorneycroft, his Chancellor of the Exchequer, in the public spending round for 1958-9, the last before the general election of 1959. Macmillan refused to let Thorneycroft pull in the fiscal belt too tightly, which prompted Thorneycroft's resignation along with his junior Treasury ministers, including Enoch Powell, who was thought to have emboldened Thorneycroft into being so uncompromising. The amount in dispute, a mere £50 million out of a total spend of £6 billion, seemed trivial, but it was the episode later highlighted by Powell, Thorneycroft and indeed Thatcher (who later appointed Thorneycroft her party chairman) as the shameful moment when Keynesian thinking triumphed over monetarism. The analogy was, of course, stretched too far, but it does reveal Macmillan's determination, for electoral and policy reasons, to avoid anything smacking of right-wing retrenchment. His staged response to the dismissals as 'little local difficulties' also showed his early mastery of 'soundbites'.

Macmillan was at the height of his power between 1957 and 1959. He held back on modernising policies which he knew would create shock waves until after the general election was safely won. For the time being, he exuded reassurance and calm, but also a toughness that surprised his Cabinet, as when he saw off the resignation of Lord Salisbury (the premier's grandson) in March 1957, ostensibly in protest at the release from jail of the pro-independence Archbishop Makarios in the British colony of Cyprus.

"I TOLD YOU THIS SORT OF STUFF WILL FETCH 'EM BACK INTO THE OLD CINEMA···"

The famous Vicky cartoon, Supermac, first published in the London *Evening Standard* on 17 November 1958. Gaitskell, top right, cowers. The doorman is Lord Hailsham, party chairman, celebrated for ringing a rallying bell at the recent party conference *(Centre for the Study of Cartoons and Caricature, University of Kent)*

The lesson Macmillan absorbed from Suez was that Britain should never again uncouple itself from the United States, and, trading on his wartime relationship with Eisenhower, he immediately set to work rebuilding their previous bond. His strategy for dealing with Suez was to ignore it: no enquiries, no recriminations, no discussion. Macmillan drew attention away from the Middle East by his tour of the Commonwealth in 1958 and his visit to Moscow in 1959. At the latter, his intuitive understanding of the media was seen in his donning a large white fur hat. This was the image everyone remembered long after the substance was forgotten. Just before the 1959 general election, Eisenhower shamelessly bolstered the Conservative cause by taking part in a joint broadcast with Macmillan from Number 10, illustrating vividly the total rehabilitation of Britain in the world community and the utter irrelevance of Suez.

Macmillan felt confident as the election approached. His own standing ran high, helped ironically by a cynical cartoon by Vicky in 1958 in the *Evening Standard* which dubbed him 'Supermac', a name immediately latched on to by his supporters as a term of approval, even reverence. Heathcoat Amory, Thorneycroft's more biddable successor as Chancellor, produced a tax-cutting budget in 1959, and the Tories were able to trade on the spread of affluence and consumer goods – televisions, washing machines, cars, even holidays abroad – to almost all sections of society. 'You've never had it so good', Macmillan had earlier intoned in 1957 (albeit not in those exact words). It became a slogan that was joined at the 1959 election by another, reminiscent of the red-scare tactics of old, 'Don't let Labour ruin it'. An extensive press and poster campaign, the most sophisticated in party history thanks to the advertising agency – Colman, Prentis and Varley – helped ram the message home. Labour offered little incentive for the electorate to switch allegiance: Hugh Gaitskell had succeeded Attlee as leader in December 1955, but proved no more able to lead a united party, nor one offering policies capable of persuading a settled electorate to switch its strong allegiances.

In the general election that Macmillan called for October 1959, the proportion of the country voting Tory dropped marginally from 49.7 per cent to 49.3 per cent, but the numbers of voters, due to more taking part, rose by nearly half a million, and the Conservative majority rose to over 100. The party won 365 seats to Labour's 258 and the Liberals' 6. It was the only time in the twentieth century that a party was elected three times in succession with increasing numbers of MPs, and was a spectacular vindication for Macmillan's style of leadership since 1957. Questions began to be asked whether Labour, at least with its current organisation and brand of policies, could ever win again, so out of tune did it appear to be with the heartland of Britain. One political socialist wrote a book entitled *Must Labour Lose?* As Macmillan's and the Tories' ratings rose still higher in 1960, and the party took a seat from Labour that March in a by-election in Yorkshire, it appeared that he would carry all before him.

With the recovery from Suez confirmed by the general election, Macmillan could now embark on the bolder half of his premiership, which he always knew would make enemies in the party. He pushed for more rapid progress to self-government in the Empire, heralded by the appointment of Iain Macleod as Colonial Secretary in October 1959 and his speech in Cape Town in February 1960 in which he spoke of a 'wind of change' sweeping through Africa in favour of black majority rule. (The right-wing, pro-empire and anti-immigration Monday Club took its name from the day that Macmillan delivered his speech.) At home, he opted for the corporatist policy of bringing representatives of industry and the unions together with government to agree and plan common objectives, so putting to an end, he hoped, years of futile dispute between capital and labour. These ideas bore fruit in the National Economic Development Council and the National Incomes Commission of 1961–2. This strategy proved a blind alley, however, due in part to the unions' inability to see the broader picture, and was tried unsuccessfully subsequently by both the Wilson and Heath governments. Macmillan established a variety of inquiries, of which the best-known were the Robbins inquiry into higher education (which prompted a huge expansion of universities) and the Buchanan inquiry into urban traffic (from which little changed, though railways were rationalised after the Beeching Report). Local government was reorganised, with the Greater London Council replacing the London County Council in 1963.

In April 1961 Macmillan opened discussions about the possibility of Britain joining the European Economic Community (EEC). Always a keen European, Macmillan was concerned that Britain had earlier missed the opportunity of joining the original six EEC nations who signed the Treaty of Rome in 1957. With party opposition coming in particular from the farming interest and the pro-Commonwealth lobby, Macmillan trod

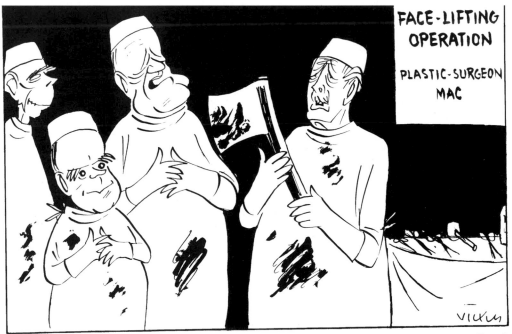

"WONDERFUL JOB, SIR! THE PUBLIC WAS GETTING A BIT BORED WITH THE SAME OLD FACES ..."

'The Night of the Long Knives' as depicted in this Vicky cartoon, first published in the *Evening Standard* on 13 July 1962. Home, Macleod and Butler in attendance *(Centre for the Study of Cartoons and Caricature, University of Kent)*

Macmillan's grouse-shooting became an object of satire by the early 1960s. The Tory Prime Minister enjoys the open air with Christopher Soames, Minister of Agriculture, during a shoot in Yorkshire in 1961 *(Hulton/Getty)*

Sir Alec Douglas-Home, with some scepticism, watching himself on television *(Hulton/Getty)*

stealthily. Macmillan saw British entry as the cornerstone policy of his second term. So when President de Gaulle vetoed Britain's entry in January 1963, his foreign and to some extent his domestic policies were suddenly in tatters. He had hoped to rejuvenate his government by his dismissal of seven Cabinet Ministers in the so-called 'Night of the Long Knives' reshuffle of July 1962. But not even this brave, even foolhardy, move gave Macmillan the lift or the fresh image for his government he sought.

Hard though Macmillan swam, he could not prevail against a tide flowing ever more strongly against him. The end of the 1950s heralded one of those periodic cultural shifts which are as hard to predict as they are to explain. The weight of intellectual opinion, offended by Suez, began turning away from the government. Bookshops suddenly became full of volumes critical of government policy, the state of Britain and its institutions. As in the late nineteenth century, concern spread that Britain's competitors, Germany, the United States, Japan and France, were doing much better economically, and that Britain's economy and political class were stagnant.

Macmillan himself began to look old and out of touch, an image accentuated by the advent of John F. Kennedy as President of the United States from January 1961. Macmillan began to be parodied as an aristocrat fit just for shooting grouse on moors in the north. In December 1959 Hugh Greene took over as Director-General of the BBC and quickly established a regime far less deferential to government. The satirical magazine, *Private Eye*, the television comedy *That Was The Week That Was* and the review *Beyond the Fringe* all date from, and encapsulate the mood of, these times. The year 1962 was particularly damaging for the government, with the most days lost through strikes since the general strike in 1926 and the loss of Orpington in Kent to the Liberals in a celebrated by-election. Then in 1963 came the Profumo scandal, which was badly handled by a prime minister who appeared both gullible and incompetent. Macmillan loyally if credulously backed his War Minister, Profumo, who subsequently admitted he had lied to the House of Commons about his affair with the prostitute Christine Keeler. The episode contributed to an aroma of distrust and decay.

Macmillan's continued leadership had been called into question, but it was a breakdown of his health that made him finally decide to resign. The leadership contest that followed, described in Chapter 6, took place during the week of the annual party conference at Blackpool in October 1963. Macmillan fought from his hospital bed to thwart Butler's last hopes of inheriting the crown for which he yearned. From a highly charged contest, the Earl of Home emerged as a compromise candidate who, in an earlier guise, had been Neville Chamberlain's Parliamentary Private Secretary during the Munich crisis.

Not since 1902, with Salisbury, had a prime minister sat in the House of Lords, and a rushed by-election saw the new leader reincarnated into the Commons as Sir Alec Douglas-Home, the third Etonian Tory leader in a row. He was handicapped by two of the ablest Conservative ministers, Macleod and Powell, refusing to serve under him, and the government then went on to alienate many supporters by Heath abolishing resale price maintenance. Despite a valiant year of fighting, it succumbed to Labour in the general election of October 1964. Not even a 'dash for growth' under Maudling, the new Chancellor, succeeded in wooing voters back to the cause. What was remarkable about the election, discussed on the next two pages, however, was how close the Conservatives in fact came to winning it. Labour achieved less than 1 per cent more of the popular vote, winning just 317 seats to the Tories' 304. Douglas-Home clung on as opposition leader for another nine months before being pushed aside. An era of Tory dominance, in electoral terms the most emphatic in its history, thus came to an end. Labour dismissed the period 1951–64 as 'thirteen wasted years', which was overly harsh and ignored the many achievements and modernisations carried through; Labour's own record of office in 1964–70, moreover, showed that it, no more than the Tories, possessed all the solutions to Britain's underlying problems.

ALEC DOUGLAS-HOME'S DEPARTURE 1964

Alec Douglas-Home received politics' equivalent to a hospital pass in rugby when he succeeded Harold Macmillan as premier in October 1963. The Tory party had already been in office for twelve years, and the next general election could not be more than twelve months away. The country and the media were growing tired of the Tories, their strongest policies had been enacted, and some of their most able lieutenants were burnt out or refusing to serve.

Yet Alec Douglas-Home brought the Tories back to within a whisker of beating Harold Wilson's Labour Party in the October 1964 general election. He battled hard for a year, preparing his party for the election, and worked tirelessly during the campaign. Party apparatchiks, deciding that his aristocratic appearance and oddly shaped head were a liability on television, saw that he would best serve the party by travelling around the country in person. Face to face, few could resist his charm.

Unpublished diaries provide a vivid portrait of the emotional last hours of Tory rule after thirteen years. Alec and Elizabeth Douglas-Home arrived back at Downing Street at 9.30 p.m. on election day, Thursday 15 October, from Perth. They gathered around a television in the corner ('white') drawing-room with their staff to listen to the first results.

A moment of belief that they could win came with the retaining of Billericay:

immediately 'everyone rushed for the drink'. The 'garden room girls' (Number 10's secretarial team) were following the news two floors below, all dressed in blue and all nervous: 'They were glued to the television damning Harold Wilson for all they were worth, as were the drivers, messengers and detectives.' But as the night wore on, the news turned bad. Elizabeth Home, ever thoughtful, went up in the lift to the third floor to give the switchboard girls a drink.

Before dawn, and believing they had lost, the Homes retired to bed. Yet the news that greeted them the next morning, Friday 16 October, was not discouraging: Labour had still to secure the magical figure of 316 seats needed for a majority, and the morning's results were going less well for Labour. A lunch party for a dozen, including Cabinet ministers Ted Heath and Reginald Maudling, was held on Number 10's first floor.

In the early afternoon, after a tantalising period when Labour remained fixed on 315 seats, the target was passed, and Labour finished up with an overall majority of four. As one diarist wrote, 'Many spirits fell again when Sir Alec had to go off to the Palace. As he went out [into Downing Street] everyone booed. Poor Lady Home was taking photos out of the window – it must have hurt her horribly and I hate them for it, especially as loud cheers accompanied Mr Wilson's arrival at 4 p. m. As if defeat was not enough, in the middle of the afternoon we heard China had exploded her first atom bomb.' News of the fall of the moderate Soviet leader, Khrushchev, also began to circulate. To the stunned and exhausted figures in Number 10, it must have appeared as if a brave new socialist era had truly dawned.

Trapped upstairs, with Wilson now ensconced in the Cabinet room believing that his predecessor had left the building, the Homes decided to make their getaway by the back door. Slipping down the grand staircase like furtive refugees, they passed the Cabinet floor, now in the hands of 'the enemy', and at the door to the garden were met by some of the staff. It was customary for the outgoing prime minister to write a letter of good wishes to the incomer. Sir Alec, having written in his own hand 'To the Prime Minister', handed the letter to Jane Parsons (the head of the Garden Room girls), which 'nearly finished her'. In the room directly above, the official team, which only hours earlier had ministered to Alec Home, were now helping plan Harold Wilson's new government. The Homes stole silently and unnoticed across the Number 10 garden to the gate in the back wall and out into Horse Guards Parade.

So rushed was their departure that Elizabeth Home and her secretary, Lorne Roper-Caldbeck, had to return to the flat on Monday 19 October, after a weekend at Chequers, to complete the packing. It was a race against the clock, but they were helped by the Number 10 staff; the affection the Homes had inspired after only a year in Number 10 was extraordinary. Lady Home saw their enforced

Douglas-Home leaves Downing Street during the ill-fated 1964 general election campaign *(PA)*

departure as a 'splendid opportunity to throw out unvalued possessions', including a large store of her husband's medicines. While she was doing so, Mary Wilson, although still living in Hampstead Garden suburb, was asked up to the flat by Lady Home. She looked 'very miserable and was on the verge of tears. What a prospect it must all be for her!'

The building was already bubbling with gossip, above all about Marcia Williams seizing the room adjoining the Cabinet room for her office. In a final act of defiance, the Homes' secretaries left their Tory posters in the room in the flat that they had used as their office. Of all transfers of power since 1945, the 1964 transition was the most polarised and aroused the most mutual animosity and suspicion.

This passage is adapted from Anthony Seldon's Number Ten: The Illustrated History.

It is easy to understand the Tories electoral success during 1951–64. As the Liberal vote never exceeded 6 per cent, the real battle was between only two parties, with the century's high point in the two-party system coming in 1951 when Labour and the Conservatives won 97 per cent of the popular vote between them. The middle classes voted solidly (over 75 per cent) for the Tories in the general elections, but over half the Conservative voting strength came from the working classes, who felt their interests were better served by voting for them. The three successive Tory leaders who won the elections (Churchill, Eden and Macmillan) were all very popular figures at the time the contests took place: in contrast, Attlee in 1951 and 1955 appeared uncharismatic and jaded, and Gaitskell, his successor, had little chance against the known, experienced Macmillan in 1959. Indicatively, the young Harold Wilson, who succeeded Gaitskell after his death in January 1963, proved the leader to capture the mood and the popular imagination in the 1964 election.

The Tory dominance was not only down to its superior leaders. The Tories were better organised and funded for much of the period, and exploited more successfully the new propaganda tools of television and advertising. The Tories' programmes for office also chimed more sonorously with the electorate. In the 1951 election Labour's attempt to play the 'blue-scare' card backfired, whereas the Tories' promise of freedom and an end to austerity suited a nation weary of rationing and controls. In 1955 and 1959, they had a solid record in office to present to the electorate. The public wanted growth, welfare and full employment: the Tories duly delivered them. Economists will long debate whether the economy was strong despite rather than because of Tory economic policy, but there is no doubt that the Tories benefited from it electorally. By 1964, however, Labour, whose policies in the 1950s had appeared radical and unclear, now appeared to offer more of what the electorate wanted. The Conservatives had little fight to offer in their manifesto, *Prosperity with a Purpose*, which had a defensive tone absent from their three preceding manifestos.

Electoral circumstances also worked in the Tories' favour in the 1950s elections. Boundary changes coming into operation in 1950 cost Labour perhaps twenty-five seats, while the new postal vote scheme may have cost them another ten. Above all, the Conservatives benefited, as they had for much of their history, from the support of the most powerful voices in society, the press proprietors, opinion-formers and captains of industry and finance. By 1963–4, even they were beginning to tire of the Conservatives and to believe that, in Harold Wilson, Britain had found the man the nation now needed.

THE HEATH BLIND ALLEY: 1965–75

To dismiss Heath's ten-year leadership as a blind alley may seem harsh. He had more hinterland than most Tory leaders in the twentieth century, being a musician and a conductor of deep learning and some talent, a committed yachtsman who sailed to success in Australia's Sydney to Hobart race in 1969, and a writer with more feeling for language and his audience than many politicians turned authors. He was singly unfortunate to come to the leadership at the end of one long period of Tory ascendancy, to have a party divided over economic and industrial relations policy, and at a time of widespread international student and labour unrest, of the 'troubles' beginning again in Northern Ireland, and of war in the Middle East leading to a quadrupling of oil prices.

Yet a blind alley his leadership was. He lost three of the four general elections he fought, a record almost as poor as Balfour's. He was bright, energetic and tenacious, but he lacked many of the qualities of leadership, including charm and ease of communication: the often fierce loyalty he aroused in close subordinates was not reciprocated among a wider audience. He never won the party's affection when leader (though he had been highly popular when first elected an MP in 1950), and he presided over a steep fall in party membership. For all his extensive work rethinking policy in opposition, he advanced it little in office beyond Macmillan's positions of 1961–3, and he eschewed

attempts to lead the party in the fresh direction identified by Mrs Thatcher, rebuffing those, especially after February 1974, who attempted to articulate these ideas. He was indeed more open to the ideas of civil servants (and was often closer to them personally) than he was to the party, to intellectuals or commentators. Most telling of all, many of his policy achievements during 1970–4 were undone during the years after his fall from power in

Edward Heath aboard his yacht *Morning Cloud* at Cowes in august 1971 *(Hulton/Getty)*

February 1974, save in one main area, taking Britain into the EEC, which had been the cause of thirty years of division within the party.

None foresaw such an unhappy record when in August 1965 Heath beat Maudling (just) and Powell (easily) for the leadership of the party in its first electoral contest among MPs. He was selected as the candidate most likely, with his classless background and fine intellect, to match Wilson in debate and broad appeal. His early years as leader were not helped by his being the first in many years to come to power when the party was out of office, but he imposed his authority on the party by consolidating in 1965 the biggest policy review in its history, which at its height involved thirty separate committees or working groups. With the likelihood of Wilson calling an early general election, the findings were published quickly, enabling the party to boast at the March 1966 general election that it had 131 specific policy proposals, in a programme entitled *Action Not Words*. The electorate was as uncomprehending of the verbiage as it was unimpressed by the ideas, and accorded Wilson a landslide majority of ninety-six. Although the Tories were ahead in the polls for much of the ensuing four years, Heath had a hard time, and the quality of his leadership was repeatedly questioned. Policy review work resumed at a great tempo, but the final reworking of policy in the manifesto for the June 1970 general election, *A Better Tomorrow*, departed little in broad substance from the rushed work of 1965. Much was made early in the year, following a conference of the shadow cabinet at the Selsdon Park Hotel in south London, about Heath taking the party in a more ideological, right-wing direction. A new 'Selsdon group' was formed on its back. In fact, the conference, convened to approve the overall policy, was not heralding any right-wing strategic shift, in part because the shadow Cabinet was fundamentally undecided on the key issue of the day, economic and incomes policy.

One of the *Action Not Words* posters from the unsuccessful 1966 campaign. Deteriorating trade union relations would help bring down both Wilson's government in 1970 and that of Heath four years later *(Bodleian Library)*

Two of the most talented figures of their generation: Reginald Maudling and Iain Macleod at the 1965 conference *(Bodleian Library)*

Edward Heath, Margaret Thatcher and Lord Hailsham in the garden of 10 Downing Street shortly after the victory in June 1970. Few would have expected Mrs Thatcher, the new Education Secretary, to be at the party's helm within five years. The future 'iron lady' already brandishes some metal *(Hulton/Getty)*

Heath's government, ironically in view of all the preparation over the previous five years, did not know where it was going, in fact, on many other key issues. Even without the crises in the Middle East and Northern Ireland, the Cabinet, which remained unusually leak-free and loyal, would have struggled to know where exactly it was steering Britain – except into Europe, Heath's pet project. The second rebuff of British entry by de Gaulle, to Wilson in 1967, made Heath even more determined to succeed, and he was helped immeasurably by loyal colleagues and by Chief Whip Francis Pym's insistence on a free vote. Heath's dream was fulfilled on 1 January 1973.

Heath was badly weakened by the death only one month after the 1970 general election of his ablest lieutenant, Macleod, whom he had made his Chancellor of the Exchequer. His successor, Anthony Barber, lacked many of his qualities and political feel. In Heath's first eighteen months, the strongly anti-union Industrial Relations Act was passed, and a host of measures passed to free up the economy. But when unemployment reached the psychologically important figure of one million in January 1972, Heath lost confidence in the pro-capitalist policies he had been pursuing since the election. Too much has been made of his embarking on a complete 'U-turn' in 1972, but the Industry Act of 1972, which afforded considerable potential for intervention in industry, marked a real change in direction; and the government also became actively involved in managing prices and incomes. The trade unions were not to be pacified, however, and, with the oil price rises in the autumn of 1973, and the miners spoiling for a fight to kill off the 'anti-union government', Heath called an election in February 1974 (which he was sure he would win) to seek a mandate to deal with the industrial crisis, hoping he would keep everyone focused on the core question 'who governs Britain?' The answer in the election was inconclusive. The Tories won more votes but fewer seats than Labour. Heath failed to do a deal with the Liberals to form a government, and when they turned him down he tried with the Ulster Unionists. When they also rejected his overtures, he left Wilson to form a minority Labour government. In a second general election in October 1974, Wilson won a small overall majority and Heath suffered a third and final defeat. Four months later he was gone. For Heath, it was a bitter and undeserved end. He was not much missed. There never was a Heath Tory party.

F I V E

THE THATCHER PARTY: 1975–2003

T he principal objective of most Tory MPs after the second general election defeat in 1974 was to find a leader who was 'anyone but Ted'. They did not expect to find a leader who was to dominate the party for the next thirty years: the first fifteen as its leader, with conspicuous electoral and policy success; the second as a brooding if diminishing presence, a figure who anointed, and then became disappointed by each successor until her ghost was finally laid to rest by Michael Howard. No other leader in the party's history had such a long direct influence on it.

THE UPHILL JOURNEY: 1975–9

While many of Heath's senior colleagues in the Shadow Cabinet stayed loyal to him, it became clear throughout 1974 that they were increasingly isolated from the party in Parliament and in the country. Heath's refusal to allow any debate on economic policy of differing viewpoints to his own precipitated Keith Joseph, popularly if erroneously regarded as the most brilliant senior figure in the party after Macleod's death, to found with Margaret Thatcher and outside support, the Centre for Policy Studies (CPS) in mid-1974. This was an alternative think-tank to the Conservative Research Department and it tapped into the monetarist and liberal economic thinking which was increasingly

Margaret Thatcher with her intellectual mentor, Keith Joseph *(PA)*

capturing the attention of the intelligentsia and opinion informers in Britain, and which had been promulgated since 1957 by the influential Institute of Economic Affairs. The CPS offered a very different solution from Heath's to the economic problems racking Britain, holding, above all, government responsible for inflation by allowing too much money to circulate (i.e. the doctrine of monetarism). Whereas Heath (like Macmillan before him) had seen government as the solution, Joseph and his colleagues saw ever-larger government as the problem.

When Joseph backed down in late 1974 as a challenger to Heath, Thatcher quickly declared her interest, espousing the liberal economic ideas she had first become attracted to in the late 1960s. At first her candidacy was not taken very seriously – she was too junior, a woman, not clubbable, too intense – but her cause was bolstered considerably by Airey Neave (later murdered by the IRA in 1979) agreeing to become her campaign manager. Edward du Cann, a popular figure in the party, withdrew late in the day for personal reasons, leaving the field clear for her to challenge Heath head-on. Heath treated her challenge with characteristic disdain, confident he would easily beat her. In the first ballot (under the new rules introduced by Alec Douglas-Home) Heath won 119 votes to Thatcher's 130. He immediately stood down and went into a sulk, her supporters said, from which he never fully recovered. Central Office was so sure of a

Heath victory, Ramsden records, that the press department was not manned on the evening the result was declared – leaving a Polish porter to field questions all night long from the international press. For the second ballot, support flowed to her from the party in the country and the Tory press. Some had not yet fully understood the new brand of policy she was espousing, but they liked the fact that she had conviction. These were worrying times: the very fabric of the state was under attack, and she exuded confidence that she had the answers. In the second ballot, she won 146 votes, Willie Whitelaw 79, James Prior 19, Geoffrey Howe 19, and John Peyton 11. On 11 February 1975, Mrs Thatcher duly became leader of the Conservative Party.

Heath's departure from front-bench politics, and the refusal of his loyalist colleagues Geoffrey Rippon and Peter Walker to serve, initially damaged her ability to heal the rift caused by the election. But it did at least clear the air. Whitelaw's acceptance of the post of deputy leader greatly helped her to reach sections of the parliamentary party that would otherwise have been out of her reach, and he helped persuade most of her front-bench team to serve. But a scepticism among them about her personally, and her new brand of policy, was to endure throughout the Opposition period; only with sackings and reshuffles in 1981–3 was she able to stamp her mark fully on her team.

The Thatcher shadow Cabinet in 1979. Carrington and Whitelaw are on her right, Joseph and Angus Maude on her left. Prior, Thorneycroft, Howe and Hailsham sit opposite. Airey Neave, murdered by the IRA just before the 1979 election, sits in the middle at the top (Camera Press)

Don't just hope for a better life. Vote for one.

VOTE CONSERVATIVE ☒

A coiffed Mrs Thatcher is sold as a positive asset in the 1979 election *(Bodleian Library)*

Thatcher had first to win arguments with her parliamentary colleagues about the future direction of Tory policy. Most were still wedded to the Keynesian prescriptions offered by Heath, and came later to be termed the 'wets'— as opposed to the 'dries', those who followed the free enterprise, anti-state policies espoused by Thatcher, Joseph and also Howe, whom recently released archives at Churchill College, Cambridge, reveal to have been an even more effective champion of the new thinking than Joseph. Charles Moore, Mrs Thatcher's official biographer, believes Joseph's prime importance was to encourage others to question convention. All three were prepared to drive forward anti-inflationary, monetarist policies even at the cost of seeing unemployment rise to levels hitherto thought unacceptable. Thatcher set up a number of policy groups, the first fruit of which was *The Right Approach*, published in October 1976, followed a year later by *The Right Approach to the Economy* and then the manifesto itself in 1979. All the time the party was edging itself in a more monetarist direction, but stealthily, and without alienating the party's traditionalists, nor saddling it with the kind of detailed commitments which were seen to have handicapped Heath in the 1966 and 1970 elections.

Thatcher also tightened her personal control over the party. She made Thorneycroft, hero of the 1958 Treasury crisis, her party chairman, with a brief to restore the membership, morale and finances lost during the Heath decade. He did not fail her. Together they purged the organisation of Heath loyalists. She appointed Angus Maude, sacked by Heath, chairman of the Conservative Research Department, Joseph to take charge of policy development (as chairman of the Advisory Committee on Policy) and Howe to work with Joseph on developing the new economic policy. Following earlier precedents, an advertising agency was employed, Saatchi and Saatchi, whose mainly negative campaign on Labour's record in office since 1974 was encapsulated in the telling slogan 'Labour isn't Working'. The troubled record of Labour under Wilson until

1976 and then James Callaghan, the persistent union troubles and the climax of the 'winter of discontent' in 1978–9, convinced voters that the fresh faces now leading the Conservative Party deserved their support. A missed opportunity to call an election in the autumn of 1978 may have cost Callaghan victory. The Tory vote in the May 1979 general election rose from 35.8 per cent in October 1974 to 43.9 per cent, resulting in a very workable majority of forty-three. Britain had its first woman prime minister. It remained to be seen in exactly what direction she would lead the country.

THE THATCHER PREMIERSHIP: 1979–90

Mrs Thatcher began cautiously. She appointed a Cabinet that largely mirrored the views of her parliamentary party, which was more 'wet' than 'dry'. Yet in the area she cared about most, economic policy, she refused to compromise. Installing her fellow radical Howe as Chancellor, she began her assault on the economic foundations of the postwar consensus. Howe's early budgets were marked by a radicalism that left her opponents reeling. Her central aim was to control inflation through the edicts of monetarism, and a pretty pure form of monetarism at that. While ortho-dox Keynesian economists urged repeatedly that public spending needed to rise to reduce grow-ing unemployment, Thatcher and her monetarist crew persisted with their argument that inflation had to be tamed first, even at the cost of high unemployment. Only then would economic recovery be built on solid foundations.

In the first year of her government the wets stuck by their new leader, despite their growing private incredulity at her policies. Yet by the end of the 1980s, as both inflation and unemploy-ment rose and Britain fell deeper into recession, sniping at her leadership began to break out into

Margaret Thatcher with her loyal husband Denis on the steps of 10 Downing Street on 4 May 1979
(Hulton/Getty)

the open. Mrs Thatcher fought back. At the 1980 conference she threw down the gauntlet to her critics: 'U-turn if you want to', she taunted them, 'the Lady's not for turning'. She continued the assault in January 1981 with her first reshuffle, sacking Norman St John-Stevas, one of her most overt critics. Despite her resolve, the situation in the country showed little sign of improving. Unemployment spiralled and in April riots broke out in Brixton and Liverpool. Mrs Thatcher's critics linked this social unrest to the government's economic strategy. Spurred on by the growing criticism, the wets regrouped, rebelling in a critical July Cabinet meeting to block further cuts in public expenditure. Mrs Thatcher refused to back down. She bided her time before launching a second Cabinet reshuffle in September. This time she was more ruthless and sacked her most stubborn opponents, Mark Carlisle, Ian Gilmour and Christopher Soames, and demoted others, including Prior. Her own type were promoted, including Leon Brittan

Survivors are brought ashore at Bluff Cove on the Falklands, from *HMS Galahad* after an Argentinian air attack on 29 June 1982 *(PA)*

The Thatchers and Cecil Parkinson, party chairman, celebrate the party's overwhelming victory in 1983. The party won an overall majority of 144 (Camera Press)

and Norman Tebbit. The reign of the wets had finally drawn to a close.

Mrs Thatcher's supporters insist that by the time of the 1982 budget the economic position was finally beginning to turn, justifying her tough policies, although her government remained extremely unpopular in the country. Yet all this was to change. In April 1982 Argentina, led by the dictator General Galtieri, invaded the Falkland Islands, a British dependency 6,000 miles away in the South Atlantic. Mrs Thatcher has faced harsh criticism from the left for her determination to restore British rule in the Falklands, but at the time the demands for action came from all quarters. Even Michael Foot, the Labour leader, declared that Britain had a 'moral duty, a political duty and every other sort of duty' to win back the Islands.

After a difficult debate in the House of Commons, Foreign Secretary Lord Carrington and two junior ministers decided to resign. In a bid for unity, Thatcher appointed Francis Pym, an arch-wet, as the new Foreign Secretary. International diplomacy then took centre stage. For Mrs Thatcher, however, diplomacy was all very well so long as the end result was the unconditional withdrawal of Argentinian forces. To make this point clear, she authorised the dispatch of a military task force, capable of retaking the Islands by force if necessary. Diplomatic efforts rumbled on but Galtieri refused to accept an unconditional withdrawal, and Mrs Thatcher would settle for nothing less. Hostilities began on 25 April, and several weeks of intense fighting followed. British victory was by no means assured and defeat would have destroyed not only British prestige but also, very likely, Mrs Thatcher's political career. These were tense times. Finally, however, on 14 June Argentina surrendered and Mrs Thatcher's popularity surged.

A year later the Tories won the 1983 general election by a landslide. The Falklands victory had certainly played a role, not least in bolstering her self-confidence and authority in the party; but so had the growing economic recovery and, most significantly, the state of the Opposition faced by Mrs Thatcher. Following the 1981 breakaway by the Social Democratic Party (SDP), the Labour Party had swung to the left, alienating the mass of moderate voters. With the Opposition hopelessly divided and Labour under Foot utterly ineffectual, Mrs Thatcher's hegemony was assured. Radical reform and new-found boldness now burst forth.

It was in Thatcher's second term that the policy of privatising state assets came into its own. While privatisation began gingerly during the first term, with government shares in British Aerospace, BP and Britoil sold off, the policy was now radically accelerated. In November 1984 British Telecom became the first public utility to be sold and was followed by British Gas in 1986 and British Airways and Rolls-Royce in 1987. Thus was spreading of share ownership added to the Tories' traditional policy of encouraging home ownership, which was given added wings when Thatcher's policy of allowing council house tenants to buy their own homes also gathered pace. Mrs Thatcher's Conservative Party was thus able to establish itself as the party of 'popular capitalism', with many people owning their own homes and buying shares for the first time. Implicit in this policy was that assets would be sold off at attractive prices. When these assets inevitably increased in value, grateful voters returned the favour at the ballot box. The support she received from the working classes was one of the defining features of her leadership of the party.

The second term was also marked by Mrs Thatcher's epic struggle with the unions, or more specifically with Arthur Scargill, President of the National Union of Mineworkers (NUM). Mrs Thatcher believed that the unions had become far too powerful and too politically motivated, and that their insistence on maintaining inefficient working practices was holding back the British economy. In 1980 and again in 1982 her government had introduced new legislation that chipped away at the unions' legal privileges. She had absorbed the lesson of Heath's 1971 Industrial Relations Act: don't try to do everything in one go. A further Act limiting union powers followed in 1984. In 1980, when confronted by the threat of a miners' strike in response to plans for pit closures, Mrs Thatcher backed down. She was not yet ready for a confrontation. The pits stayed open. The issue returned in March 1984 when plans to close around twenty 'uneconomic' pits were presented by the National Coal Board (NCB). This time there would be no government climbdown.

Knowing that a confrontation with the miners was almost inevitable, Mrs Thatcher's government had secretly built up emergency stockpiles of coal to ensure power stations could remain open even if strikes forced the pits to close. Once Scargill announced his intention to lead the miners out on strike, the government publicly refused to become involved, claiming it was a dispute between the NUM and the NCB. Behind the scenes, however, Mrs Thatcher did everything she could to advise and support the NCB, including insisting on a forceful police presence at pickets, to counteract attempts by striking miners to intimidate their colleagues into joining the strike. The strike lasted from 12 March 1984 to 3 March 1985 and cost the country over £2 billion, but enough miners kept working to prevent an NUM victory. Crucially for Mrs Thatcher, Scargill's

Mrs Thatcher's foe, Arthur Scargill, President of the National Union of Mineworkers, rallying miners in London during the miners' strike in 1984 *(PA)*

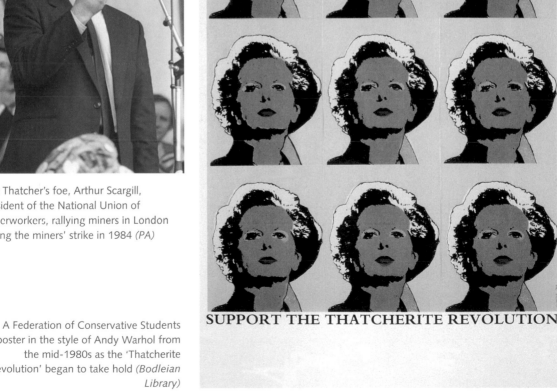

SUPPORT THE THATCHERITE REVOLUTION

A Federation of Conservative Students poster in the style of Andy Warhol from the mid-1980s as the 'Thatcherite Revolution' began to take hold *(Bodleian Library)*

miners ultimately returned to work without winning concessions. The strike had failed and the belief that democratically elected governments could not survive in office without the support of the NUM had finally been shattered. It was, without doubt, one of the greatest triumphs.

Mrs Thatcher's boldness extended to her attitude towards Europe. When she came to office, Britain was the largest contributor to Europe's budget, even though British income was below the EEC average. In 1980 she had seized upon this fact as manifestly unfair and eventually negotiated a reduction, which lasted for three years. In 1984 an increasingly self-confident and aggressive Mrs Thatcher was determined to find a permanent solution. To the fury of her European partners, beginning at the Stuttgart EEC summit in 1983, Mrs Thatcher simply refused to discuss EEC business until a permanent British rebate was agreed. A year later the Europeans finally gave in. Mrs Thatcher had her rebate and once again felt vindicated. Critics claim she could have reached a solution more amicably, which would have led to less bitterness among fellow leaders. But Mrs Thatcher was unrepentant. Toughness worked, she insisted. And, of course, 'Europe bashing' did little harm to her support back home, especially among an increasingly Euro-sceptic party and press.

Mrs Thatcher's second term also saw a breakthrough in Irish policy, which followed increasingly bold and lethal attacks on British targets by the IRA. These included the murder of the Queen's cousin, Lord Mountbatten, in August 1979 and the 1982 bomb at Horse Guards Parade. In October 1984 the IRA almost succeeded in killing Mrs Thatcher and the Cabinet by bombing the Grand Hotel at Brighton. Despite these atrocities, negotiations with the Irish government finally bore fruit in the Anglo-Irish Agreement, signed in November 1985. Condemned as treacherous by many Unionists, who feared it brought a united Ireland a step closer, the agreement aimed to strengthen cooperation between the British and Irish governments, particularly regarding security. With hindsight the agreement can be seen as a bold initiative on the government's part, the first step on the long road that led to Major's breakthroughs and eventually to the Good Friday Agreement of 1998. Neither Salisbury nor Bonar Law would have approved of what she did: it was one of the few occasions where she went against the party's right wing.

Yet, for all her achievements, the second term was not all plain sailing for Mrs Thatcher. Some colleagues became increasingly restless with her domineering style of government (she was often dubbed 'presidential'), and her pronounced right-wing views. One minister in particular was determined to push matters to a head. His name was

A young Michael Heseltine. His departure from Mrs Thatcher's Cabinet over the Westland affair was a significant moment in her leadership (Hulton/Getty)

Michael Heseltine. The catalyst for a confrontation between the two was a dispute over the troubled Westland company, Britain's only helicopter manufacturer. Facing bankruptcy, Westland had received the offer of a lifeline from an American firm, Sikorsky; but Heseltine, then Defence Secretary and a keen European, wanted to organise a European-backed rescue. Mrs Thatcher felt this was not an issue for the government and was happy to allow the American bid to go ahead. There followed a pungent battle of wills between Heseltine and the Prime Minister, lasting several months. It culminated in Heseltine dramatically walking out of Cabinet in January 1986 and announcing his resignation to the waiting media.

Mrs Thatcher's supporters claimed that Heseltine resigned because he was unable to prevail over Westland and, knowing that further promotion under her was unlikely, was looking for an excuse to leave the government. Heseltine, however, lambasted Thatcher's style of government. He claimed that he had been denied his constitutional right to a Cabinet debate on Westland and had been subject to dirty tricks designed to discredit him, including the leak of a confidential law officer's letter. The latter was a very serious charge. Had it been proved that Mrs Thatcher was involved in the leaking, she would have certainly resigned. No hard evidence of this emerged at the time, however, and she survived. Loyalists dismissed Westland as Heseltine's personal vendetta, but other MPs began to reflect on just how domineering Mrs Thatcher had become.

By mid-1986, as the prospect of an election loomed, the party united around their leader. Helped by growing signs of economic recovery, Mrs Thatcher's popularity received a much-needed boost and she won a historic third general election victory in 1987. Conservative support fell slightly in comparison with 1983, in part because Labour was beginning its long march back to sanity under Neil Kinnock, who succeeded Foot as

Willie Whitelaw was the rock of Mrs Thatcher's government until his retirement in 1988 *(Hulton/Getty)*

leader in 1983. But, with a majority of 101, the result was still a triumph for Mrs Thatcher, and was a high watermark for the party. She was determined that her revolution would continue, with renewed impetus.

In the third term of the Thatcher government, the Prime Minister's radical agenda extended to social policy. The 1988 Education Reform Act saw a Thatcherite push to raise standards in schools by establishing a National Curriculum and key 'attainment targets' for students. Funding for schools was reorganised in an attempt to provide incentives to improve quality, giving schools the chance to 'opt out' of local authority control and receive money directly from central government. Mrs Thatcher also turned her attention to reform of the NHS, while stressing that health care would remain free and universally available. These parameters necessarily limited the radicalism of the reforms, which were aimed principally at introducing some element of Thatcherite free-market economics into the monolithic NHS. With hindsight, what seems remarkable about Mrs Thatcher's reform of social policy, especially in contrast to her economic and industrial relations policies, is its timidity. She rejected introducing education vouchers or expanding means testing to pay for welfare benefits. She left the welfare state substantially unaltered.

Ultimately the third term is less a story of radicalism renewed than of stagnation and decay. John Campbell, a Thatcher biographer, interestingly rates her first term her best, and her third, by a mile, her worst. By the late 1980s Mrs Thatcher, who in the early days of her leadership had been renowned for her astute political antennae, had grown increasingly out of touch with both her party and the country. She badly missed Whitelaw, who retired in January 1988, a real turning point.

This trend can be seen with undeniable clarity in her determination to press ahead with the community charge, popularly known as the 'poll tax'. The principal complaint against the poll tax was that, unlike the 'rates' that it replaced, it was a flat-rate tax whereby everyone, regardless of their income or wealth, paid the same. Local councils would set the level of the tax and all voters would then have to pay. Mrs Thatcher hoped that high-spending (read Labour) councils would set a high rate of tax and would consequently suffer at the polls. Yet this logic proved flawed. Although a few councils managed to deliver low poll-tax bills, the vast majority of the population found themselves substantially worse off. Instead of blaming their local councils, however, voters chose to blame the central government, or more specifically Mrs Thatcher. The Conservatives' popularity plummeted and protests turned violent in central London. Yet, once again, the lady was not for turning and, to the horror of her colleagues, now anxiously thinking towards the next election, she stuck steadfastly to her tax. Had she really chosen the right issue on which to fight, they asked? Was she losing her touch, as also appeared to be the case over her odd decision to oppose German reunification?

Initially she had been close to her principal lieutenants: Howe, her first Chancellor and then Foreign Secretary and Nigel Lawson, who replaced Howe as Chancellor in

1983. Yet by the late 1980s these relations had come under strain. The principal policy issue over which they disagreed was Europe. Lawson and Howe believed that, if the British government was to have any hope of influencing the future shape of the EU, it was vital to adopt a positive approach. This would include allowing the pound to join other European currencies in the Exchange Rate Mechanism (ERM). Mrs Thatcher, however, had grown increasingly sceptical towards Europe over her premiership and felt vexed that she had agreed to sign the Single European Act 1986 – one of the very few decisions for which the right blame her. She gave a staunchly Euro-sceptic speech in Bruges in September 1988, and feared the ERM would be the first step towards a European super-state and the demise of Britain as a sovereign nation. Again and again Lawson and Howe pleaded with Thatcher to embrace Europe and set a date for ERM entry, but each time she refused.

Exacerbating their policy differences was growing personal bitterness. Howe felt particularly spited by the Prime Minister, who would regularly ignore or patronise him in front of colleagues. In July 1989 Howe's discontent turned to outright anger when, without any warning, Mrs Thatcher reshuffled her Cabinet and demoted him to Leader of the House of Commons. He bided his time, partially placated by the title of Deputy Prime Minister, until it became clear that this title came with little power attached. A challenge to her leadership from a 'stalking horse', Old Etonian Sir Anthony Meyer, came and went. Meanwhile in October 1989 matters with Lawson came to a head. Mrs Thatcher's economic adviser, Alan Walters, was known for his exceptional hostility to the ERM and these views, completely at odds with Lawson's official policy, came to appear in the media with increasing frequency. On 26 October Lawson protested to Mrs Thatcher that the situation had become intolerable. One could not have two mouthpieces for government economic policy, he said. He demanded that she sack Walters. Mrs Thatcher refused and so Lawson walked out on her and the government.

Mrs Thatcher's government never recovered from Lawson's shock resignation. She stumbled on as leader for another year, becoming increasingly withdrawn and relying on the views of her closest Number 10 aides. Two stood out: Bernard Ingham, her Press Secretary, and Charles Powell, the Foreign Affairs Private Secretary. Isolated in Cabinet, the Downing Street bunker became her refuge. Finally, incensed by her anti-European tirades, Howe followed Lawson and resigned from the government. In a stinging speech in the Commons, which surprised many with its directness, Howe poured scorn on Thatcher's style of leadership and her attitude towards Europe. He ended by calling

The poll tax riot in Trafalgar Square in March 1990 *(PA)*

suggestively for 'others to consider their own response' to the situation. The very next day, Michael Heseltine announced that he would challenge the Prime Minister for the leadership. The 152 votes he secured in the subsequent contest forced the leadership election to a second round and Mrs Thatcher's support rapidly evaporated. She withdrew from the race rather than face a humiliating defeat. Her eleven and a half years as Prime Minister and fifteen years as leader of the party had drawn to a tragic close.

MARGARET THATCHER'S DEPARTURE 1990

The Conservative victory of June 1987 gave Mrs Thatcher a third successive general election win, a feat unprecedented in the twentieth century for any premier. Yet, in little over three years, she had fallen from power, pushed out of office by the very people, her Cabinet ministers, who owed their political preferment to her.

The economy, which had been booming in the mid-1980s, went into decline following the stock market crash of October 1987. Concern was compounded by the unpopular introduction of the community charge or 'poll tax', differences over entry into the European Exchange Rate Mechanism (instituted in October 1990), and Geoffrey Howe's resignation from his Cabinet post on 1 November 1990. Poor by-election results had unnerved Tory MPs, as had Howe's bitterly anti-Thatcher resignation speech on 13 November, described later by her as his 'final act of bile and treachery'.

The first ballot of Tory MPs, in a Byzantine electoral process, was to be held on 20 November. Proposed by Douglas Hurd, her Foreign Secretary, Mrs Thatcher was seconded by John Major, her Chancellor, despite the fact that, as one of his aides, Judith Chaplin, wrote in her diary, 'I get the feeling he isn't that keen'. On the afternoon of Sunday 18 November, Mrs Thatcher flew to Paris for a European conference, assured by her courtiers she would beat Heseltine in the first round. As she flew across the English Channel, she was not comforted to read that day's newspapers, with many commentators saying it was time for her to go.

That weekend even ardent Thatcherites sensed things might be slipping away from their champion. If she failed to win the first ballot – dreaded prospect – who would be best placed to take over, challenge and defeat the arch anti-Thatcherite, Heseltine? Hurd they deemed to be too European. It was Major who emerged as the figure best placed to carry the Thatcherite torch forward and the man most likely to unify the party. On Monday 19 November Jeffrey Archer, who had an uncanny habit of popping up at pivotal moments, drove to Major's Huntingdon home, where he was recuperating in bed from a wisdom-tooth operation. Archer meticulously and pointedly spread a copy of every newspaper over Major's bed and set about persuading him that there was a broad backing for him, should a second ballot be necessary.

Voting in the first ballot took place on Tuesday 20 November. The result, announced at 6.30 p.m., gave Mrs Thatcher insufficient votes, according to the rules, for an outright victory over Heseltine: she had 204 votes to Heseltine's 152. The news was broken to her in her private rooms in the British Embassy in Paris. A second ballot would thus be necessary, duly called for a week later. She returned to London just before midday on Wednesday 21 November, fired up to beat off any challenge. But by now even ultra-loyalists were sensing the game might be up. That afternoon she toured the tea room and corridors of the House of Commons to drum up support. It was a pathetic scene. Even Denis, her husband, told her, 'Don't go on, love'. But she was not yet ready to listen. She called Hurd. Would he nominate her for the second ballot? Good. She phoned Major. You'll second me? There was a long pause – 'it was a very long period of silence', he later recalled. He agreed to back her, 'but I resented the way she didn't ask, but presumed on my support'.

She now set herself the task of stiffening support among her senior ministers. She was sure she would do it. One by one she saw them in her room in the Commons on the Wednesday evening. Almost to a man they conveyed the al-most uncannily consensual view that, though they person-ally supported her, they did not believe she was in a position to win: 'weasel words', she wrote, 'whereby they had transmuted their betrayal into frank advice and concern for my fate.' She returned to Number 10, confused and upset. That night she decided what she had to do, and at 7.30 a.m. on the Thursday morning, 22 November, she phoned Andrew Turnbull, her Principal Private Secretary, to tell him that she would resign. At Cabinet that morning, with tears in her eyes, she announced her decision to go, in the interests of party unity, and she urged her ministers to unite behind the figure best placed to defeat Heseltine. It was a sombre affair. Expressions of appreciation were intoned; she sensed that they were relieved she was going,

yet every single one pretended otherwise. She retreated that weekend to lick her wounds, shocked and deeply saddened.

Tuesday 27 November saw the second ballot, in which Major defeated Hurd and Heseltine. Mrs Thatcher was delighted by the result and danced a jig of joy at the top of the stairs of Number 11, where the Majors were living. Mrs Thatcher had had the luxury of some days to compose herself before she left Number 10 for the last time on the morning of Wednesday 28 November. Some one thousand bouquets had poured into Number 10 from the public over the previous five days, and she was in sparkling form at a farewell party for 200 guests in Number 10's Pillared Room on the Tuesday evening. Her personal staff presented her with a first edition of Rudyard Kipling's poetry; 'Life begins at sixty-five', she quipped in her speech. At 9.30 the next morning she left Number 10. 'We are leaving Downing Street for the last time after eleven and a half wonderful years', she said, 'We are very happy that we leave the United Kingdom in a very much better state than when we came.' At 9.35 a.m. her chauffeur-driven Daimler arrived at the gates of Buckingham Palace and she stepped out to tender her resignation as one of Britain's greatest prime ministers in history.

A tearful Mrs Thatcher leaves Downing Street in November 1990 after eleven and a half years in office. Denis loyally follows (PA)

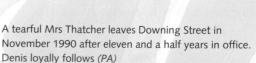

Mrs Thatcher and President Reagan forged a strong partnership and friendship during the 1980s
(PA)

To her supporters, of whom there are very many, Margaret Thatcher left Britain a renewed and invigorated force both at home and on the world stage. She reversed years of national decline. She made Britain again the essential ally of the United States, largely due to her personal relationship with President Reagan, and helped end the Cold War. She turned around the economy and finally tamed the over-powerful unions, who had protected their own interests at the expense of the country's well-being for far too long. She radically overhauled the British state, taking power away from bureaucrats and putting it in the hands of the electorate, who came to enjoy a wealth and a standard of living that they had never known before. On coming to power she found Britain in tatters, and she gave it back its pride and confidence.

Her critics, however, are less kind. They point above all to her intensely divisive nature and question the efficacy of many of her policies. The 'economic miracle' is largely a myth, they insist, suggesting that recovery was inevitable and that monetarism only prolonged the recession of the early 1980s. Even when recovery came it proved unsustainable and was over-egged by Lawson with her acquiescence, which then led to the harsh recession of the 1990s. While a few became rich under Mrs Thatcher, many missed out on growing prosperity, and the gap between the rich and the poor, and north and south, widened considerably. Local government was badly weakened, and power, despite privatisations, was concentrated in central government as never before. The party lost support in Scotland, from which it never recovered, and membership and party organisation ran down badly under her – though she was at her best in her big conference speeches. She encouraged and cemented an ill-considered Euro-scepticism, which continues to plague the Conservative Party and indeed the country to this day.

Not even her detractors could deny, however, that Thatcher was a very major force in the party's, and nation's, history. Her great failing as a party figure occurred not when she led it, but afterwards. Although her refusal to let go of the reins may have been understandable in human terms, not least because she felt she had been stabbed in the back by an ungrateful Cabinet, she failed to appreciate the difficulties she would create for her successors by not withdrawing in a dignified and gracious way into the background. An international job, or work for charitable or other good causes, would have won her respect and admiration. Not even her most ardent supporters, however, can argue that she added one iota to her stature, or helped the party, by her continued interference and sniping, or by her not stopping her acolytes and admirers from making undermining noises in her absence. While her departure from Number 10 in November 1990 was sad for the party, the way she chose to conduct herself in the years that followed was far sadder still.

MAJOR'S TROUBLED PREMIERSHIP: 1990–7

John Major has unjustly been called the worst Tory prime minister of the twentieth century. Richard Thorpe, biographer of Eden and Douglas-Home, calls it the worst Tory period in office since the 1832 Reform Act. Ridiculed by Labour (especially after Blair became its leader in mid-1994), by the press and, less understandably, by his party, the time is ripe for a reappraisal of his record. It is true that he led the party to one of the worst defeats in its history in 1997. But in 1992 he led it to an unexpected victory, in which it won the most votes, over 14 million, in the party's history and it was the only time last century when a party won four elections consecutively. How can these two milestones have been achieved by the same man? What can be said in defence of Major's leadership?

Since he led the party only when in government, it is harder than with most to evaluate Major as a Tory *party* leader, because he had no record as leader of the party in opposition. He loved the

WHAT DOES THE CONSERVATIVE PARTY OFFER A WORKING CLASS KID FROM BRIXTON?

THEY MADE HIM PRIME MINISTER.

No wonder John Major believes everyone should have an equal opportunity.
CONSERVATIVE [X]

The party made much of John Major's Brixton roots during the 1992 general election (*Bodleian Library*)

One of the hard-hitting campaign adverts in the 1992 campaign, raising the spectre of 'Labour's Double Whammy' (Bodleian Library)

party in the country, and he was regarded with real affection by many constituency activists. But he did not love his parliamentary party, nor his Cabinet, nor they him. Major belonged to no single school of conservatism, had no mentors among past Tory leaders or theorists (though he would look back to Baldwin with affection), and had no interest in redefining Toryism – though, in articulating some of his homespun personal beliefs, he did chime with some of its essential propositions. In his resistance to change to the constitution, however, he did echo one of Disraeli's three great themes. Of the party organisation, he was a gradual reformer, encouraging consultation with members and overseeing an overhaul of Central Office under his party chairmen, Chris Patten, Norman Fowler and Brian Mawhinney. But his grand plans for making the party more democratic, on which he spoke at length in his final day as party leader, were left unenacted. If the balance of verdict on his leadership of the Tory party is negative, with a reduced and ageing membership and with the party at a historic low ebb in terms of electoral success, although seeing some revival on 1 May 1997 in local government, one can not say it was for want of his trying to arrest the long-term decline that pre-dated his arrival at Number 10 in the party's appeal to activists or voters. He also carried the centre of the party mostly with him and played a key role in the 1992 general election which killed off 'old Labour'.

Major by temperament and choice was a conciliator. Before he became Prime Minister, he had found Mrs Thatcher's style of leadership personally distasteful. His chairmanship of Cabinet and Cabinet committees, in contrast, allowed ministers to express their views, and guided them to a conclusion in line with his intentions. Rather than have dissent in Cabinet, he preferred to delay decisions until he could reconcile differences. He had close allies in Cabinet, principally Chris Patten (1990–2), Douglas Hurd (1990–5), Michael Heseltine (1995–7), and Tony Newton throughout, but he did not have a 'kitchen Cabinet' of regular close aides, and resorted to an ad hoc inner Cabinet only in the run-up to both general elections and during particularly difficult periods, such as late 1994. The worst that can be said of his unassertive style of leadership was that it may have encouraged divisions to grow, whereas a strong line earlier may have resolved some issues sooner. The best is that he avoided the highly personalised, 'denocracy' style of government (a reference to Blair's 'den', or office, at 10 Downing Street) followed by Thatcher and later by Blair as harshly criticised in the Butler Report of July 2004.

The circumstances that confronted Major as Prime Minister were not propitious. One can judge performance only against such background. Great leaders throughout history have been made by great opportunities – war, depression, or a widespread shift in public mood that the leader can articulate. The historical opportunity for *any* leader who succeeded Mrs Thatcher in November 1990 was, in contrast, unusually restricting. He faced far tougher Labour leaders than did Mrs Thatcher. She served opposite James Callaghan on his way out, a frankly inadequate Michael Foot, and a young if improving Neil Kinnock; Major faced Kinnock in his prime, John Smith, and Tony Blair, the most effective opposition Labour leader in the party's history. Neither did Major have, like Mrs Thatcher, a coterie of sympathetic interpreters of his policies and position in the media and intellectual life – the *sine qua non* of a successful modern premiership. Instead, he had the opposite, with obvious results.

While he was served by some outstanding officials and ministers, the pool of political talent at his disposal after eleven years in office, and still more so after many able Tories lost their seats in 1992, was restricted. The seventy former ministers on the backbenches were often bitter and unbiddable. Those who knew they would not receive jobs – including many hardened Euro-sceptics – saw little reason for being either loyal to Major or understanding of his plight. The hunger for power, one of the party's two secret weapons, was fatally lost in these years.

The ideological background for Major in the 1990s was similarly unpromising. Mrs Thatcher was able to adopt an intellectually coherent platform. By the time Major became Prime Minister, the battle for ideas had been won, as had the Cold War, and the 1990s offered fewer certainties. Yet demand was still there for a big idea – 'what is Majorism?' – but in the 1990s fresh portmanteau ideas, certainly on the right, were not to be had. Major and his government received little credit for his completion of the Thatcherite agenda in economic and social policy, discussed below, taking it into areas from which she had shrunk; it tended to be seen as almost cheating, a mere footnote or coda to her premiership.

Few premiers enjoy favourable inheritances; none claim them. Major's in 1990, however, was difficult. In the in-tray were the Gulf crisis, deepening recession, which hit Tory heartlands hard, the poll tax, and a party already deeply unpopular, and divided over Europe. It also contained unexploded bombs such as arms trading with Iraq, the growth of shady lobbying companies, and some Tory MPs whose behaviour would soon flower over the pages of a press avid for stories of Tory 'sleaze'. He felt strongly the lack of a ready understanding of the problems he inherited from Thatcher, so reluctant was the press at large to admit to her having faults. His first years were overshadowed by the recession and the consequent problems in the public finances (which he could have done

Major meets soldiers from the 3rd Battalion of the Desert Rats in Saudi Arabia before the first Gulf War in 1991 *(PA)*

Kenneth Clarke, Major's Chancellor of the Exchequer 1993–7, enjoys a musical moment *(PA)*

more to master). His later years suffered from a small and dwindling parliamentary majority at the mercy of eccentric backbenchers, and of having to steer the Maastricht Treaty through in 1993 in very different circumstances from the acclaim that had greeted his original deal in 1991. Mrs Thatcher had to contend with the ineffectual carping from Heath: Major had to contend with Thatcher's lethal undermining.

Sleaze, neither initiated nor encouraged by Major, brilliantly exploited by New Labour, duly became one of the defining issues of his premiership, and proved a daunting subject to handle. Major responded by establishing the Scott and Nolan Inquiries, to the fury of his right, and then, when parliamentary pressures prevented him endorsing their reports to the full, he was castigated by the centre and left. How might Mrs Thatcher, or Blair, have managed the issue? Yet again, many more condemned Major over sleaze than came forward with practical and workable solutions. Much chortling followed revelations of his affair with Edwina Currie from those who judged him harshly all along.

Nor did he have the time to develop his admittedly inchoate ideas. Where Heath had five years in opposition to plan, Mrs Thatcher four years and Blair three, Major had barely one week, after it seemed likely he would win in November 1990, to plan his policies and the personnel he wanted to serve him. Once in office, he again lacked the time to develop his ideas. For a cricketer, he was placed from the outset on the back foot, and only rarely did he have the chance to play forward.

In electoral terms, Major suffered from the emergence of New Labour, which stole the Tories' other secret weapon: adaptability. In place of the Labour Party of old, for which ideological purity often meant difficulties in adapting to changing voter preference, Major faced the supreme 'flexi-party', willing to adopt almost any policy and position to appeal to centre-ground voters. Labour was no longer frightening to many Tory voters. The 'New Labour New Danger' slogan ultimately failed because too few believed in any danger. The most difficult problem of all that he faced was that, with polls and by-elections pointing continually to the likelihood of heavy defeat, there was little incentive for his own parliamentary party to follow his lead when an alternative – any alternative – offered a better prospect of a revival in fortunes.

Tory hegemony throughout history depended on the backing of the powerful interests in the country – the City, business and the press, as well as the professions. The last were alienated by Mrs Thatcher and never fully returned. Significant elements of the first three flew in the 1990s. In contrast, the interest that in electoral terms had handicapped Labour since the 1970s and before, the trade unions, were deliberately distanced by Blair. There were no powerful interests for Major to slay, or the equivalent to those whose vanquishing added so greatly to Mrs Thatcher's stature – a bloated state sector, inefficient nationalised industries, over-mighty trade unions. If Major's equivalent to the Falklands War was the 1991 Gulf War, which did not end in such emphatic fashion, the equivalent of the 1980s victory in the Cold War, where the popular forces of liberal democracy triumphed over corrupt statism, was Bosnia in the 1990s, without such clear moral absolutes, and where the Tory party was itself split down the middle, as was the West, on how to respond. A truly considerable leader might have been able to rise above his unfavourable background. Major could not. But then no one, least of all the authors, have ever claimed that he was such a first-order leader.

Major's premiership was not without its achievements, more so than the governments of A.J. Balfour (1902–5), Eden (1955–7), Heath (1970–4) or indeed Labour's

Callaghan (1976–9). A case can even be made for saying he achieved more than Wilson in 1964–70, even allowing for Wilson's landslide victory in 1966. The Major government's agenda consolidated Thatcherism, succeeded in privatising coal (1994) and rail (with the 1996–7 sale of Railtrack and franchises), as well as pursuing other radical policies such as the sale of the nuclear industry (1996). The government introduced welfare reforms which, for the first time since 1945, allowed for welfare costs to fall as a proportion of national income. The march of reform continued through institutions such as the Stock Exchange and the army, and through a mini-revolution in education. Even in 1997 the government was still producing policies that followed a radical Conservative approach, such as basic pension plus.

In hard, measurable terms the government produced a strong economic record, even though it over-egged the economy before the 1992 election. The Major years – after the recession of 1990–2 – saw consistently low inflation (below 4 per cent for four years); steady economic growth at 2–3 per cent, which showed no sign of overheating or slackening, and repeated praise from international organisations such as the OECD.

The last Tory Cabinet of the twentieth century rally behind John Major at the 1996 party conference. William Hague is on the far left (Corbis)

There was a minor renaissance of culture and sport through National Lottery funding (1994) and unsung improvements to public services through the Citizens' Charter (1991). In foreign and defence policy the Major government adapted surprisingly smoothly to the post-Cold War world, with a clear appraisal of priorities and capabilities. A steady and resolute leader over Iraq, in Bosnia, against a majority of his Cabinet, he argued for increasing British troops and, though still too cautious, he helped pave the way for the coming of peace. He made mistakes; the worst by far, in party and electoral terms was not leaving the ERM before being forced out in September 1992.

Major's leadership style was exactly what was required for the times. Conservative unity on Europe, which fractured in the mid- to late 1980s, showed that Mrs Thatcher's style of leadership and negative stance on the EU were no longer tenable. Major had the difficult task of managing strong and complex currents of parliamentary and public opinion which moved decisively in a Euro-sceptic direction in the 1990s. Many criticised his policy on Europe: yet a hardline pro or anti policy would have torn the goverment assunder. Across a range of other policy issues, his non-doctrinaire approach suited the tenor of the times. Instead of, like the right, wishing that the public sector would go away or, like much of the centre-left of his party, considering it sacrosanct, he took a case-by-case approach to reform. Major's pragmatic and humane approach offered a real way forward in Northern Ireland, as Blair himself acknowledged at the Good Friday Agreement press conference. Ireland is a prime example of where the accusation that Major lacked all principles or consistency falls apart.

Failed leaders see little of their policy survive. This will not happen with Major. What, then, will last of the Major years? A consensus on the role of the state in the economy which anticipated the Bank of England reforms of May 1997; the National Lottery; public service reform; and stable economic growth with low inflation, perhaps the fabled 'end of inflation'. A further possible legacy is a consensus on what makes for the desirable characteristics of state provision in health and welfare; a consensus on taxation and distributive justice; and a cautious European policy based around the principles of his 1994 Leiden lecture. Though it does not like to acknowledge it, Labour after 1997 followed many of Major's leads, not the least on Ireland and Europe.

As a human being, he was often sorely tested. Much of his pleasure in being Prime Minister was taken away by the barrage of criticism, and the difficulty he found in handling it. Yet he remained a dignified and polite premier, respected by many despite the press ridicule, and lacking arrogance or disdain for people in his personal dealings, even after more than six years in Downing Street. He was perhaps the first Conservative premier fully to believe in race and sex equality and in progress towards homosexual equality. His command of detail enabled surprisingly positive negotiating outcomes, for instance at the EU council in Edinburgh in December 1992. He showed occasional, perhaps underused, political courage and a gambler's nerve, as in defying his handlers in the 1992 and 1997 general elections and in launching the 1995 leadership election, discussed on the following two pages.

Major was neither nonentity nor failure. His will be judged an important if unruly and bedevilled premiership at the end of the Conservative century, completing some parts of an earlier agenda while in some key respects helping to define a Conservatism for the twenty-first century. It is not a bad legacy, as he himself might have put it.

THE WILDERNESS YEARS: 1997-2003

The leaderships of William Hague (1997-2001) and Iain Duncan Smith (2001-3) have been widely criticised, not least by the party itself. Mistakes were certainly made, above all inconsistency on strategy. Labour's weaknesses were not clearly enough identified. It was allowed to set the agenda on traditionally strong Tory areas like law and order, defence and choice in public services. But one should not be too harsh on the leaders; never in its history had Labour been as electorally strong or as unified as it was under Blair after 1994. Indeed, he rallied behind him many of those very powerful forces in the press, industry, and opinion-formers, as well as the middle classes, which had traditionally coalesced around the Tories during their periods of ascendancy. It is easy to criticise the leadership since 1997, but harder to see even the most inspired leader in the party's history making much more of a dent electorally on Labour.

The 1997 defeat was a terrible starting point, the worst performance for the party in votes since 1832 and in seats since 1906. The party lost four and a half million voters, from 14.1 million in 1992 to 9.6 million in 1997, with the share of the popular vote falling from 41.9 per cent to 30.7 per cent. It was left without any seats in Scotland and Wales, and was largely denuded of seats in the large cities and metropolitan areas of England. The parliamentary party was more than halved: it lost 178 seats, and retained just 165 MPs.

Major announced his resignation as party leader on 2 May 1997, the day after the general election. Five candidates were nominated for his succession: Kenneth Clarke, William Hague, Michael Howard, Peter Lilley and John Redwood. Heseltine was ruled out due to health problems, and Michael Portillo and Malcolm Rifkind could not stand

BACK ME OR SACK ME: MAJOR'S LEADERSHIP GAMBLE, 1995

Life went from bad to worse for John Major in late 1994 and early 1995, with opinion polls still poor and party dissent rising. He was becoming sick to death of the constant bickering. By June, Tory MPs were circling around the Prime Minister, speculating that he would either have to resign altogether or be dragged through an ignominious leadership contest in the autumn. At a meeting with the Eurosceptic Fresh Start Group, Major was shouted down after making a speech defending his 'wait and see' policy on the single currency. The meeting was the last straw, bringing to a head months of backbench unrest and widening divisions within the party. On the flight back from a 'G7' meeting in Halifax, Canada, Major resolved to force the issue by resigning as party leader and submitting himself for re-election. Some of his closest advisers recommended that he simply soldier on, but Douglas Hurd and Kenneth Clarke strongly supported the plan. It was one of the riskiest decisions of his premiership, but he believed that the gamble might yet enable him to make a fresh start and regain the initiative ahead of a general election.

On Thursday 22 June 1995, Major called a press conference in the garden of Number 10. The Cabinet and the 1922 Committee had just been informed, his campaign manager, Lord Cranborne (Leader of the House of Lords), already appointed, but to the rest of the world, including the assembled press corps, Major's announcement came as a bolt out of the blue. 'I am not prepared to see the party I care for laid out on the rack any longer', Major declared, 'The Conservative Party must make its choice . . . In short it is time to put up or shut up.' Although some of his senior colleagues thought he might be defeated, he was not in any doubt that he would win. Never before in history had a party leader triggered a leadership contest in this way. Major would continue his duties as Prime Minister even though he had resigned as party leader. He had to win a simple majority of the 329 Conservative MPs as well as being 15 per cent ahead of any rival if a second round was to be avoided. He knew that anything less than 200 votes would weaken him, probably fatally. It was a brave decision to have taken.

Central Office had to remain neutral, while the Chief Whip, Richard Ryder, and the Whips' Office were scrupulous also in not taking sides. Under Cranborne, the campaign team quickly took shape, with Ian Lang and Douglas Hurd becoming the chief lieutenants. In the first forty-eight hours of the 'campaign', Major gained the initiative and wrong-footed his opponents. The team assumed a challenger would emerge and that it would most likely be Norman Lamont, who had been on bad terms with Major since before his departure from the Cabinet in 1993. With the former Chancellor failing to rally enough support, however, it soon became clear that a member of the

Cabinet, Welsh Secretary John Redwood, was to mount a challenge. A hardened Euro-sceptic, Redwood had been unhappy with Major's handling of Europe and the single currency, and claimed he was also disgruntled at the fact that Major had not consulted him personally prior to his announcement. Redwood pleaded with Michael Portillo to support him, but Portillo vowed to enter the race only if it went to a second round. In the meantime, he pledged his loyalty to Major.

Redwood's campaign drew the support of the majority of Euro-sceptic MPs, including the storm troopers of the Euro-sceptic cause, the 'Whipless rebels', as well as others who had been thorns in Major's side since at least 1992. They were ridiculed as the 'Vulcan's barmy army' by some of Major's team and the press, a reference to Redwood's physical appearance allegedly resembling a Vulcan. Redwood's battle cry was 'No Change, No Chance'. Both sides campaigned vigorously between 29 June and 3 July, but it was Major's team that was the more organised and better financed. Most of the press refused to endorse Major, however, and the Sun, which had been steadfastly anti-Major since 1992, dubbed the contest as 'Redwood vs Deadwood'.

Decision day came on 4 July, American Independence Day. At 5.10 p.m. Sir Marcus Fox, Chairman of the 1922 Committee, announced the result to Tory MPs in a committee room of the House of Commons: '218 Major, 89 Redwood, 20 abstentions'. Major had surpassed his hurdle of 200 supporters, but not as convincingly as many in his team would have liked. Major was personally disappointed that he had not reached 220, but he had seen off Redwood's challenge. What carried the day for him was a brilliantly orchestrated plan whereby key figures told waiting television cameras that he had grabbed a great victory. A great victory duly became the agreed line on the extraordinary contest. 'I believe [it] has put to rest any question or any speculation about the leadership of the Conservative Party up to and beyond the next election . . . The message that I would give to every Conservative . . . is that the time for division is over', Major declared on the doorstep to Number 10. His gamble had secured the former up to a point, but it certainly had not guaranteed the latter.

Major holds a press conference in the rose garden of Number 10 in June 1995, announcing the leadership election *(PA)*

as they had lost their seats. Clarke forged a ticket with Redwood, which Tory historian John Barnes says echoed that between Austen Chamberlain and Bonar Law. It was not to be. Clarke and Redwood made it to the final round, but no further, and one can only speculate how such a powerful and pungent duo might have performed. It certainly would not have been dull. On 19 June, Hague with 92 votes to Clarke's 70, became the youngest leader of the Conservative Party since Pitt in 1783.

Hague made positive contributions as leader. The leadership rules were changed to enable the whole party membership a say rather than just the MPs. Party finances were restored and were in the black again by 2001. He brought the party round to accepting a more collegiate line on Europe, which was a Euro-sceptic one, thereby quietening years of open warfare: the party did well in the 1999 elections for the European Parliament party partly as a result. He invested considerable effort in local government, which saw some recovery, and he manoeuvred out almost all Major's Cabinet members who remained after 1997, promoting younger and fresher faces in their place to present to the electorate. He performed well against Blair in Parliament, especially at Prime Minister's Questions, keeping up his party's morale with his sparring. His main failing was his switching strategic direction on policy rather than sticking to just one course. 'Caring, compassionate Conservatism' combined with social liberalism from 1997 to 1998 was thus followed by 'kitchen table Conservatism', designed to be in touch with the views of

A 16-year-old William Hague making his first conference speech in 1977 with Mrs Thatcher looking on (*Hulton/Getty*)

the ordinary voter. Then from 1999, in another switch, policy became more populist, with leadership support for Tony Martin, the Norfolk farmer who shot dead an intruder, and a more anti-European Union line. Hague himself admits that 'what went wrong was the amount of switching in our policy direction'.

The 2001 manifesto, *Time for Common Sense*, was launched as 'the most ambitious for a generation', and offered tax cuts (£8 billion), less state involvement in health and education, and ruled out joining the single currency at least for the next Parliament. The result saw a sliver-thin recovery to 31.7 per cent of the national vote and 166 seats (a net gain of 1 per cent and one seat). This contrasted with a 4 per cent gain between 1945 and 1950, and 4.5 per cent between 1966 and 1970, after those two earlier Labour landslides. Hague announced the day after the election that he would stand down, soldiering on as leader until a leadership election could take place under the new rules over the summer.

The main candidates were Clarke, David Davis, Duncan Smith and Portillo. Among the MP elections the victor in the first ballot was Michael Portillo but, when he wandered incautiously too far in the direction of social liberalism, he faded, and Clarke emerged as winner in the final round by a small margin over Duncan Smith. In the membership ballot, however, Duncan Smith triumphed over Clarke by a ratio of three to two, and he was announced the victor on 13 September 2001 (inauspiciously two days after 9/11).

A 40-year-old William Hague making his last speech as party leader, with Ffion looking on, resigning on the morning after the party's second successive heavy defeat in June 2001
(PA)

Kenneth Clarke, the disappointed loser, congratulates Iain Duncan Smith on his election as party leader two days after 9/11 *(Corbis)*

Duncan Smith leaves Central Office after being defeated in a vote of confidence in his leadership in October 2003 *(Hulton/Getty)*

Clarke refused to serve under him, and Portillo decided to bow out of politics. Duncan Smith, to the surprise of some, appointed a broad-based shadow Cabinet and set in train a major rethink of policy, drawing heavily on international experience. Oliver Letwin proved one of his most inspiring appointments as shadow Home Secretary, and Howard as shadow Chancellor. Theresa May caught the media's attention as party chairman. Duncan Smith succeeded in establishing a new truce over Europe by effectively ruling out discussion. But his two-year leadership was overshadowed by international affairs, with the Afghanistan war following 9/11, then the war in Iraq, which Duncan Smith supported uncritically but which kept the spotlight on Labour, not the Tories. The media meanwhile appeared more interested in the feuds in Central Office than in policy announcements. Eventually, a series of unpopular decisions and botched relaunches (such as the 'quiet man' in October 2002), and failure to shift the opinion polls significantly against Labour led to pressure on him to stand down. A final straw was the Brent East by-election in September 2003, when the Liberal Democrats came from third to take the seat off Labour, while the Conservative vote collapsed. In October 2003 Duncan Smith lost a party vote of confidence in his leadership (by 75 to 90 votes), triggering a leadership election.

A HOWARD TORY PARTY?

Howard emerged as the undisputed successor. No other candidate was prepared to stand against him. He thus became the first leader since voting for the leadership began in 1965 to emerge without any competition. By general agreement, including that of the Prime Minister, the Tory party now again had a formidable leader, one with the intellect, experience and debating skills to lead the party again back into a new period of Tory ascendancy. With so many cards held by the government, however, which is still in possession of a massive majority, the journey back out of the wilderness will not be easy. But if anyone can do it for the party, it is Howard.

Michael Howard emerges as the new party leader without a contest on 6 November 2003 *(Corbis)*

S I X

THE TORY BODY POLITIC

Since the early nineteenth century, the figures that have shaped the party have done so from locations across Britain's cities, towns, country estates and in its conference halls. As a testament to the influence of the aristocracy in Tory politics, party luminaries and foot soldiers alike have met in some of the most splendid buildings and settings in the country. This chapter will explore the places where many of the party's most historic decisions, meetings and conferences have occurred. From the first gentlemen's clubs in Pall Mall to the rise of the once formidable Conservative Central Office, we shall see how the party's headquarters evolved to the present day. Meanwhile, in the countryside, the great houses and estates belonging to party leaders and benefactors provided the venues and backdrops for serious discussion and more frivolous entertainment. We will finish at the seaside, where the annual party conference played host to some of the most dramatic events in the party's history.

PARTY HQ

The heart of the party's organisation, Conservative Central Office, emerged in response to a series of political crises and electoral defeats which threatened the party's very existence as a major force in British politics. With the survival of the party at stake when the franchise was extended in 1832, 1867, 1884 and 1918, the party had to build and sustain an organisation that could adapt to the era of democratic politics. The jealously guarded autonomy of local Conservative associations, competition from other parties and policy disputes would often make life difficult for organisers at the centre.

CARLTON CLUB ORIGINS, 1830–70

The loose grouping of Tory peers and Members of Parliament in the seventeenth and eighteenth centuries had no need for a central organisation other than the Whips' Office buried deep in the Palace of Westminster. If leading parliamentarians needed to meet and discuss tactics outside the palace precincts, they would do so informally in the established London clubs such as White's, Brooks's and Boodle's. The advent of electoral reform

The Houses of Parliament before the fire of 1834, by Havell *(Hulton/Getty)*

The entrance to the first Carlton Club, which was bombed in the Blitz. Pall Mall, London *(Hulton/Getty)*

changed all this. Within a week of the Duke of Wellington's government's fall in November 1830, a small group of leading Tories met in the house of Joseph Planta MP in Charles Street, off St James's Square. Known as the 'Charles Street Gang', the group met periodically to 'direct the operations of opposition'. In June 1831 they agreed to set up a fund to provide an organiser's salary, meet the cost of premises, manage the press and fight elections. By the beginning of the following year, they were still finding it difficult to mobilise support and raise funds for a losing battle against the Whig reformers. With the Tory cause in trouble, Wellington encouraged the gang to create a more formal club to bolster support in the country. At the Thatched House Tavern in St James's Street in March 1832, Lord Kensington duly agreed to lease 2 Carlton House Terrace, for a new club, and a formal committee was established to recruit members with an annual subscription of £10. The 'Carlton Club', as it soon became known, acquired 500 members within a month, many of whom were parliamentarians and gentry, known supporters of Wellington's Tories. With a severe defeat in the post-Reform Act general election in December 1832, the club became a refuge and rallying point for the surviving rump of 175 Tory MPs.

As the dust began to settle after the constitutional crisis of 1830–2, Wellington believed the Tory Party's best course of action was to adjust to the realities of a reformed electoral system and an enlarged electorate. Within a few years of its foundation, the Carlton Club was being referred to as 'the headquarters of the party organisation', particularly after Parliament was destroyed by the fire in 1834, leaving Tory politicians nowhere to meet, except at the Carlton and each other's houses, before Parliament took possession of Charles Barry's new Palace of Westminster in 1852. From a suite of rooms inside the club, MPs, peers and a few officials set to work coordinating their activities in Parliament with that of mobilising the party's support in the country in the run-up to elections. Although provincial Tories preferred to retain control themselves of many constituency affairs, social contacts between the party in London and the rest of the country were to prove a unifying force. By 1835, the wealth and standing of the club was such that it was able to occupy elegant new premises on Pall Mall designed by Sir Robert Smirke. With a general election approaching in the same year, the new party leader, Sir Robert Peel, placed the club's electoral activities on a permanent footing with the creation of an election committee under the supervision of Francis R. Bonham. Bonham recruited candidates, sought subscriptions and reported gossip to his leader. His efforts paid off in 1841, when Peel's new Conservative Party won its first outright election victory since Wellington's old Tory Party lost office eleven years beforehand.

When Peel and Bonham broke with the party in 1846 over the repeal of the Corn Laws, the organisation which had been so carefully constructed fell for several years into a state of disrepair. Some protectionist Conservatives set up alternative headquarters in Old Bond Street. Like the parliamentary party itself, the Carlton Club was bitterly divided, which distracted it from running an effective organisation. It was left to Benjamin Disraeli, who emerged in 1849 as the de facto leader of the anti-Peelite Conservatives in the Commons, to pick up the pieces. This he did with the assistance of Philip Rose and Markham Spofforth, both partners in the London firm of solicitors, Baxter, Rose, Norton & Co. The firm's Victoria Street premises became in practice the party's first proper offices in 1853, although the Carlton Club remained the party's social and political hub. Despite all these efforts, by the 1860s the Conservatives were being challenged by the far more effective organisation of the Liberal Party. With the doubling of the electorate to around two million after the Second Reform Act in 1867 and the Conservatives' defeat at the hands of the Liberals the following year, it became clear that the party would need an entirely new structure and headquarters to fit the new age.

TORY CLUBLAND

Belonging to a club has come to be seen as a badge of allegiance in Conservative circles. The Carlton Club was not the first Tory club in the country. Popular support for Pitt's stand against revolutionary fervour emanating from France in the 1790s gave rise to the formation of 'Pitt clubs', King and Constitution clubs in large towns and cities across Britain. The White Lion Club in Nottingham, renamed the True Blue Club in 1797, was renowned for its displays of patriotic sentiment. By the time of the Carlton Club's foundation, an array of Tory-sympathising clubs had thus sprung up around the country, providing venues for political discussion and activity. It was the Carlton which was to become the pinnacle of Tory respectability in smart London circles and a rival to the Whig Reform Club, founded a few years later. It soon became the place for any aspiring Conservative to be seen and heard, as Disraeli himself recognised when he became a Conservative in 1835. Membership was to be his first move up the greasy pole. 'Whips, election committees, provincial grandees, Tadpoles and Tapers – all the principals, stage hands, prompters, designers of the great party political drama congregated in its precincts', was how party historian, Robert Blake, described the scene at the Carlton in the mid-nineteenth century. Such was the increasingly exclusive status of the Carlton Club that, by the turn of the century, a new generation of London clubs, such as the Constitutional, St Stephen's, Junior Carlton and Conservative Clubs, had come into existence.

Although the Carlton Club ceased to be the home of the party's headquarters in 1853, it remained at the heart of the party. The club's grand surroundings in Pall Mall, where it remained until destroyed by an air raid in October 1940, would provide the home for some of the most significant decisions in the

The CLUBMAN

INCORPORATING THE CONSERVATIVE CLUBS GAZETTE

VOL. 1. No. 3.   4ᴰ   MAY, 1948

SWINTON—the new Conservative College of the North.   (See pages 4 & 5)

POLITICS · CLUB NEWS · SPORT

Front cover of the May 1948 edition of *The Clubman*, one of many publications published for the hundreds of Conservative Clubs across the country (*Bodleian Library*)

party's history, none more so than the meeting that took place on 19 October 1922 which brought down Lloyd George's Coalition Government and the leadership of Austen Chamberlain along with it (the background to this tumultuous event is explained in Chapter 3). The atmosphere in the club on that day was electrifying, particularly after Stanley Baldwin's impassioned speech. With the motion to fight the 1922 general election as an independent party carried by 185 to 88, the history of the Conservative Party took a significant fresh turn. No event in the club's history since can compare with that autumn day in 1922. Most often, the club is a place of intrigue and political manoeuvrings in the

Margaret Thatcher sits at the feet of former Prime Minister Harold Macmillan on his 85th birthday at the Carlton Club in London, 7 February 1979. Despite her servile position, she had little time for the old man's policies (Hulton/Getty)

Conservative Party, with its members more prone to concern themselves with good food and drink rather than high-octane political debate.

Some of the party's grandest social events have taken place at the club, including banquets, parties and well-heated and even drunken exchanges. Carlton Club members did not take kindly to political turncoats or adversaries in their midst. When most Peelites either stayed away or left the club after the split in 1846, one Peelite member, who was to go on to become Prime Minister, continued to enjoy its dining facilities. According to one newspaper report, several angry and tipsy Conservative MPs informed William Gladstone that 'he ought to be pitched out of the window in the direction of the Reform Club'. But the club could be tolerant if members remained good Conservatives. Indeed, almost any form of misconduct would be tolerated. Sir John Cave-Browne-Cave was one of the club's most committed alcoholics, who on one occasion had to be restrained after attempting a duel with an armchair. Another Victorian member, Charles Agar, would never leave the club at night and was often found by staff hiding behind his newspaper in a dark corner. For others, the club was an extension into adult life of public school. In 1853 the Duke of Buckingham complained to the club's committee about 'the unfair way in which members helped themselves to rice pudding'.

After the destruction of the old Carlton Club in 1940, the club moved to 69 St James's Street where it stands today. Unlike many gentlemen's clubs in the latter twentieth century, the Carlton resisted moves to admit women members. When Margaret Thatcher became leader of the party in 1975, the club invited her to become its first 'honorary' member, which she accepted, but it presented the Carlton with something of a dilemma. Soon the club had to open its doors to 'lady associate members', although they were barred from entering the public rooms on the ground floor 'designed for members and their gentlemen guests' and from attending or voting at general meetings. Change looked to be on the way when in 1998 William Hague became the first Tory leader to call publicly for full membership for women in the club. Since 1998 a majority of members have voted for change, but not the required two-thirds of the club's membership in support of the move. In 2001 Iain Duncan Smith became the first leader to decline membership of the club in protest to the club's position on women members. There that which did so much to propel the Conservative Party into prominence has failed to open its doors fully to the very gender who helped to sustain its existence for more than a century.

THE RISE OF CONSERVATIVE CENTRAL OFFICE, 1870–1911

By 1870 Disraeli was convinced that the old structures of party organisation had to be replaced with an entirely new and much more professional body. Disraeli charged John Gorst, a young barrister and MP, with the responsibility for organising a central office for the party. Its first home was to be a modest set of offices in 53 Parliament Street, a stone's throw from the Houses of Parliament. Disraeli gave his new 'Principal Agent' a relatively free hand. Within two years, Gorst had begun to transform the way the party organised itself for elections: keeping a register of approved candidates which could be made available to constituencies, stimulating local grass-roots activity and bringing the headquarters of the National Union of Conservative Associations, which Disraeli had created in 1867, under the same roof. The progress made by the new Central Office and the renewal of party fortunes under Disraeli helped the Conservatives win the 1874 general election, their first convincing victory in more than two decades.

In 1874 Central Office moved to the more spacious St Stephen's Chambers along Westminster Bridge Road. Once again the Liberal Party had stolen a march on Conservative organisation when it formed the National Liberal Federation in 1877, which sought to capitalise on local campaigning innovations, such as Joseph Chamberlain's caucuses in Birmingham and other major cities. A period of stagnation followed Gorst's resignation as Principal Agent. Following the unexpected defeat of the party in 1880 and the death of Disraeli the year after, the first serious power struggle over the heart of the party's organisation occurred. Lord Randolph Churchill, a perennial thorn in the side of the new leader in the Commons, Sir Stafford Northcote, attempted to secure for the National Union of Conservative Associations 'its legitimate influence in the party organisation'. His aim was to democratise the party and transfer control of policy, finance and candidate selection to the National Union, making Central Office its servant in the process. Churchill was stopped firmly in his tracks by Lord Salisbury, party leader in the Lords, and lost out in his mission for 'Tory democracy'.

Sir John Gorst, Principal Agent 1870–4 and 1880–2, caricature by Sir Frances Carruthers Gould (*National Portrait Gallery*)

After 1885 Central Office received a new impetus, with the arrival of a new 'Principal Agent'. Armed with only six members of staff and three secretaries, Richard Middleton, a former naval man, known as Captain Middleton or 'the Skipper', took Central Office into the twentieth century with zeal. It forged a strong relationship with the party in Parliament, ably overseen by Aretas Akers-Douglas, the Chief Whip, and with the growing party in the country. Middleton's partnership with the new leader, Lord Salisbury, ensured a real unity of purpose and determination in the activities of Central Office. Salisbury's daughter records in her biography of her father how, after the close of a House of Lords sitting, '[Salisbury's] brougham would draw up at St Stephen's Chambers and, seating himself at Captain Middleton's table . . . he would go through the last reports from the constituencies, weigh the qualifications of proposed candidates, or discuss with Whip and Agent the latest teacup-storm among some section of his supporters.' Central Office was imbued with a new sense of professionalism, reflected in its first publications, in particular the fortnightly *National Union Gleanings* (later *Gleanings and Memoranda*), which provided speechwriters and sympathetic journalists with a sculpted analysis from a Conservative perspective on developments in British politics. Middleton's achievement was to interlock each part of the party organisation with Central Office with the sole aim of building solid Conservative majorities in Parliament, which he did with distinction in the elections of 1886, 1895 and 1900. The Skipper's operation out of St Stephen's Chambers was looked upon by successive generations of party organisers as a golden age of Conservative Party organisation.

R.W. Middleton, Principal Agent 1885–1903 *(Conservative Research Department)*

Momentum was again lost when Middleton stood down in 1903, which, coinciding with a serious dispute over policy, had a debilitating effect on party organisation after 1903. Salisbury's and Balfour's comparative neglect of organisational matters after the landslide victory of 1900 was compounded when Joseph Chamberlain attempted to capture the

National Union to push for greater party democracy and promote Tarrif Reform between 1903 and 1905. Unlike Randolph Churchill, Chamberlain succeeded in using the National Union for his own purposes, though Central Office remained loyal to Balfour, the party leader, as it had done in the early 1880s. Middleton's successors as Principal Agent, however, lacked his calibre and clout, all of which contributed to the party's heavy defeat in 1906.

After two more successive defeats, Central Office was given its first major overhaul. The post of 'Chairman of the Party Organisation' was created for an 'officer of Cabinet rank', who under the party leader 'should be responsible for the management of the affairs of the Party'. Other reforms included the appointment of a treasurer and the establishment of an advisory board, comprising heads of committees from the National Union, to advise the chairman on wider political developments. The post-1911 reforms revived Central Office after nearly a decade of neglect. The new chairman, Sir Arthur Steel-Maitland, immediately set about rebuilding bridges with the voluntary party, improving Central Office's facilities, expanding its staff and dividing its work into proper departments. A press bureau was also set up to feed stories to supportive newspapers. The 1911 Parliament Act reduced the maximum time between general elections from seven to five years, and the injection of funds and revitalisation positioned the party well for a general election in 1915.

FORMIDABLE MACHINE, 1926–79

Following the disruption of the First World War, a trebling of the franchise in 1918 and the fall of Baldwin's first government in 1923, Central Office was left reeling, requiring yet another period of reorganisation. J.C.C. Davidson's appointment as chairman in 1926 transformed the fortunes of Central Office, instituting reforms to rationalise and streamline its work, which had expanded in the 1920s to foster the growth of women's and trade unionists' organisations. By 1928, 180 people worked in Palace Chambers on Bridge Street, where Central Office had moved to in 1922, with a further 63 staff in regional offices across the country. One of Davidson's achievements was to recruit eminent figures from outside the party, particularly from advertising, the civil service and even the intelligence services. One such recruit was Joseph Ball, an officer from MI5, who was appointed the first Principal Publicity Officer in 1927. As we shall see in Chapter 10, Ball went on to play a seminal role not only in propaganda but also directing the Conservative Research Department, another of Davidson's main innovations.

Left: The doorway of Central Office at Palace Chambers, 1938, with the Palace of Westminster beyond *(Hulton/Getty)*

Below: J.C.C. Davidson, party chairman 1926–30, poses at work *(Hulton/Getty)*

The pinnacle of Central Office's success perhaps came in the decade after the defeat of 1945. During the Second World War the office had moved to Old Queen Street, where the Research Department had established its own headquarters, and then again to new premises in Abbey House on Victoria Street in 1946. It was here that Lord Woolton, chairman between 1946 and 1955, built his formidable political machine. Affectionately referred to as 'Uncle Fred' by Office staff, Woolton had run one of Manchester's largest stores, Lewis's, before rising to prominence as Minister of Food during the Second World War. Woolton instituted a far-reaching reform of Central Office and expanded it to nearly 250 members of staff within five years. The propaganda and media operation was enhanced

Lord Woolton, party chairman 1946–55, surveys campaign posters for the 1955 general election with party officials in Central Office (then located in Abbey House) shortly after Churchill stood down *(Corbis)*

with a new broadcasting department, while concerted efforts were made to reach out to a much larger audience than the rapidly growing party membership, which had already risen to nearly 3 million by 1952. The Research Department was relaunched as a separate body, remaining in Old Queen Street, and was to prove its value by supplying shadow Cabinets and MPs with high-quality information.

In June 1958 Central Office was on the move again. With its elegant and rather imposing front, No. 32 Smith Square embodied the prestige and power of Central Office, which Woolton had done so much to augment. Central Office and its ancillary bodies at the heart of the party remained strong throughout much of the 1950s and the early 1960s, with only a few changes being implemented by successive chairmen and directors (as the principal agents were now known). Following the narrow defeat of 1964, the Office supervised the party's first formal leadership election, ensured better training and salaries for agents in constituencies and stepped up membership drives, all of which contributed to the return to power six years later. Following the Heath era,

Margaret Thatcher brought Lord Thorneycroft back out of retirement to recharge Central Office's batteries, and he proved the most effective chairman since Woolton, ably assisted by Baroness Young from 1976. Once again the party machine had come to the aid of a new leader, facilitating greatly Mrs Thatcher's recovery of the party's fortune.

HIGHS AND LOWS, 1979–2003

Central Office often led other parties' organisations in pioneering new forms of organisation and campaigning techniques. After 1979, a new marketing department was set up to modernise communications, gleaning much from the Republican Party's campaign techniques in the USA. An influx of younger and commercially savvy staff in the 1980s, such as Anthony Garner and Tony Garrett, enabled party headquarters to adopt new and more sophisticated methods of propaganda and recruitment. The use of

information technology, direct mailing and opinion polling was far more advanced than anything the party's opponents were to develop until the early 1990s, when Labour began to tap into the expertise of the US Democrat Party. There was an increasingly regular turnover of party chairmen, but most of them made their mark, notably Cecil Parkinson and Norman Tebbit with their election successes in 1983 and 1987. The period also saw reversals. One was the absorption of the Research Department into the Central Office machine in 1979, ending its semi-detached status, which denied the party its own internal 'think-tank' and intellectual hub. Rising costs incurred by increasingly expensive campaigns combined with depleting funds from falling membership became a major concern for successive

32 Smith Square, the site of Conservative Central Office between 1958 and 2004 (PA)

Margaret Thatcher and Norman Tebbit waving to the crowd below Central Office after the party's third successive election victory, June 1987. They had many differences during the campaign *(Hulton/Getty)*

chairmen and treasurers. As Mrs Thatcher's premiership began to unravel, so too did the organisational prowess of Conservative Central Office. After the fourth successive victory of 1992 during which Chris Patten was chairman, financial difficulties resulted in Central Office shedding seventy jobs in 1994, a sizeable chunk of its permanent staff. The party even had to resort to mortgaging 32 Smith Square soon after the 1997 general election.

Cecil Parkinson's return from political retirement to the chairmanship after the 1997 defeat provided some stability in the immediate aftermath. Hague turned to Archie Norman, the former Asda boss and newly elected MP, to 'overhaul and modernise'

Central Office as its new chief executive in the summer of 1998. Norman embarked on a rationalisation programme which involved a £3 million cut in spending, redundancy for 40 per cent of staff and the closure of several regional offices. The news that these included leading figures such as the former campaigns manager, Tony Garrett, who had worked for the party for twenty-seven years, caused inevitable upset with staff and association chairmen. Norman undertook a major restructuring of departments and oversaw the creation of a 'war room', a copy of New Labour's innovation at its Millbank headquarters. There were some initiatives, including the creation of the One Nation Unit in 2000, which Hague charged with drawing up proposals for tackling poverty and encouraging family life; but little of its work filtered through to party policy at election time. For all William Hague's attempts at a fresh start, disagreements over party policy and clashes of personality saw Central Office become the focus for discontent within the party as it tumbled to another humiliating defeat in June 2001.

While Iain Duncan Smith's first chairman, David Davis, was criticised for failing to make an impact on a demoralised Central Office, Theresa May equipped herself well as the first woman to chair the party. Internal battles between the modernising wing of the party, led by supporters of Michael Portillo, and traditionalists remained the hallmark of Central Office after the 2001 election. Clashes of personality and disagreements over policy it seemed would not go away.

BETTER TIMES? 2004–

A genuinely fresh start would occur only after November 2003. Michael Howard's decision to appoint Liam Fox and Maurice Saatchi as co-chairmen, with the former attending to the grassroots and media operation and the latter overseeing Central Office itself, raised eyebrows at first, but soon began to pay dividends. The streamlining of departments and restructuring of activities

Theresa May, the first woman to become party chairman (2002–3), with her trademark leopard-skin shoes *(PA)*

Lord Saatchi and Dr Liam Fox, party co-chairmen since November 2003, with Central Office staff wave goodbye to Smith Square in July 2004, after 46 years of good and bad memories *(Hulton/Getty)*

within the office has placed the party again on a much firmer footing. Howard made clear that the party would make a clean break from Smith Square. Following a good showing in the local government elections in June 2004, Central Office was given a new lease of life when it moved into state-of-the-art offices in 25 Victoria Street. It was hoped that the move would draw to a close a decade of defeat and infighting that had done so much to tarnish what was once one of the most formidable party machines in the Western world.

TOWN AND COUNTRY

Outside the precincts of Westminster, Conservatives have assembled in some of the finest buildings in the country, to conduct serious political business and to enjoy good company in luscious surroundings. They were not unique in this respect: Whigs and Liberals would also rendezvous in smart locations in and around London; but the grandeur, lavishness and sheer scale of mass rallies, political salons and country-house parties distinguished the Tory party from the early nineteenth century onwards. As the power and influence of the landed classes declined in the twentieth century, the party's social scene lost much of its Victorian and Edwardian grandeur, but the Tories' appetite for intrigue and plotting remains to this day a feature of life in both town and country.

POLITICKING

After 1921, prime ministers of all parties would retreat to Chequers, the Buckinghamshire estate bequeathed to the nation by the Lee family. But before then, Tory leaders, especially in the nineteenth century, were of such independent means that they could turn their elegant London homes and country houses into political salons and meeting places. Peel's grand town house at No. 4 Whitehall Gardens and his estate, Drayton Manor in Staffordshire, witnessed some of the high drama surrounding the party's split over the Corn Laws. In the 1840s and '50s, Lord Stanley invited senior Tories to Knowsley in Lancashire, which was set in beautifully landscaped gardens designed by Capability Brown, to discuss tactics in opposition. Disraeli dismissed Knowsley as one of the 'ugliest homes in England', although he was rather more complimentary about Stanley's splendid house in St James's Square. Disraeli himself would often chair important shadow-Cabinet meetings at his London home at 19 Curzon Street, but it was to his beloved Hughenden Manor in the Chilterns that he retreated for solace, reading

Hughenden Manor, Disraeli's Buckinghamshire estate from 1848, in *Morris's Views*, 1879 *(Mary Evans)*

Winston Churchill bricklaying with daughter Mary at his home in Chartwell, Kent in 1928 *(Hulton/Getty)*

and writing. Unlike most leading Conservative figures in the nineteenth century, Disraeli did not inherit a fine country pile. Disraeli believed that the acquisition of Hughenden, made possible only through the benevolence of his patron, Lord George Bentinck, was the key to advancing up the party's hierarchy. No. 20 Arlington Street, in St James's, was another favourite location for Tory circles to meet later on in the century. Lord Salisbury could entertain over a thousand people in the five-storey house and many more at his huge estate of Hatfield, Hertfordshire (as we shall see on page 154).

In the twentieth century, fewer Conservative leaders were to reside in large country estates. Bonar Law was not an aristocrat but the son of a manse who became a businessman. Winston Churchill bought Chartwell in 1924 for its magnificent views over the Weald of Kent. Until his death in 1965, Chartwell's rooms and gardens bore the imprint of a statesman who was never happier than when he entertained guests and family, or when he was painting, landscaping and writing. 'A day away from Chartwell is a day wasted', Churchill once remarked. From his study in Chartwell, Churchill worked on his budgets as Tory Chancellor between 1924 and 1929; and during his years in the wilderness in the 1930s he convened meetings of advisers and military personnel to discuss the growing crisis in Europe. High-level meetings in the war and when he was Prime Minister in the early 1950s frequently took place at Chartwell, to the occasional consternation of Ministers and officials. Home had his home, the Hirsel, in Scotland as his retreat, and Macmillan Birch Grove in Sussex, where he entertained President Kennedy.

Blenheim Palace, the birthplace of Winston Churchill and home to the Duke of Malborough, was perhaps the grandest of all platforms for leaders to address the party faithful. Bonar Law's speech on Irish Home Rule at the Unionist rally of July 1912 was one among many events to take place at Blenheim. The great municipal halls of Birmingham, Liverpool, Glasgow and other industrial cities were centres of provincial power in the Conservative Party until the 1950s. Although Joseph Chamberlain established his reforming credentials as a Liberal Mayor of Birmingham, his alliance with

Macmillan addressing the party faithful at Swinton College in 1949 *(Hulton/Getty)*

the Conservatives after 1886 encouraged many of his supporters to switch sides, helping to make Birmingham City Hall a bastion of Conservatism in the early 1900s. His impassioned speech calling for Tarrif Reform at the City Hall in May 1903 was a pivotal moment in the party's history. Another building which became important to Conservatives in the twentieth century was Swinton Castle in Masham, Yorkshire. In 1948 Lord Swinton, a distinguished Conservative Cabinet minister in the interwar years (and briefly after), donated part of his family home to the party to form a college which, in the words of R.A. Butler, would enable 'keen party members [to] sit at the feet of the leaders of modern Conservatism'. The weekend schools at Swinton College formed part of a highly successful political education campaign launched after the war for tens of thousands of party members and aspiring candidates. After twenty-nine years of loyal service, the college closed in 1977.

Aside from party leaders, the homes of other senior figures in the party would become political salons and headquarters for leadership campaigns. In the 1980s and '90s, No. 8 Lord North Street, the home of Jonathan Aitken, became one of the most vibrant Tory salons in Westminster. The street has long been associated with political intrigue and was also home to Harold Wilson as Prime Minister and the Institute of Economic Affairs. Only walking distance from the Palace of Westminster and Central Office, Aitken would assemble an array of guests for champagne parties and the more sober meetings of the Conservative Philosophy Group. Among those who attended were President Richard

Nixon, as well as many of the thinkers, journalists and politicians who were to influence Conservative politics in the Thatcher and Major years. When John Major invited his critics to 'put up or shut up' in June 1995, his campaign team operated out of Alistair Goodlad's house in the street, much to the bemusement of the media, who assumed that the team met in the official campaign headquarters in Cowley Street, just around the corner. Meanwhile telephone lines were being installed by supporters of Michael Portillo elsewhere in Westminster in anticipation of a second round in the contest. They were not needed, but two further leadership elections in 1997 and 2001 ensured that several smart London homes of Tory MPs would become hives of campaigning.

ENTERTAINING

Combining business with pleasure has always been a way of life in politics. Even in bad times, politicians and their faithful try to lift their spirits with good living. Ever since the days of Pitt and Wellington, high society has always been welcome in the villas, country piles and elegant town houses of the Conservative elite. According generous hospitality to royalty, fellow politicians, leaders of commerce and industry and patrons of the arts has been part of the course. The political house party is one such event, which has featured prominently in the Tory calendar since the late 1800s. One of the most celebrated Tory hostesses from the Victorian era was Lady Londonderry, whose weekend house parties saw political careers made and broken. The Duke of Devonshire was another grandee who delighted in welcoming Conservative leading lights to Compton Place, his seaside residence in Eastbourne, where he was instrumental in bringing together the Chamberlains and the Cecils in the 1890s.

The great political house parties of the nineteenth century began to fade after the First World War, as the decline of the aristocracy's political influence and the mass

Balfour, badminton racket in tow, with Lady Londonderry at a house party in Hertfordshire, a few weeks before war was declared in 1914 *(Hulton/Getty)*

ENTERTAINING AT HATFIELD

The Jacobean splendour of Hatfield House in Hertfordshire, ancestral home to the Cecil family, provided the setting for many a garden party, dinner and entertainment for both Tory grandee and grass-roots member when Salisbury was party leader. The 20,000-acre estate, which contained the main house of 127 rooms, numerous outbuildings, extensive gardens and even a racing track, was his pride and joy. The Salisbury household, with its forty servants, laid on entertainment on a massive scale. Visiting heads of state from the Kaiser of Germany to the Shah of Persia would be welcomed in lavish style, as was Queen Victoria, the Archbishop of Canterbury and writers including Lewis Carroll, Robert Browning and Matthew Arnold. On one occasion nearly 5,000 distinguished guests attended a garden party in honour of a visit from the Prince of Naples, many of whom had travelled to Hatfield from King's Cross in special trains.

Like other great social occasions, such as Ascot and the Derby, gentlemen would dress in the standard attire of top hat and tails and the ladies in long, laced dresses and florid hats, with elegant umbrellas. Festivities included watching trick-shooting, equestrian displays and, if guests were lucky, demonstrations of Lord Salisbury's scientific innovations. In 1877, visitors to Hatfield were startled to discover the main rooms covered with telephone cords. As one family member recorded, guests were even more bemused when they heard Salisbury's voice 'resounding oratorically from selected spots within the house, as he reiterated with varying emphasis and expression: "Hey diddle diddle the cat and the fiddle; the cow jumped over the moon"'. Salisbury was happy for his guests to mingle and amuse themselves rather than dragoon them around from

Nancy Astor entertaining George Bernard Shaw at Cliveden in August 1941 (Corbis)

extension of the franchise heralded a new era of mixing politics with sociability. Cliveden was one of the notable exceptions. In the interwar years, the Conservative Party's first woman MP (and the first elected woman MP to sit in Parliament) played hostess to some extraordinary parties. The family home of Lady Nancy Astor, Cliveden, set among 375 acres of landscaped gardens in the Thames valley, was a wedding present from her father-in-law, the millionaire newspaper proprietor William Waldorf (Viscount Astor). Among Lady Astor's guests at Cliveden were King Edward VII, President Roosevelt, Rudyard Kipling, Henry James, T.E. Lawrence, George

one room to the next, a form of entertaining which he called 'the great cause of Guest Emancipation'.

The soirées and weekend garden parties served an important purpose for Lord Salisbury. 'The family learnt everything by discussion', recalled one guest, adding that politics, religion and foreign affairs 'were discussed in every passage and doorway of the house'. They also allowed him to reach out to the growing leagues of the party faithful. The gardens and parks of Hatfield also hosted a series of meetings of the Primrose League, founded in 1883. In 1879 over a thousand members of the London and Westminster Working Men's Constitutional Association, which was also founded to mobilise the Conservative working-class vote, travelled up to Hatfield to hear Salisbury espouse the virtues of Empire and national unity, and castigate Gladstone's Liberal alliance with the Irish Nationalists.

Hatfield House, the ancestral home of Lord Salisbury (Corbis)

Bernard Shaw and Charlie Chaplin. By the 1930s, Cliveden had established itself not only as the stately home for Conservatives to mingle with society but also to influence thinking in troubled times. The 'Cliveden set' believed appeasement was the right way to contain Hitler's rise in Continental Europe, and rejoiced when Neville Chamberlain returned from Munich in 1938 announcing 'peace in our time'. Winston Churchill, who would occasionally visit Cliveden along with the rich and the famous, evidently disagreed, and also found the rather decadent lifestyle of the Astors something of a bore. There was little love lost between them. 'Winston,' said Lady Astor to Churchill at the breakfast table in Cliveden, 'if I were married to you I'd put poison in your coffee.' 'Nancy,' replied Churchill, 'if I were married to you, I'd drink it.'

An insight into the life can be seen in *The Remains of the Day*, the Kazuro Ishiguro novel made into a popular film. Cliveden is now an exclusive hotel.

CONFERENCE SEASON

The Conservative Party has not always headed to the seaside for the annual party conference. Brighton did not host its first conference until 1875, Scarborough was not used until the 1920s, Bournemouth and Margate did not host the annual gathering until the 1930s. Only from the early 1960s did the party conference regularly meet in the three 'big B' seaside towns.

Reflecting the strength of Conservative and Unionist support in Britain's great industrial cities and other large provincial cities and towns, the party initially assembled annually in the municipal halls of Liverpool, Newcastle, Nottingham and Leeds as well as in London. The first conference of the National Union of Conservative and Constitutional (later Unionist) Associations was held in London in 1867, attended by only six delegates and one chairman, Disraeli's Principal Agent Sir John Gorst. Disraeli conceived the National Union as a body to bring together the voluntary side of the party, but he never intended it to influence policy or the direction of the party's leadership. As the years passed, the National Union and its conference played a much more significant and, at times, highly controversial role. The rank and file have used the conference as a vehicle with which to press the leadership into taking various courses of action. As it grew in importance, the annual party conference became the venue for some pivotal moments in the party's history. We conclude with five such conferences. We omit the one conference that directly influenced the party leadership. Richard Kelly, the authority on

Bonar Law addressing the 1911 annual party conference in Leeds only a few days after his election as leader
(*Hulton/Getty*)

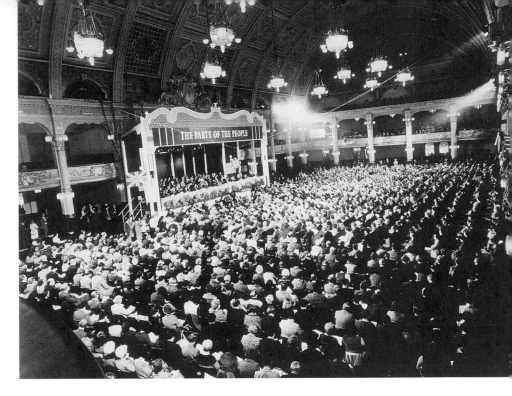

The 1977 annual party conference in Blackpool, two years before Mrs Thatcher's first election victory *(Bodleian Library)*

Tory conferences, has argued that the 1950 conference, which encouraged the leadership to accept a target of 300,000 houses built a year, was in fact unexceptional.

Disraeli's Crystal Palace Speech, 1872

Although Disraeli failed to attend the first conference, he decided to use its stage in 1872 for his powerful declaration of Conservatism. Following his address to a gathering of Lancashire Conservatives at the Free Trade Hall in Manchester, Disraeli declared to the sixth conference of the National Union at Crystal Palace that the 'Tory Party, unless it is a National Party, is nothing'. His speech, though short on policy detail and prescription, marked the end of a long period of playing second fiddle to the Palmerston moderate coalition of Whigs, Peelites and Liberals, while projecting the Conservatives as the party of power. Disraeli's call for the party to represent the 'maintenance of the empire of England', the preservation of national institutions and 'the elevation of the condition of the people' has echoed down the years.

Fighting for the Union, Liverpool 1921

The prospect of Irish Home Rule split Gladstone's Liberal Party in the late nineteenth century, but it was the Conservative Party that was to be thrown into chaos between 1911 and 1914 when it fought in vain to defend Ireland's position in the Union. Bonar Law's highly provocative speech to the conference in London in 1912, demanding resistance to the measures proposed by Liberal Prime Minister Asquith, stirred up diehard sentiment in the rank and file. But it was Bonar Law's successor, Austen Chamberlain, who, having had to come to terms with the inevitability of Irish self-government, faced the tempestuous conferences in 1921. It was the party managers' misfortune that the conference was held in Liverpool, a highly sectarian city, on the eve of the signing of the Anglo-Irish Treaty. Chamberlain supported the treaty, but many in the hall did not, and there was a strong possibility that the conference would formally oppose the leadership over the issue. As the debate on Ireland drew to a climax, fights and scuffles broke out in the main conference hall between rank-and-file members representing various sectarian corners of the city. In the end, Chamberlain's speech did enough to calm nerves and reassure the party of the merits of the treaty; but the division and violence of the 1921 conference, which received relatively little coverage in the days before radio and television, contributed to his demise the following year.

Leadership Convention, Blackpool 1963

Harold Macmillan's untimely resignation as Prime Minister and Tory leader during the week of the party conference in October 1963 precipitated a leadership crisis that was to be played out in full view of the party faithful and the wider public on their television screens. The conference was immediately transformed into an American-style party

R.A. Butler applauded after his speech to the 1963 annual conference, but it would not be enough to clinch him the leadership. Iain Macleod applauds to his right, while the two other contenders, Lords Hailsham and Home, are to his left (PA)

A scene of devastation at the Grand Hotel, Brighton, following the IRA bombing in 1984 *(Hulton/Getty)*

convention with activists adorning badges and waving banners in support of their chosen candidate. The routine platform speeches of the prime contenders were now invested with far greater significance. The volume, length and tone of the applause of the amassed party faithful in the hall became an important barometer of opinion and those with influence. In the end, Butler's performance was poor, Macleod's well-received, and Maudling's indifferent; and Hailsham's backfired spectacularly. Yet it was Home, whose speech in many ways was the least inspiring of them all, who was eventually invited by the Queen to form a government. With all other factors weighed in the balance, Home was considered by the 'magic circle' (later castigated by Macleod) to be the least unpopular Tory to lead the party, unlike his rivals, who had divided party opinion in Blackpool.

Terrorist Atrocity, Brighton 1984

Late into the night of 12 October 1984 a large IRA bomb exploded in the Grand Hotel, Brighton, where many prominent Conservatives were staying for the party conference. The intention was to murder Margaret Thatcher and as many members of her government as possible. The IRA's plot failed, but five people were killed, including Anthony Berry MP, and the wife of John Wakeham, the Chief Whip, who was himself seriously injured. Norman Tebbit, Mrs Thatcher's Industry Secretary, was also badly hurt along with his wife, who was paralysed by the bomb. Thatcher's decision to proceed with the conference showed defiance in the face of adversity. She roundly condemned the outrage in her speech the following day, which even her detractors thought showed her steel. Despite the shock waves that resonated throughout the party and the political establishment in the aftermath of the attack, Mrs Thatcher went on to sign the Anglo-Irish Treaty the following year, much to the disappointment of the Unionists in Northern Ireland.

Norman Tebbit holds aloft the Maastricht Treaty at the 1992 conference. Major, out of focus on the left, looks on, seething inside (PA)

Putting the Boot in, Brighton 1992

John Major faced the toughest party conference of his political life in October 1992. Despite the general election victory earlier in the year, his government was profoundly damaged by its forced exit from the exchange-rate mechanism (ERM) in September and divisions over Europe were bubbling under the surface. The party desperately needed a trouble-free conference to restore morale and confidence in the leadership. It was not to be. Norman Tebbit, who had retired from the frontline as party Chairman in 1987, had not intended to make another conference speech. But the need of the hour he believed called him back. As he walked slowly and solemnly to the podium, parts of the conference hall rose to cheer him on, much to the revulsion of Major, Hurd and other ministers sitting on the platform. Revelling in the affirmation, Tebbit invited audience participation, evincing shouts of 'No' to a succession of questions: did they want to be citizens of a European Union, to see a single currency, to let other countries decide immigration controls? After his rallying speech, Tebbit walked into the body of the hall, waving amid ecstatic applause. It was an act of humiliation for the leadership. But it also unleashed pent up frustrations which divided the party for the next ten or more years.

SEVEN

THE GREAT AND THE GOOD

The Conservative Party would not have risen to become one of the most successful parties in the Western world were it not for some very remarkable leaders. Leaders of the Conservative Party have frequently been at the helm of the nation. Since William Pitt 'the Younger' became Prime Minister in 1783, twenty-three of his thirty-eight successors have been either Tory or Conservative. But they are only the select few among the great and good of the party. Its achievements in office and in opposition owe much to the brilliance of others: those who made a difference from positions of power and influence inside the Cabinet, shadow Cabinet as well as the often powerful Whips' Office and 1922 Committee. This chapter highlights just some of the men and women who did so much to improve the fortunes of the Conservative Party throughout its long history.

LEADERS

The epithet of 'great Conservative leader' can be applied to only a select few among the party's twenty-six leaders since the late eighteenth century: Pitt, Liverpool, Peel, Disraeli, Salisbury, Baldwin, Churchill, Macmillan and Thatcher. These were the defining leaders who summed up successful ages in the Tory party's history. They all combined, albeit in different ways, 'a disposition to preserve' with an 'ability to improve' – a dual role to which Edmund Burke believed all Conservative statesmen should aspire. None of the other nineteen leaders were able in the same way to command or to define the party, which took its character from their personal styles, priorities and policies. The electoral success the party enjoyed under them was very much a personal pledge of confidence in and support for the leader, all of whom in their different ways were powerful communicators.

GREAT COMMUNICATORS

The power of speech in politics can easily be underestimated: well-chosen words can often make the difference between victory and defeat in a vital House of Commons debate. Pitt and Peel could command the House with their oratory, but it was Disraeli, Baldwin and Churchill in particular who displayed the ability not only to gauge the mood of the chamber, but also to win the argument through their speeches. Disraeli could easily humiliate his opponents (on both sides of the House) by the force of his razor-edged rhetoric. Only in Gladstone did he meet his match. 'In terms of total mastery of the House of Commons, you can't beat Baldwin', remarked Bill Deedes, who, as a young lobby correspondent for the *Morning Post*, reported on one of Baldwin's last speeches as

Winston Churchill makes a radio broadcast to the British public from the White House, Washington DC in 1943
(Hulton/Getty)

Baldwin with his trademark pipe in 1930 *(PA)*

Prime Minister in May 1937, observing that the interwar leader used nothing more than scribbled notes on the back of an envelope for his inspiration. Churchill's speeches after May 1940 will always be remembered as some of the most effective ever made by any British Prime Minister. Macmillan, Thatcher and Hague were also highly able and often entertaining performers in the Commons. Ever since Disraeli's seminal address at Crystal Palace in 1872, Tory leaders have often used the platform of the party conference to both reassure the troops and project their vision for the party. Mrs Thatcher's conference speeches, most notably 'the Lady's not for turning' speech in 1980, enhanced her authority over the party as she made it clear she would not deviate from her chosen course.

Articulating the Conservative cause in a way that chimed with the times was a skill that only the most successful of the party's leaders possessed. Despite his suspicion of mass politics and the spread of democracy, Lord Salisbury's cultivation of 'Villa Toryism' tapped into an appetite for Conservative politics among the growing suburbs of middle-class Britain at the turn of the twentieth century. Stanley Baldwin, in the new age of the mass electorate, grasped the need to convey a Conservative appeal beyond the traditional heartlands. As Philip Williamson has pointed out, Baldwin's 'Englishness' chimed with the public mood. Through his skilful use of the new media of radio and newsreel, Baldwin's reassuring 'fireside chat' manner on a range of issues warmed the country to his leadership and to the party during the troubled times of the interwar years. His meticulous preparation included taking advice from the BBC's first Director-General, John Reith. Baldwin's pipe became his trademark, featuring prominently in newspaper photographs and newsreels and even on the radio: the strike of a match would regularly punctuate his flow of words. Twenty years later, Harold Macmillan established himself as one of the most natural performers of the early television age. Macmillan made brilliant use of party political broadcasts to get across his message, which was again of reassurance but also talk of the better life which the Tories alone could provide.

THE LONG AND SHORT OF TORY PREMIERSHIPS

SIX LONGEST-SERVING CONSERVATIVE PRIME MINISTERS (SINCE 1783)

1. *William Pitt: 18 years, 343 days (1783–1801; 1804–6)*

2. *Earl of Liverpool: 14 years, 305 days (1812–27)*

3. *Marquess of Salisbury: 13 years, 252 days (1885–6; 1886–92; 1895–1902)*

4. *Margaret Thatcher: 11 years, 209 days (1979–90)*

5. *Winston Churchill: 8 years, 240 days (1940–5; 1951–5)*

6. *Stanley Baldwin: 7 years, 82 days (1923; 1924–9; 1935–7)*

SIX SHORTEST-SERVING CONSERVATIVE PRIME MINISTERS (SINCE 1783)

1. *George Canning: 119 days (1827)*

2. *Viscount Goderich: 130 days (1827–8)*

3. *Andrew Bonar Law: 209 days (1922–3)*

4. *Sir Alec-Douglas Home: 362 days (1963–4)*

5. *Spencer Perceval: 2 years, 221 days (1809–12)*

6. *Duke of Wellington: 2 years, 320 days (1828–30)*

DRIVERS OF IDEAS

Political imagination is another essential quality that has enabled successful Tory leaders to adapt the party to the aspirations of each new age. They have also encouraged new thinking and tapped into the most fertile intellectual forces of their generation, often leaving much of the intellectual and policy groundwork to their senior lieutenants – Churchill and Thatcher being the prime examples. The latter ensured that the party digested innovative policy ideas that werc being developed by a growing band of think-tanks on the free markets right into the 1970s. With Keith Joseph and Geoffrey Howe spearheading intellectual renewal inside the party, Thatcher relentlessly pursued a strategy which, though deliberately short on detail, enabled her to carry the party into government bubbling with ideas and confidence.

Churchill has often been criticised for his lack of interest in policy renewal during and after the war, which was driven by Eden and Butler, but he managed to hold his team together and became a champion for its new policies in the 1950 and 1951 general elections. The need for periodic recasting of the party's appeal was shown by Peel, whose Tamworth Manifesto in 1835 represented the earliest attempt to draw together Conservative principles and beliefs into a moderate and reforming programme for government, rejecting the reactionary Toryism of the Reform Crisis.

RISK TAKERS

Many Tory leaders have taken great risks to get to the top job but often become risk-averse once they are there. Some of the clearest examples of leaders defying opinion in their own party for the sake of advancing its position in the country come over the extension of the franchise in the late nineteenth century. When Gladstone's Liberal government failed to pass the Second Reform Bill through Parliament, Disraeli and Derby formed a minority administration to reshape the bill and re-establish the Conservative Party's reforming credentials with the 1867 Reform Act. With several leading Cabinet ministers resigning and the potential for a huge backbench revolt, Derby exclaimed: 'This is the end of the Conservative Party.' But, with Disraeli's skilful manoeuvring, the gamble paid off. Despite losing at the subsequent election, the party had asserted itself as an alternative government after over thirty years of almost continuous opposition. Lord Salisbury too grasped the opportunity to shape the measures designed to broaden the electorate. By amending the 1884 Third Reform Act and 1885 Redistribution Act, Salisbury wisely predicted that the Conservative Party would have to draw its strength from the rapidly expanding suburbs. His foresight and tactical brilliance paved the way for the suburban middle classes to become the bedrock of its electoral strength in the twentieth century. Thatcher's decision to forsake the policies pursued by postwar Tory leaders was a similar 'leap in the dark' which allowed the party to power ahead with confidence and enjoy a long period of dominance.

In contrast, those leaders who do not 'make the weather' can be bold but not in ways that cement new periods of hegemony. Heath took Britain into the EEC in 1973, undeterred by opposition within his own party. He persevered and, in his eyes, grasped a historic opportunity, which had eluded Harold Macmillan before him, of opening a new chapter in the history of the party and the country. John Major's leadership in initiating the peace process in Northern Ireland was another course of action which was beset with danger and earned him little electoral reward. Despite setbacks along the way, above all from his own right wing and from the Tory press, his determination to move the process forward between 1993 and 1997 was both imaginative and courageous.

LEADING FROM THE FRONT

Taking command of a crisis or leading the country through war gives prime ministers of all parties opportunities to make a mark denied to those who served in settled times. Many of the key nine Tory leaders exploited such events to their lasting political advantage. It took the ingenuity of Pitt to galvanise support for the wars against Napoleon at the turn of the nineteenth century, while the Duke of Wellington, hero of those wars, resolved one of the most contentious disputes in British politics, Catholic emancipation, in 1829. It had sounded the death knell for Wellington's Tory predecessors, particularly Canning, and landed the old Tory Party in serious trouble. Disraeli showed steady and determined leadership during the Eastern Crisis of 1875–8, culminating in his negotiating triumph at the Congress of Berlin in 1878.

Baldwin's resolution of the General Strike in 1926 was achieved through a combination of delicate diplomacy, shrewd decision-making and a public stance which inspired confidence and reassurance. 'I have always believed that it was Baldwin who saved the country from a real disaster in 1926', remarked the young backbencher, Harold Macmillan. If it were not for his skills in managing another crisis – that of the abdication of Edward VIII – the survival of the monarchy in 1936 could even have been in doubt. Margaret Thatcher's determination to prevail in the Falklands war in 1982 transformed the fortunes of her premiership and her party. Again it was the wartime leadership of Winston Churchill that transformed him from one whose career up to 1939 has been described as a failure into the party's and nation's most revered leader in adverse times. 'I have nothing to offer but blood, toil, tears and sweat', Churchill told the House of Commons soon after becoming Prime Minister in May 1940. In taking command of Britain's war effort in the darkest days of the war, Churchill lifted the morale of the nation and paved the way to victory.

RALLYING THE NATION

England has saved herself by her exertions, and will, I trust, save Europe by her example.

William Pitt 'the Younger', speech to the House of Commons after the Battle of Trafalgar, 1805

For my part I do not believe that the country is in danger, I think England is safe in the care of men who inhabit her; that she is safe in something much more precious than her accumulated capital – her accumulated experience; she is safe in her national character, in her fame, in the traditions of a thousand years, and in that glorious future which I believe awaits her.

Benjamin Disraeli, speech to the House of Commons, third reading of the Reform Bill, 1867

To me, England is the country, and the country is England.

Stanley Baldwin, speech to the Royal Society of St George, 1924

We shall defend our island, whatever the cost may be. We shall fight on the beaches. We shall fight on the landing grounds. We shall fight in the fields, and in the streets, we shall fight in the hills. We shall never surrender!

Winston Churchill, speech to the House of Commons after Dunkirk, June 1940

We have ceased to be a nation in retreat. We have instead a new-found confidence – born in the economic battles at home and tested and found true 8,000 miles away . . . Britain found herself again in the South Atlantic and will not look back from the victory she has won.

Margaret Thatcher, speaking after the recapture of the Falklands Islands, July 1982

LIFE OUTSIDE POLITICS

'Conservatives do not believe that the political struggle is the most important thing in life', wrote Lord Hailsham. Most of those who have risen to the apex of power in the party have invariably excelled and distinguished themselves in other walks of life. Almost all of the party's leaders enjoyed interests outside politics, which gave them a much-needed hinterland. Literature and writing was one of them. Disraeli once famously remarked, 'When I want to read a novel, I write one.' Indeed, his literary output as a novelist is the

Churchill painting a beach scene from the Surf Club in Miami, Florida in 1946 (*Hulton/Getty*)

most prodigious of all the party leaders. Disraeli wrote twelve novels in his life, beginning with *Vivian Grey*, published at the age of 21, and ending with *Endymion*, when he was 76, one year before his death. His trilogy – *Coningsby*, *Sybil* and *Tancred* – was among the best-selling works of his generation and provide an enlightening insight into his thinking on society, religion and, of course, politics. Balfour's philosophical tracts, including his best known book, *A Defence of Philosophical Doubt*, were considered scholarly but,

Baldwin enjoying the library in his country home, Astley Hall (*Mary Evans*)

unlike in Disraeli's case, did little to advance his reputation at large, let alone within his party. One Tory-sympathising journal, the *Pall Mall Gazette*, chastised the Edwardian leader for 'shivering in philosophic doubt on the steps of a metaphysical bathing machine'. Baldwin confessed that his was a 'second class intellect', but he did possess, as his cousin, Rudyard Kipling, observed, a 'literary creativity which lies at the heart of politics'. Books like *On England*, *Our Inheritance* and *The Torch of Freedom*, which were drawn from his collection of speeches, were clear and highly

Disraeli and his peacocks, reading under the verandah, at Hughenden. Engraving in the *Illustrated London News*, 1881 *(Mary Evans)*

accessible. No other twentieth-century Conservative leader can compare with Churchill, winner of the Nobel Prize for Literature, for literary output: he was also an artist of rare talent, as can be seen in the splendid illustrated book of his painting, written by his daughter, Mary Soames, who also edited the letters between him and Clementine. Anthony Eden wrote three dull volumes of memoirs, but a splendid book on his experience of the First World War and his early years, *Another World*. Harold Macmillan was a particularly well-read leader whose diaries, recently edited by Peter Catterall, are much more compelling than his laboured six volumes of memoirs. Recent leaders have continued this literary tradition, albeit with mixed results. Writing the life of Pitt 'the Younger' provided William Hague with a new lease of life after his exit from the top, while Iain Duncan Smith's literary debut, *The Devil's Tune*, encountered almost as much criticism as his period as leader.

Many Tory leaders have embraced the great outdoors in one way or another. When doctors recommended that Lord Salisbury lose weight, he took to cycling around the paths of his Hatfield estate on a tricycle. So much did he enjoy this new pursuit that he constructed a proper asphalted cycle track, and was constantly accompanied by a groom to prevent him from toppling over. Other leaders were successful sportsmen. Balfour was a keen golfer, while Edward Heath capped his prowess as a conductor by excelling at sailing. Alec Douglas-Home is the only Tory leader to have played first-class cricket. Lord Dunglass, as he was called in his youth, played for Middlesex in the 1920s and toured South America with the MCC in 1926–7. In all he played ten first-class matches, and

FOUR WIVES AND A HUSBAND

Aspiring leaders must have tolerant, support-
ive and able spouses if their careers are to take
off. The sacrifices they have to make, as do their
children, are limitless.

MARY ANN DISRAELI

Disraeli would not have made it so far up the
'greasy pole' without the help of several women
in his life. The wife of his family solicitor,
Sarah Austen, supported his literary ambi-
tions, while his love affair with Henrietta
Sykes, a vivacious and wealthy lady who moved

Mary Ann Disraeli by W.H. Mote, 1839 *(Mary Evans)*

in the highest political circles, was instrumental
to his entering Conservative politics after
failing to be elected as a Radical and an
independent in the early 1830s. It was his
marriage to Mary Anne Wyndham Lewis in
1839 that gave Disraeli the attention and
security that he desperately craved. A wealthy
widow twelve years his senior, she paid off all of
his debts and became his emotional anchor.
Utterly devoted to his political career, she would
often check his many letters for mistakes. On the
night of his victory over the 1867 Reform Act
she welcomed him home with a bottle of cham-
pagne and a pie from Fortnum & Mason's.
Queen Victoria was the other main woman to
command Disraeli's loyalty and affection,
remarking that he was 'full of poetry, romance
and chivalry'.

LUCY BALDWIN

Lucy Baldwin also proved a model Tory leader's
wife. The daughter of a scientist and mother to
their four daughters and two sons, she loyally
supported her husband's rise to the top. She was
never far from his side, even accompanying him
into the recording studios for his BBC
broadcasts with knitting kit in tow. She loyally
entertained all manner of guests at Number
10 on Thursday evenings. On one occasion he
returned to Downing Street from the Commons
to hear a performance by the visiting White
Russian Cossack Choir, while on another he
was greeted with a display of traditional
quilting work by the wives of Welsh miners.

Lucy Baldwin with her husband, after voting in the St George's by-election in March 1931 *(Popperfoto)*

Dorothy Macmillan addressing the Conservative Women's Conference in 1958 *(Bodleian Library)*

Tall, elegant and always smartly dressed with fur, Lucy was very active within the women's organisation of the party.

DOROTHY MACMILLAN

Lady Dorothy Macmillan, daughter of the Duke of Devonshire, was another generous hostess. Garden tea parties were her particular forte – a regular occasion in the Tory social calendar when her husband was Prime Minister. She took great pleasure in preparing and serving food and drink at numerous parties. Harold wrote that she 'always arrived [at Number 10] in a Ford or Austin van filled with vast quantities of vegetables and flowers and packages of all kinds'. He was mortified when he learned in 1929 that his beloved Dorothy had been having an affair with Robert Boothby, a raffish fellow Tory MP.

Denis and Margaret Thatcher on their wedding day in December 1941 *(Hulton/Getty)*

DENIS THATCHER

'I have been married to one of the greatest women the world has ever produced. All I could produce – small as it may be – was love and loyalty', Denis Thatcher remarked on his fortieth wedding anniversary. It was the Conservative Party that brought the Thatchers together. As an activist in Kent, Denis was on the selection committee that adopted the 23-year-old research chemist, Margaret Roberts, as the Conservative candidate for Dartford in 1949 (which she lost in the general election the following year). After their marriage in 1951, Denis, a highly successful businessman, became the cornerstone of his wife's career, providing her with the financial security that enabled her to read for the bar and run for the more winnable seat of Finchley. As her political career took off, Denis became the most loyal and discreet of consorts. A driven workaholic and with few interests outside politics, Margaret Thatcher depended on her husband for wise and calming advice. He claimed never to have commented on her speeches, preferring

Macmillan knew that their youngest daughter, Sarah, was Boothby's. Some, like Anthony Howard, argue that the thirty-year affair put a steel into his backbone that drove him all the way to the top. The marriage held together throughout, and Lady Dorothy was her husband's most loyal supporter in office.

took twelve wickets with an average of 30.25 runs. John Major may well have gone on to enjoy a life playing cricket were it not for a leg injury he suffered in a car accident as a young man. As it was, he has had to satisfy himself with an encyclopaedic knowledge of the game. His lifelong enthusiasm for it, which he shared with Baldwin, would be a source of relief during his more troubled times as Prime Minister. On leaving Downing Street for the last time as Prime Minister on 2 May 1997, he revealingly set off for the Oval to find solace in cricket. Country sports have traditionally been a favourite pastime for Tory leaders. Macmillan's adventures in the grouse-shooting season are well known,

to be a 'shadow on the wall; out of sight, out of mind if necessary . . . but there to help'. It was Denis, though, who had the last word during the dramatic departure of November 1990. 'Darling, I don't want you to be humiliated', was his advice when it became clear that his wife's fifteen-year reign over the party was drawing to an ignominious close. His death in 2004 left her bereft of the best friend she ever had in life.

SANDRA HOWARD

Many wives of Tory leaders have added a touch of glamour and panache to their husbands' careers, but few more so than Sandra Howard. The daughter of an RAF wing commander, she was married three times, the first to a nephew of Alec Douglas-Home, before she tied the knot with Michael Howard in 1975. Sandra enjoyed a glittering career as a model in the 1960s, often posing for Vogue *and* Harpers & Queen *in front of the lenses of David Bailey and Norman Parkinson. A jet-setting socialite, she became acquaintanced and friends with Frank Sinatra and other show business stars on both sides of the Atlantic. Loyally at Michael Howard's side during his rise through the ranks in the 1980s and early 1990s, she confessed to being more than 'demob-happy' when her husband stood down from the front bench in 1999. Unlike many consorts, she has never been afraid to enter the fray herself, often writing letters in her husband's defence to newspaper editors who criticised him. She has also found political life 'addictive' and returned to the limelight with relish when Michael Howard emerged in November 2003.*

as is Home's fly-fishing. They are likely to be the last Tory leaders to enjoy field sports for some time. Other leaders have found enjoyment in the company of creatures great and small. 'What is a terrace without them?', Disraeli once quipped, pointing at the peacocks in his beloved Hughenden. His Buckinghamshire estate was also home to a collection of wildfowl including two swans he named Hero and Leander. Baldwin claimed he was all too happy to return to his Worcestershire home in order to 'lead a decent life and keep pigs', while Churchill was also fond of pigs (who, he said, regarded men as equals) as well as poodles, budgerigars and tropical fish.

LEADING LIGHTS

The Conservative Party is littered with careers of individuals who might have become leader, but for one reason or another never made it to the top. Most held several great offices of state in their careers and some were to have a lasting influence on the party's direction.

LEADING STATESMEN

Maintaining Britain's position as both a power broker in Europe and architect of the largest empire in the world was a central preoccupation of Tory governments in the late eighteenth and nineteenth centuries. Before entering Number 10, George Canning and Lord Salisbury had already distinguished themselves as formidable Conservative Foreign Secretaries. An ardent opponent of the French Revolution and disciple of Pitt's, Canning forged a distinctively 'liberal' foreign policy which helped to stabilise European politics in

the aftermath of Waterloo and the fall of Napoleon. Lord Salisbury dominated foreign policy in the last third of the nineteenth century, being Secretary of State for India twice and Foreign Secretary four times between 1878 and 1900 (an office which he held for most of the time he was Prime Minister). His greatest triumph came in 1878 when he accompanied Disraeli to the Congress of Berlin. Although it was seen as a personal triumph for Disraeli, who famously proclaimed 'peace with honour' after successfully containing Russia's imperial ambitions, the Treaty of Berlin bore the stamp of Salisbury's personal input.

Conservative Chancellors of the Exchequer had the great responsibility for managing what was once the largest economy in the world. Frederik 'Prosperity' Robinson's liberalising measures paved the way for a period of industrial and commercial growth in the 1820s. In the later nineteenth century Stafford Northcote under Disraeli and Michael Hicks Beach under Salisbury, both encouraged the

A caricature of Lord Salisbury as Secretary of State for India in 1874 (first published in *The London Sketch Book*) *(Hulton/Getty)*

Spy cartoon of W.H. Smith in 1887. Son of the founder of the W.H. Smith's stationery chain, he was financial secretary of the Treasury between 1874 and 1877, before becoming First Lord of the Admiralty and a Cabinet Minister *(Hulton/Getty)*

expansion of free trade, low levels of taxation and a reduction in the national debt (though the last was thrown off course by the huge expense of the Boer War at the end of the century). Northcote also reformed the civil service, while Charles Ritchie, Chancellor under Balfour, enacted the 1888 Local Government Act which introduced democracy to municipal government.

Perhaps the most important Conservative statesman in the late nineteenth century was Richard A. Cross, Home Secretary in Disraeli's 1874–80 government. A middle-class Lancastrian, Cross was the architect of that government's pioneering social and union legislation. W.H. Smith, son of the founder of the bookseller, held many senior posts under Disraeli and Salisbury, including First Lord of the Admiralty and Leader of the House of Commons. Both Smith and Cross were mocked by their aristocratic colleagues, including Lord Randolph Churchill, who dubbed them as 'Marshall and Snelgrove' (after the popular department store). Smith's tenure at the Admiralty also provided inspiration for the satirical character of 'Sir Joseph Porter' in Gilbert and Sullivan's *HMS Pinafore*.

Conservative foreign secretaries in the twentieth century presided over Briton's last decades as a great power and then over its retreat from empire. Arthur Balfour and Austen Chamberlain may have failed as party leaders, but they subsequently redeemed themselves on the international stage. Chamberlain's diplomacy, in particular, led to the triumph of

the Locarno Treaties in 1925, for which he was rewarded with the Nobel Peace Prize. Eden's career profile went in reverse: a generally successful long period as Foreign Secretary albeit under Churchill's shadow, only to have his reputation wrecked by his period as Prime Minister (1955–7). Geoffrey Howe completed the dismantling of Britain's empire, negotiating the handover of Hong Kong to China, and Douglas Hurd provided a steady hand at the rudder at the end of the cold war.

Geoffrey Howe, Chancellor of the Exchequer, Foreign Secretary and Deputy Prime Minister in Mrs Thatcher's governments between 1979 and 1990 *(Palace of Westminster Collection)*

FAMILY CONNECTIONS

TWO GREAT DYNASTIES: CECILS AND CHAMBERLAINS

The Cecil family has been the most influential dynasty in Conservative politics. Robert Cecil, the 3rd Marquess of Salisbury, was the pre-eminent family member, leading the party between 1885 and 1902. Salisbury's 1900–2 administration contained so many members of his family that he was openly accused of nepotism. The 'Hotel Cecil' comprised Salisbury's eldest son, Lord Cranborne, who was appointed Under-Secretary at the Foreign Office, and his two younger sons, Lord Robert Cecil and Lord Hugh Cecil, who also had colourful careers in

politics ahead of them. The 5th Marquess, 'Bobbety', was so restless he provoked Churchill to say that the problem with the Cecils is they are always 'either ill or resigning'. Briefly leader in the Lords during Churchill's and Eden's incapacity through ill-health in mid-1953, he crucially resigned in 1957. The most recent Cecil to scale the heights was Lord Cranborne, dismissed by Hague as Shadow Leader of the Lords in 1998.

There were only two months between 1890 and 1940 when there was not a Chamberlain serving in the party hierarchy. Joseph Chamberlain began his career as a Radical Liberal Mayor of Birmingham, where he pioneered slum clearance and transformed municipal politics. As a Liberal Unionist he joined forces with Salisbury's administration after breaking with Gladstone's Irish Home Rule policy in 1886. He served as Colonial Secretary between 1895 and 1903, when he became a champion for Tarrif Reform. The result was dangerously to split the party and precipitate its fall from government after nearly twenty years in government. His sons Austen and Neville followed in their father's footsteps, though they went straight into the Conservative Party. Austen Chamberlain was one of only two party leaders in the twentieth century not to become Prime Minister, while his half-brother, Neville, is remembered more

The 5th Marquess of Salisbury, 'Bobbety', in August 1953, then acting Foreign Secretary *(Hulton/Getty)*

Winston Churchill with Christopher and Mary Soames (to his right), Clementine (to his right), and grandson Nicholas Soames standing to Churchill's left (now a Tory MP and shadow Cabinet Minister) at Westerham in 1954. Chartwell was just a short distance from Westerham village (*Corbis*)

for his controversial policy of appeasement than for his substantial achievements in the domestic arena. Had he not been a casualty of the First World War, Norman Chamberlain, cousin of Neville and Austen, might also have become a distinguished minister.

FOLLOWING IN THEIR FATHER'S FOOTSTEPS

Pitt 'the Younger' famously followed in his father's footsteps as Prime Minister. The Earl of Chatham (Pitt 'the Elder'), Whig Prime Minister between 1766 and 1768, groomed his son for office from his early days. Lord Randolph Churchill was one of the party's leading mavericks as founder of the Fourth Party in the 1880s, while his son Winston crossed the floor from Conservative to Liberal in 1904 and back again in 1924. Both Winston Churchill's son, Randolph, and grandson, Winston, entered the House as Conservative MPs though with less obvious success. Stanley Baldwin directly succeeded his father, Alfred, as MP for Bewdley in 1908. The Hogg family has been represented in Parliament almost continuously since 1835. The most recent descendant, Douglas Hogg (son of

Churchill's son, Randolph, campaigning in Devonport in 1950 (Hulton/Getty)

Thatcher's Lord Chancellor, Quintin Hogg or Lord Hailsham) has sat in the House of Commons since 1979, rising to become Major's Minister for Agriculture in the mid-1990s. His wife was Major's Head of Policy in Number 10 from 1990–4, while his grand-father, Lord Hailsham, was also Lord Chancellor (in the late 1920s and 1930s).

A MARRIAGE MADE IN POLITICS

Love and politics do occasionally go hand in hand in the Conservative Party. The first Conservative woman Member of Parliament, Nancy Astor, succeeded her husband as MP for Plymouth Sutton in 1919, while the formidable party chairman in the 1920s, J.C.C. Davidson, made way for his wife to succeed him as MP for Hemel Hempstead in 1937. In the last thirty years there have been three principal married couples to sit on the front and backbenches. Nicholas and Ann Winterton have sat together on the backbenches since 1983, representing adjoining constituencies in Cheshire. Peter Bottomley first entered Parliament as a

LEADING INTELLECTS

The most philosophically minded Conservatives tend not to be the most successful politicians – Edmund Burke, A.J. Balfour, Lord Hugh Cecil, Enoch Powell and Keith Joseph fall into this category. Robert Rhodes James proved a much better historian than minister, and Lord Hailsham (junior) arguably a more influential polemicist than Lord

Chancellor. His seminal book *The Case for Conservatism*, published in 1947, inspired a generation of Conservatives in the postwar period, as did the early work of Enoch Powell. A scholar in the classics, and a professor of Greek at Sydney University at the age of just 26, Powell is regarded as perhaps the party's greatest intellect in the twentieth century, but as a minister he was a disappointment.

Enoch Powell by Graham Jones (*Palace of Westminster collection*)

Sir Douglas Hogg arriving for a Sunday morning
Cabinet meeting during the General Strike in May 1926
(Hulton/Getty)

Andrew Mackay and Julie Kirkbride, one of several
married couples to sit on the Conservative benches in
the House of Commons *(PA)*

Conservative MP in 1974, rising through the junior ministerial ranks, but he was soon overtaken by his wife, Virginia, whose rapid promotion culminated in her reaching the Cabinet in 1992. Andrew Mackay, Deputy Chief Whip in John Major's government, married Julie

Kirkbride shortly after she entered the House of Commons in the 1997 general election. As Mackay's front-bench career in opposition faded, his new wife's took off as she became shadow Secretary for Culture, Media and Sport under Michael Howard in 2003.

Perhaps the productive useful brains in the Tory party have been those who could develop ideas into working policies. As chairman of the Unionist Social Reform Committee before the First World War, F.E. Smith played a crucial role laying the groundwork for the social and economic reforms of Baldwin's 1924–9 government. R.A. Butler, as we have seen, was the leading architect of a raft of forward-looking policy initiatives during and after the Second World War. After the 1997 defeat, Peter Lilley, David Willetts and Oliver Letwin, three of the most rigorous and analytical minds of the party in the last decade, sought to move forward the party's thinking on the welfare state, social policy and the public services beyond the Thatcherite agenda.

The distinguished Lord Chancellor and one-time party
chairman, Lord Hailsham (centre) *(Camera Press)*

F.E. Smith (Lord Birkenhead) addresses the Unionist Rally at Blenheim Palace in 1912 *(PA)*

LEADING ORATORS

George Canning made his name as a formidable platform speaker in the early 1800s. Lord Randolph Churchill whipped up enthusiasm for his campaign for 'Tory democracy' at the early conferences of the National Union in the 1880s while Joseph Chamberlain's populist appeal as a conference speaker contrasted with the lacklustre performances of his party leader, Arthur Balfour. As an orator, as in so much else besides, Winston Churchill

eclipsed his contemporaries. After the war, few could match Enoch Powell's oratory, most renowned in his counter-productive 'rivers of blood' speech in 1968, warning of the dangers of immigration. Both Iain Macleod and Michael Heseltine were able to communicate the party's message with flair from the conference platform and both became the conference darlings of their generation. Michael Heseltine became famous with the party faithful for his barnstorming, Labour-bashing performances at the party conference, in the late 1970s and early 1980s. Heseltine knew how to lampoon his opponents, which he did with renewed vigour on his return to the front bench in the 1990s. When Labour MP Gordon Brown made reference to his growing enthusiasm for 'post neoclassical endogenous growth theory', Heseltine

Michael Heseltine in mid-flow at the 1979 annual conference *(Bodleian Library)*

chastised the then shadow Chancellor and his special adviser, Ed Balls, at the Tory party conference in 1996, saying that the idea wasn't 'Brown's, it was Balls!' Since the party lost office in 1997, few leading figures in the party have emulated their oratorical prowess.

MOVERS AND SHAKERS

Aside from the stars of the Tory front bench, there are the 'men in grey suits': the Whips and leading members of the backbench 1922 Committee. The gentlemen of the Whips' Office (the first woman Tory Whip was appointed only in 1996) have often managed the affairs of the parliamentary party with a degree of cunning and invention that eluded their more high-profile ministerial colleagues. Until the 1911–14 reforms, the Whips' Office shared much of the responsibility for fund-raising and campaigning with the Principal Agents in Central Office. Directly appointed by the party leader, the Whips are the means of securing the loyalty and support of backbench MPs. A vital channel of communication between the leadership and the parliamentary party, the Whips' Office is also a well-travelled route to the top for many of the party's leading lights. The behaviour, opinions and peccadilloes of each and every Tory MP are carefully monitored by the Whips who often hold the key to promotion.

The Whips' Office is home to some of the darkest arts in the political trade in enforcing discipline among its backbenchers. Robert Wallace, a Conservative MP in the 1890s, was often astounded by the 'dexterous blending of menace, cajolery and reward'. 'On any signs of individual action in their party', said Wallace, 'they can put the pistol of Dissolution to their heads and say, "Your vote or your life; if you do not come to heel, we will blow your Parliamentary brains out."' One century on, the rebellious behaviour of malcontents on the backbenches and a dwindling majority would require some pretty drastic tactics. In his diary of life in the Whips' Office in the 1990s, Gyles Brandreth revealed the lengths to which his colleagues would go to ensure the government's survival. These would range from ferrying in the desperately ill in ambulances for crucial divisions and painful arm twisting of potential rebels and mavericks. David Lightbown was one of the largest Conservative MPs to serve in the Whips' Office. During a particularly tight vote on the ratification of the Maastricht Treaty in November 1992, Brandreth noted that 'Lightbown, all twenty stone of him, pursued one of the rebels into the lavatory and was so engrossed in the task of "persuading" his prey to do the decent thing, he missed the vote himself!'

FIVE GREAT CHIEF WHIPS

Sir Thomas Freemantle

Sir Thomas Freemantle was Peel's Chief Whip between 1837 and 1844. After the Reform Act of 1832 and the party's disastrous defeat in the general election of that year, Peel transferred his energies to managing the rump of 175 MPs in the House of Commons. Under Peel's supervision, Freemantle introduced many of the practices which the Whips Office follows to this day, including a weekly Whip's letter with details of forthcoming votes and the formal organisation of pairing (whereby MPs would pair off with backbenchers from other parties to maintain the balance of numbers in divisions). Freemantle also arranged for Peel to meet regularly with his backbenchers personally to explain his advice on voting and the reasoning behind it. He was an adroit operator and highly trusted among the backbenches. Its effect was to increase the cohesion of the party in the division lobbies while the new pairing system enabled the Chief Whip to prepare the numbers for key votes days in advance. As a result of Freemantle's work, the party enjoyed its first period of real unity in the post-Reform Act era.

Aretas Akers-Douglas

Few did more to build Salisbury's Conservative Party than Aretas Akers-Douglas, Chief Whip between 1885 and 1895. Having earned a reputation as an active party organiser in Kent, Akers-Douglas rapidly became acquainted with the Westminster elite. Along with the Principal Agent, Captain Richard Middleton, who also learned his trade in Kent, Akers-Douglas helped to soothe the pain caused by Lord Randolph Churchill's attempt to usurp the leadership's control over the party organisation in the early 1880s. The convincing general election victory of 1895 was in no small measure down to his achievements in the previous ten years.

Aretas Akers-Douglas, Chief Whip 1885–95 (Mary Evans)

Bolton Eyres-Monsell

Bolton Eyres-Monsell was Baldwin's Chief Whip between 1923 and 1931. Like the other

Another prime mover in the Parliamentary Conservative Party is the chairman of the 1922 Committee. Gervais Rentoul, elected MP in 1922, founded the committee in 1923 to provide information and support to new Conservative MPs. As its first chairman, Rentoul quickly established the 1922 Committee as an important conduit between backbenchers and the leadership, and in 1926 membership was thrown open to all Conservative backbenchers. As it matured, the committee became a forum for private debate, and ministers were regularly invited to address members on policy and other issues. It was

great Chief Whips, Eyres-Monsell held sway in the Whips' Office for a long period. He was instrumental in promoting the work of the new backbench 1922 Committee, which was formed to help newly elected MPs find their parliamentary feet, and helped ensure that the committee earned greater credibility in the eyes of the leadership than the various groups that had preceded it. He also had an important influence in the formation of independent backbench committees, ensuring that the swollen ranks of the parliamentary party (412 after the landslide victory at the 1924 election) were consulted on the wide range of policies that Baldwin's second administration implemented. Eyres-Monsell's greatest achievement was perhaps to help contain the number of Baldwin's critics within the party in 1930–1.

David Margesson

Eyres-Monsell's successor, David Margesson, is regarded by many as the doyen of Conservative Chief Whips of the twentieth century. His reign in the Whips' Office between 1931 and 1941 was under four Prime Ministers – Baldwin, MacDonald, Chamberlain and Churchill. Not only did he have to contend with the largest-ever parliamentary force in the twentieth century, totalling 470 in 1931, but he also successfully cooperated with Labour and Liberal MPs who supported the National Government. He established himself as a strict disciplinarian running a slick machine from the Whips' Office. Margesson kept open the channels of communication with the appeasers, thus preventing a more serious rift in the parliamentary party. Margesson's managerial qualities were recognised by Churchill, who appointed him Secretary for War in May 1940.

Edward Heath

As Chief Whip for Anthony Eden and Harold Macmillan in the years 1955 and 1959, Heath proved himself one of the most effective and highly regarded Chief Whips of the postwar era. His major achievement as Chief Whip was to limit the damage caused by the Suez crisis in 1956 among the backbenches. Although Eden fell, Macmillan was so impressed with Heath's handling of the affair that he invited him to dinner on his first night in Number 10, cementing one of the closest relationships between a Prime Minister and a Chief Whip since the war.

during the War Coalition after 1940 that it came fully into its own. Chaired by Alexander Erskine-Hill, the committee became an important medium for Tory backbenchers to express their anxieties about the war efforts to ministers of Churchill's Coalition Government. The chairman became one the most senior and respected figures in the party and was to regularly meet with the leader along with the Chief Whip. John Morrison, chairman between 1955 and 1964, played a key role in the leadership crisis of 1963 in taking soundings of backbench preferences, which in the end favoured Lord Home.

Sir Gervais Rentoul, first chairman of the 1922 Committee *(Topfoto)*

The furore over the way the 1963 crisis had been resolved resulted in the committee's chairman assuming responsibility for the conduct of leadership elections after 1965. With these new powers in place, committee chairmen were not afraid to voice their dissatisfaction with the performance of the front bench and indeed the leadership. Edward du Cann remains the longest-serving chairman (1972–84). He was an important figure in the fall of Heath in 1975, as well as being one of the few senior backbench Tories Mrs Thatcher listened to early on in her leadership. As the respected student of Parliament, Philip Norton has written, 'The 1922 Committee did not start life as a king maker; but that is what it eventually became.' Both John Major and Iain Duncan Smith were given rough rides during their regular meetings with the committee, but the most dramatic moment came with the demise of Margaret Thatcher. Although support from her Cabinet fell away after the first leadership ballot in November 1990, it was the chairman of the 1922 Committee, Cranley Onslow, who had the unenviable task of informing her that she no longer enjoyed the full confidence of the parliamentary party.

EIGHT

WRECKERS, REBELS, ROGUES AND ECCENTRICS

This chapter opens the doors to the Tory hall of infamy – a place where the stubborn, the rebellious and the disgraced have come to reside after dragging their party into defeat or disrepute. Yet some rebels brought the party to its senses, rescuing it from even greater perils. Like other parties, the Conservatives have had their fair share of eccentrics who have added a splash of colour to the often humdrum life of party politics.

DESTRUCTIVE PERSONALITIES

Rarely has the party suffered defeat at the hands of the electorate without one of its leading figures being at the centre of a divisive political storm. There are a few whose overwhelming sense of personal ambition and conviction came at the expense of party unity, often exacerbating the crises which beset the party. Two personalities in particular wrought immense damage on the fortunes and prestige of the Conservatives as a responsible party of government and opposition. Joseph Chamberlain and Enoch Powell forcefully pursued agendas which either harmed the party's standing or prevented it from adapting itself to the most vexed political questions of their day.

JOSEPH CHAMBERLAIN

Peel is seen by many not as the founder of the modern Conservative Party, but as its all-but destroyer. Disraeli and Salisbury certainly recognised his failings as a party leader and were determined not to repeat them. Only the forceful presence of Joseph Chamberlain at the turn of the twentieth century would propel the party into its second traumatic period of defeat and division. Following his appointment as Salisbury's Colonial

Secretary, Chamberlain pursued an expansionist imperial policy which triggered the Boer War between 1899 and 1902. 'Joe's War' revealed less the might than the vulnerabilities of the British Empire at a massive cost to the nation's finances.

Chamberlain was emboldened to press the party to adopt a policy of Tarrif Reform. While Balfour dithered, Chamberlain mobilised a national campaign to promote his cause in Birmingham in 1903. He single-handedly polarised opinion in the party, reopening the old debates about free trade and protection. Although Balfour was determined not to be 'another Sir Robert Peel', by 1905 Chamberlain's Tariff Reform League had won the backing of the party in the country, leaving the leadership unable to reconcile the opposing factions within the parliamentary party. In the run-up to the 1906 general election Chamberlain even encouraged his supporters to deselect 'free-trade' Conservative candidates. The result was one of the worst landslide defeats for the party in the twentieth century.

Spy cartoon of Joseph Chamberlain as Colonial Secretary (1895–1903) *(Palace of Westminster Collection)*

ENOCH POWELL

'All political lives, unless they are cut off in midstream at a happy juncture, end in failure', surmised Enoch Powell famously in his biography of Joseph Chamberlain. Powell was one of the party's rising stars in the postwar years, having distinguished himself as a gifted orator, impressive policy thinker and capable minister. Since the 1950s, controls on immigration had become the source of heated debate within the party. Powell had forcefully argued for tighter controls as a member of Heath's shadow Cabinet, but he broke cover in April 1968 in a speech to Conservatives in Birmingham to voice his concerns. 'We must be mad, literally mad, as a nation to be permitting the annual inflow of some 50,000 dependants . . . Like the Roman, I seem to see 'the River Tiber foaming with much blood! Powell warned. Fearing that Powell's speech would arouse racial hatred, Heath promptly sacked him from his

Powell speaking in May 1974 (Hulton/Getty)

shadow Cabinet. Within weeks Powell had amassed a large personal following in the party and the country, which he would exploit with devastating effect.

Powell became a thorn in the side of Heath's government after 1970, launching fierce attacks over Ulster, the economy and incomes policy. But it was Britain's entry into the Common Market that caused Powell to turn on his party in such spectacular fashion. By denouncing the February 1974 election as a fraud and urging people to vote Labour, Powell may well have had a decisive influence on the close election, particularly in the marginal seats of the West Midlands. Powell rejoiced in Heath's fall from power but was condemned by many in the party for treason. Powell's presence on the backbenches and in the conference hall had a poisonous influence on the febrile atmosphere of the Heath years. As Tony Howard remarked, Powell had 'dedicated himself to destroying Ted Heath and achieved it in 1974, but in doing so he killed himself rather like a Queen Bee'. Powell's Birmingham speech did nothing to endear the party to ethnic minority voters, nor for race relations, nor to produce a national policy on immigration. His stance on Europe was equally damaging and counter-productive for the party. Despite being defended in a recent biography by Simon Heffer, it is hard to see his career as being anything other than an utter waste of a brilliant talent.

THE WRECKERS

Some of the most significant rebellions in the party's history have been triggered by its high command failing to recognise or deliberately ignoring dissenting voices. The backbench rebellion against Austen Chamberlain's continuing support for Lloyd George's coalition in 1922 is a prime example. Historians agree that the events of October 1922 were vital to restoring the party as a credible alternative government after years of difficulty and division in opposition. Most other rebellions, particularly during periods in office, have however been less constructive.

THE ULTRAS, 1820S–30S

The first bout of Tory insurgence came in the 1820s and early 1830s. The High Tories, or 'Ultras' (named after their right-wing counterparts in post-revolutionary France), were a perennial thorn in the side of the governments of Liverpool, Canning and Wellington. Led by Lord Chandos (latterly the Duke of Buckingham), the Duke of Cumberland and Lord Lyndhurst, the Ultras represented the reactionary right of the landed Tory party, drawing support from areas untouched by the Industrial Revolution. With 'Protection, Protestantism and no popery' as their mantra, the Ultras were obdurately opposed to what Norman Gash has called the 'revolutionary trilogy of great constitutional reforms' (Catholic Emancipation, repeal of the Test Acts and electoral reform). Wellington eventually conceded Catholic Emancipation in 1829, but found most of his supporters rebelling in the crucial votes: he even found himself having to fight a duel with one angry Ultra. Another, the Duke of Newcastle, accused him of being 'the most unprincipled . . . and most dangerous man, not excepting Cromwell, that this country has seen for many a year'. By 1830, Wellington's Tories had descended into crisis, culminating in his resignation. The Ultras had fatally weakened Wellington's hand and in so doing enabled the Whigs to reform the electoral system on their own terms. Ultra agitation played a significant role in taking the party to crushing electoral defeats in 1830–2, ending sixty years of almost uninterrupted Tory hegemony.

EDWARDIAN DIEHARDS, 1906–14

Following the landslide defeat of 1906, once again the issue of Irish Home Rule consumed the party, as did the continuing dispute over Tarrif Reform. Between 1906 and

Edwardian diehard John Gretton, caricatured by Tom Cottrell *(National Portrait Gallery)*

COLONEL JOHN GRETTON.

1911 Arthur Balfour failed to exert control over dissident voices in the parliamentary party. A burgeoning number of 'diehard' MPs were intent on defending the party's 'true blue' principles in the face of a Liberal government which was driving forward a radical domestic agenda. Moderate opinion in the party was overwhelmed by the zeal of diehards such as Henry Page Croft and John Gretton. Increasingly fratricidal debates erupted over Tarrif Reform, social policy, and about how to respond to Lloyd George's radical 1909 Budget. Page Croft sought to rid the party of 'unbelievers' – those who took a more measured stance on Tarrif Reform – through undercover organis-ations such as the Confederacy and the Reveille. The constitutional crisis in 1910–11, precipit-ated by the 1909 Budget, was exacerbated by bitter resistance from diehards in the House of Lords. Following the struggle between the 'Hedgers', who reluctantly sought compromise, and the 'Ditchers', led by Lords Selborne and Milner, who would rather 'die in the last ditch' than pass the 1911 Parliament Act, Balfour's position became untenable. His successor, Bonar Law, an Ulsterman by descent, played to the diehard gallery by pursuing a policy of bitter resistance to Home Rule. It took the outbreak of the First World War to drag the party back to the centre ground of British politics.

SIR HENRY PAGE CROFT.

Henry Page Croft, caricatured by Tom Cottrell *(National Portrait Gallery)*

TORY PRESS BARONS, 1929–30

Baldwin had successfully brought many diehards back into the mainstream of the party in the early 1920s. But defeat in 1929 threw into question Baldwin's moderate strategy. As the depression gripped the British economy, he came under strong pressure from certain quarters in his party to adopt a protectionist policy in opposition. Spearheading the campaign was Lord Beaverbrook, proprietor of the *Daily Express, Sunday Express* and *Evening Standard* newspapers. Joining forces with Lord Rothermere, the hard-right proprietor of the *Daily Mail*, Beaverbrook launched the Empire Crusade in February 1929. Their intention was to depose Baldwin, accusing him of weak leadership in opposition and presiding over a 'semi-socialist' programme of reform in government. The Empire Crusaders gathered momentum by winning over party members and funds to their cause. Beaverbrook and Rothermere used their mass newspaper circulations to propound their ideas, thus blurring the official party line from public view. The Party Chairman, J.C.C. Davidson, warned Baldwin that 'the Rothermere, Beaverbrook . . . poison has produced a feverish condition in the party'. Baldwin despised his antagonists, refusing to bow to the 'engines of propaganda [and the] personal dislikes of two men'. By October 1930 large sections of the party were on the verge of openly repudiating their leader. The crisis was diffused when Baldwin agreed to commit the party to a limited form of protection, sensing that public belief in free trade had collapsed as a result of soaring unemployment. Having made this concession, Baldwin used the St George's by-election in March 1931 to hit back at his Empire Crusade opponents. Not until 1992–97 did the Tory press do so much again to undermine a Tory leader.

Lord Beaverbrook, newspaper proprietor and thorn in the side of Baldwin's leadership in 1929–31 *(PA)*

MAJOR'S BASTARDS, 1992–7

John Major won the party an unexpected fourth term in government in 1992, but his slender majority of twenty-one would crucially restrict his room for manoeuvre, particularly over Europe. Spurred on by Margaret Thatcher's denunciation of the Maastricht Treaty, over which many considered Major had achieved a sensible compromise position, Tory Euro-sceptics were in the ascendant after the 1992 election. Within a month of the election, twenty-two Euro-sceptic backbenchers voted against the ratification of the treaty in the House of Commons. By mid-1993, he had become exasperated with the disloyalty and damage done – even from inside the Cabinet. 'Where do you think most of this poison is coming from?', Major confided to ITN's Michael Brunson in the aftermath of the Maastricht votes. 'From the dispossessed and the never-possessed. You can think of ex-ministers who are going around causing all sorts of trouble. We don't want three more of the bastards out there.' As Major's majority dwindled after successive by-election defeats, his patience finally snapped in November 1994, when he removed the Whip from eight backbenchers who rebelled over the EC Finance Bill. Teresa Gorman, Christopher Gill, and Nicholas Budgen were among the most ardent Euro-sceptics of the eight Whipless rebels – as was the future party leader, Iain Duncan Smith. They were joined by Richard Body, who resigned the Whip in protest. The nine Whipless rebels regarded themselves as heroes and made the most of their new-found freedom, attracting support from sympathisers on the backbenches. They attacked the government and Major personally at every available opportunity, often colluding with Labour and Liberal Democrats during tight Commons votes. Major's manoeuvre had done more harm than good: the Whip was quietly restored within six months. Not even his leadership gamble in mid-1995 silenced the Euro-sceptics. Malice and resentment grew on either side, bursting into full public gaze during the 1997 election campaign, when scores of Conservative candidates defied the leadership over its 'wait and see' policy towards the euro. The rebellion had now become an open mutiny – a recipe for disaster for any party during an election. The Euro-sceptics, egged on by much of the Tory press, aided the rise of a pro-European Labour Party led by Tony Blair.

REBELS WITH A CAUSE

Aside from the most harmful rebellions in Tory history, there have been several instances when dissent helped bring about a significant change of direction which may have saved

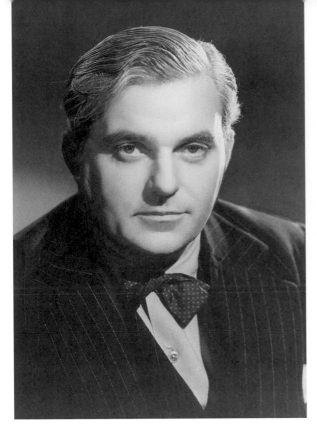

Above: Robert Boothby *(National Portrait Gallery)*

Above right: Harold Macmillan in 1932 *(Corbis)*

Right: Michael Portillo at a press conference in Central Office shortly before the party's heavy defeat in 2001 *(Hulton/Getty)*

the party from even greater harm. The most obvious example were those Tory MPs who lambasted the appeasement policy of Neville Chamberlain in the late 1930s. Between twenty and thirty Conservative backbenchers warned that the policy would only lead to further Italian and German aggression and that there was no choice but to hastily rearm. They were derided as alarmists by the party establishment, who denounced them as 'the Glamour Boys' – young and inexperienced lightweights who only craved attention. Winston Churchill's calls for action could be discredited because of his vicious attacks on the leadership over Indian

PISTOLS AT DAWN

One scandal borne not out of greed or lust but personal rivalry was a duel between two leading Cabinet ministers during the Napoleonic Wars. George Canning had been enjoying a meteoric rise under Pitt and Portland becoming Foreign Secretary in 1809. A highly ambitious Tory, Canning was swift to claim credit for military victories in the aftermath of Trafalgar, but equally determined to pin failures, such as the defeat at Corunna, on his aristocratic rival in Cabinet, Lord Castlereagh. The War Secretary himself was envious of Canning's political ascent, taking great exception to his criticisms. The rivalry took a bitter turn when Canning demanded that Castlereagh be sacked from Lord Portland's administration following the failure of the Walcheren expedition in the summer of 1809 – the heaviest blow to Britain's military prestige during the Napoleonic Wars. In the event both had to resign from office. When Castlereagh learned of Canning's scheming, he challenged him to a duel. Canning had never fired a gun in his life but could not contemplate the public shame of refusing. At 6 a.m. on a cold September morning, the two met on Putney Heath. Both missed with the first shot, but with the second Castlereagh hit Canning in the thigh, though the wound did not turn out to be serious. The affair was scandalous for the time: duelling, though legal, was no longer deemed an acceptable or honourable method of settling a dispute, let alone by two distinguished former Cabinet ministers. The Morning Chronicle summed up public opinion: 'To suppose it possible, after the disgusting exhibition they have made, to form out of their dispersed and disordered ranks a government that could stand, is the height of absurdity.' Yet, both recovered their standing and served in future Tory administrations. Although Castlereagh, an unhappy man, took his own life in 1822, Canning went on to become Prime Minister in 1827.

George Canning by Sir Thomas Lawrence (National Portrait Gallery)

HAND IN THE TILL

There have been numerous cases of financial impropriety and misconduct in British politics, but very few instances of organised corruption. The 'homes for votes' scandal in Westminster City Council in the early 1990s was a rare example of Conservative politicians being implicated for offences of this kind. One hundred a forty years earlier, one Yorkshireman used his position as a Tory MP to expand his business empire in the 'railway mania' which was gripping the country. By 1844 George Hudson controlled almost 1,500 miles of track in England. The following year he entered Parliament as Conservative MP for Sunderland. Hudson was not unusual in combining his business interests with politics: 155 other MPs were directors of the railway companies that had sprung up in the 1840s. But Hudson, who was dubbed the 'Railway King', ruthlessly used his seat to expand his empire, bribing fellow Tory parliamentarians to support his private members bills which authorised numerous railway purchases. As well as influencing politics in Westminster, Hudson became Lord Mayor of York, served on magistracies in Durham and North Riding, owned three provincial newspapers and even chaired the Yorkshire Union Bank. His ambition was to take control of every railway company, using whatever means he could, including falsifying accounts, insider share dealing and even theft. His scheme was brought to an ignominious end in 1849 when he was discovered to have stolen £9,000 from Eastern Counties, one of his companies, to bribe MPs. Forced to resign his chairmanships and pay back the stolen sums, Hudson was cast out by his fellow MPs and the party but was protected from prosecution by parliamentary privilege. Eventually he lost his seat in 1859 and fled to France to avoid his creditors.

Captain Peter Baker was elected as the youngest Conservative MP in 1950, aged 29, with an impressive record of service in the war which earned him the Military Cross. A man of boundless energy, Baker had thrown himself into the world of commerce. Like fellow MPs, Horatio Bottomley and Michael Heseltine, Baker made his mark in publishing. Baker's empire, however, became embroiled in various financial crises, prompting the young MP to resort to forgery to prop up companies facing liquidation. It was a sorry tale: Baker developed a serious drinking habit as his business interests sank into further trouble and eventually suffered a nervous breakdown. Baker admitted, 'There were whole weeks in 1953 and 1954 that I cannot remember. Often I had to check up in *Hansard* to make sure I had attended the Commons and voted.' Unlike George Hudson, Baker's fraudulent conduct did not involve bribery or corrupting the political process, but his political career ended abruptly when he received a seven-year prison sentence after being charged at the Old Bailey on six counts of forgery.

The 'cash for questions' affair in the 1990s was one of the most damaging financial scandals to affect the party in its recent history. Unlike previous cases of misconduct, the fact that a number of MPs became entangled in the furore gave the impression that a large section of the parliamentary party was more interested in personal gain than public service. In 1994 a *Sunday Times* investigation revealed that several Tory MPs, including some ministerial aides, were prepared to receive £1,000 for asking a parliamentary question. Graham Riddick initially accepted a cheque but soon returned it, while David Treddinick, after denying any involvement, was revealed to have asked his cheque to be sent to his home address. Although both apologised, they were suspended from the House of Commons, falling foul of an entrapment which had compromised their integrity. What was more damaging to

Neil Hamilton posing obediently at the Festival of Erotica in 2000 *(Topfoto)*

John Major's leadership was the backlash among fellow Tory MPs who believed that Riddick and Treddinick had been unfairly punished.

Far more serious for the party was the connection between several Conservative ministers and the owner of Harrods, Mohammed Al Fayed. In 1994 the *Guardian* alleged that Tory MPs Tim Smith and Neil Hamilton had received cash payments in brown envelopes as backbenchers in the late 1980s in return for asking parliamentary questions on Fayed's behalf. Since the mid-1980s, Al Fayed had sought to promote his commercial interests through the services of Ian Greer, a lobbyist. Greer arranged for a number of Tory backbenchers to table questions in return for cash. Tim Smith admitted that he had received a string of cash payments from Al Fayed and resigned immediately. But Hamilton denied his involvement and refused to resign his ministerial office. It was alleged in particular that he and his wife regularly enjoyed hospitality at Fayed's expense, including lavish weekends at the Paris Ritz. The affair burst into the public gaze when Al Fayed, frustrated with the government's refusal to grant him British nationality and disappointed with the lobbying effort that had been conducted on his behalf, revealed his side the the story to the *Guardian*. Three years of claim and counter-claim ensued, culminating in Hamilton's defeat at the 1997 election at the hands of the white-suited former BBC journalist, Martin Bell.

AITKEN'S 'SWORD OF TRUTH'

If 'cash for questions' had cast a dark shadow over John Major's government, then so did the fall from grace of one of the party's rising stars. Promoted to the Cabinet in 1994, Jonathan Aitken was tipped as a potential leader, but he became embroiled in a scandal which led to his imprisonment. The Guardian and a Granada Television documentary alleged in October 1994 that Aitken had exploited his connections with Saudi Arabian businessmen for his own advantage. It was claimed that when Aitken was a defence minister he had stayed at Al Fayed's Paris Ritz at the expense of a Saudi businessman involved in a major arms contract. Aitken furiously denied the allegations, offering a series of deceitful alibis which involved his wife and daughter, and resigned from the Cabinet in April 1995 to issue writs for libel against his accusers. 'If it falls to me', Aitken declared, 'to start a fight to cut the cancer of bent and twisted journalism in our country with the simple sword of truth and the trusty shield of fair play, so be it.' Like Hamilton, Aitken lost his seat in the 1997 election. In 1999 he pleaded guilty to the charges and was jailed for eighteen months, condemned by the judge for his 'gross and inexcusable breach of trust'. It was one of the most dramatic falls from grace in modern times. Aitken sought to rebuild his life after his time in gaol, turning to his faith for solace. In February 2004, he made a tentative approach to return to Parliament as a Conservative in his old seat, but was stopped in his tracks by Michael Howard. Four months later he backed the United Kingdom Independence Party in the European Parliament elections.

Jonathan Aitken as a young journalist in 1971, standing behind his editor, Brian Roberts, of the *Sunday Telegraph* (Hulton/Getty)

BEDROOM ANTICS

Infidelity and an uncontrollable libido have brought down many politicians. The governments of Macmillan and Major were in particular beset with scandals exposing the dalliance of several leading Tories. Appointed Secretary of State for War in 1960, John Profumo was believed to be a man of integrity and probity, but his weakness for the opposite sex proved his undoing. At a party at Cliveden in 1961, Profumo was introduced to Christine Keeler by the London socialite Stephen Ward, and began an affair with her. It transpired that she was also having an affair with a Soviet naval attaché, Colonel Eugene Ivanov. Profumo's relationship with Keeler lasted only a few weeks but, when the story got out in the summer of 1963, he made a statement to the House of Commons admitting he knew her but denying any impropriety. Following a rash of newspaper reports revealing the details of the affair, Profumo admitted that he had lied to the House and resigned from the government. Although there was no suspicion that Profumo had passed on state secrets to Keeler, the fact that he had lied to his parliamentary colleagues seemed to epitomise the decline of moral standards in public life. The scandal had put Harold Macmillan under severe personal strain and hastened his departure from Downing Street in October 1963. He was particularly stung by a devastating speech made by Nigel Birch, a Tory backbencher, during a debate on the affair a few months earlier:

'What is to happen now? We cannot just have business as usual. I myself feel that the time will come very soon when my Right Honourable Friend ought to make way for a much younger colleague . . . perhaps some word of Browning might be appropriate:

Christine Keeler in 1963
(Hulton/Getty)

John Profumo and his wife drive away from reporters in June 1963 *(Corbis)*

. . . let him never come back to us!
    There would be doubt, hesitation and pain.
        Forced praise on our part – the glimmer of twilight,
        Never glad confident morning again.'

The Thatcher governments were light on scandals, though Jeffrey Archer could be relied on to blur the lines between his sexually-charged novels and his real life. He won a libel case against the *Daily Star*, who had reported that Archer had slept with prostitute Monica Coghlan. His wife Mary famously came to his defence, and was described by the judge as 'fragant'. It subsequently transpired that Archer had lied about the affair and he was imprisoned, which duly produced another tome.

The sleaze-ridden atmosphere of the mid-1990s had as much to do with bedroom antics as it did with brown paper envelopes.

Jeffrey Archer in a production of his play *The Accused*, shortly before he was found guilty of perjury in July 2001 *(TopFoto)*

The first to fall from grace was David Mellor, MP for Putney, who became the first Secretary of State for National Heritage in 1992. Within months of the election, the Minister of Fun, as he was dubbed, was revealed to have been having an extra-marital affair with actress Antonia de Sancha. Alleged details were blazoned across the tabloids, from toe-sucking to adorning the blue strip of Chelsea Football Club while in the act. Posing with his family in front of the cameras, Mellor admitted his infidelity but refused to resign. Major stuck by his friend and ally, but the press bayed for his scalp. After weeks of pressure Mellor reluctantly resigned, but the affair had dragged down the government into disrepute and threw into question Major's judgement only months after leading the party to a victory. The press turned even more to Tory 'sleaze', following Major's speech to the party conference in October 1993, when he called for a return to traditional values of decency and integrity. Although he did not mention sexual morality the 'back to basics' speech was a gift to journalists. Even before the conference ended, Steven Norris, a transport minister who was married with two children, was revealed as having not one mistress but five. The next to fall was Tim Yeo, Minister for the Environment, who resigned after stories about his fathering a love child with a single mother who happened to be a Conservative councillor. There then followed a litany of cases involving adulterous and deviant backbench MPs. Back to basics was hastily dropped, but the last years of Tory rule in the 1990s were irredeemably tarred with the brush of scandal and sleaze.

ECCENTRICS

Lord Hailsham was one of the party's most likeable eccentrics in the 1950s and 1960s. He enjoyed a long and distinguished career spanning five decades, first entering Parliament in 1938 as MP for Oxford and retiring from his last Cabinet post as Margaret Thatcher's Lord Chancellor in 1987. He could be a sparkling rhetorician and was an ebullient party chairman in the late 1950s, never losing an opportunity to lambast his Labour opponents. Vigorously ringing his trademark 'Victory Bell' to open the 1957 party conference, Hailsham declaimed: 'Let us say to the Labour Party: "Send not to ask for whom the bell tolls – it tolls for them!"' During the 1964 general election campaign, Hailsham declared that if the public voted for Labour's programme it would be 'stark, raving bonkers'. While on the campaign trail in the same election, he took exception to a Labour Party supporter who was furiously waving a placard of Harold Wilson. Hailsham charged towards him, attacking the placard with his walking stick.

Nicholas Fairbairn in full tartan attire in the House of Commons *(PA)*

The most eccentric 'Tartan Tory' from north of the border was Nicholas Fairbairn, MP for Perth and Kinross between 1974 and 1995. He was a distinguished QC and former Solicitor-General for Scotland, but his approach to politics and life in the public eye was unashamedly frank and irreverent. On succeeding to Alec Douglas-Home's seat in 1974, he confessed to feeling 'rather like a hot-cross-bun in a deep freeze' in the House of Commons. In his 1973 entry to *Who's Who*, Fairbairn listed his recreations as 'Making love, ends meet and people laugh'. He later explained that 'most people, if they were honest, will admit that those were their main recreations – apart, perhaps, from Ted Heath, who would probably miss out on the first and the third.' A self-confessed womaniser, he once proclaimed that 'a sexy mistress is better than a boring wife'. Fairbairn was not universally popular on the Tory benches, but he rarely failed to reduce his colleagues to hysteria with his quick wit and sharp tongue. During one late-night parliamentary debate in the mid-1980s, Fairbairn fell asleep. Awaking suddenly, Fairbairn rose to his feet to intervene in another MP's speech. 'I must apologise to the House,' exclaimed Fairbairn, 'the greatest mistake I made this evening was not to fall asleep but to wake up. I have never heard such rubbish!' The speaker in question was a fellow Scot, the future leader of the Liberal Democrats, Charles Kennedy.

Alan Clark, the year before his death in 1998 *(TopFoto)*

Alan Clark was one of the party's most outspoken and outrageous figures in the last thirty years. Clark enjoyed a roller-coaster career climbing the ministerial ladder under Margaret Thatcher to become Minister of State for Defence Procurement, but was never entrusted with a seat at the Cabinet. His diaries, first published in 1993, provide an insight into a man driven by the excitement of the political game and not afraid of political incorrectness or courting controversy. His gaffes often landed him in trouble, but he somehow managed to retain the confidence of his beloved Prime Minister. As a junior trade minister, Clark infamously referred to Africa in a meeting with officials as 'Bongo-Bongo land'. Like Fairbairn, Clark was a philanderer finding himself incapable of resisting the lure of attractive women. He managed to seduce not only the wife of a judge but also her two daughters – known as the 'coven'. Despite this, he remained married to his wife, Jane, until his death in 1999. Clark was irrepressible, so much so that he returned to political life as MP for Kensington and Chelsea in 1997 despite disgracing his party and government in the early 1990s by being, as he put it, 'economical with the actualité' in the 'arms to Iraq' affair.

MULTI-TALENTED TORIES

The Conservative Party has been fortunate enough to draw on the services of men and women of diverse talents whose achievements are often little known today. After making his debut for Yorkshire in 1890, Stanley Jackson was described in Wisden as one of the 'five all-rounders' to watch. Jackson played 20 test matches for England and led his side to victory against Australia in 1905. In 1921 Jackson received the highest honour that a cricketer can enjoy when he became President of the MCC. Having been elected to Parliament in 1915 Jackson became a (not very distinguished) chairman of the party between 1923 and 1926. A more recent sporting legend to represent the party at Westminster was Sebastian Coe. Record-breaking long-distance runner and gold medallist in the 1984 Olympics, Coe retired from sport to make a life in politics. Successfully contesting a marginal seat in Cornwall in the 1992 general election, Coe became an active and loyal Member of Parliament – making it to the Whips' Office in

1996. Losing his seat in 1997, Coe went on to become William Hague's right-hand man as his chief of staff until the 2001 election.

The Tory party has attracted several eminent writers and journalists to its ranks over the years. John Buchan's Richard Hannay novels, such as *Thirty-Nine Steps*, were particularly popular before the Second World War. Buchan was also an ambitious Tory, famously remarking, 'Publishing is my business, writing my amusement and politics my duty.' Elected as Conservative MP for the Scottish Universities in 1927, Buchan was a keen advocate in Parliament for raising educational standards and assisting the growing numbers of unemployed in Scotland in the 1930s. He was a speech-writer for Baldwin, pioneered the work of the Education Department in Central Office and was active in recruiting graduates and undergraduates to the party. In 1935 he was appointed Governor-General of Canada. William Deedes, who is now a legend, made his name as a successful reporter in the 1930s before going on to represent the Kentish town of Ashford as a Conservative between 1950 and 1970. A more affable and gentlemanly equivalent of New Labour's spin doctors, Deedes became indispensable to Macmillan as an adviser and director of party political broadcasts and was rewarded in 1962 with a place in the Cabinet. Following his retirement from politics in 1970, he became a rarity

for an ex-Cabinet minister, by going on to edit a broadsheet newspaper, the *Daily Telegraph*. In his nineties, Deedes continues to file copy for the paper. His fellow columnist at the *Telegraph*, Boris Johnson, is the most recent high-profile poacher turned gamekeeper to enter politics as a Tory MP. Combining his career as the forthright editor of the *Spectator* with that as an MP and, since the summer of 2004, front-bench spokesman for the arts, Johnson has articulated a form of liberal Euro-sceptic Toryism that has won him friends in the party, particularly among younger supporters. According to Johnson, the Tory party of the early twenty-first century is 'the funkiest, most jiving party on Earth!'

Boris Johnson enjoys a pint in his Henley constituency *(TopFoto)*

N I N E

PARTY AND COUNTRY

The emergence of a popular organisation with an active following in the late nineteenth century brought many unforseen benefits to a party rapidly adapting to the new era of mass democracy. The rank and file have been the lifeblood of the Conservative Party in the last 130 years. From the activities of local party members to the roles played by women and the youth movement, Conservatism spread its tentacles far and wide in British society. This chapter explores the changing relationship between party and country since the early nineteenth century. The last twenty-five years have seen the party losing its appeal drastically in parts of society and areas of the country where it was once strong. Only after the Conservatives recover their strength in all corners of the United Kingdom will they re-emerge again as the party of the nation.

THE GRASS ROOTS

The grass-roots membership are the loyal foot soldiers who keep the party afloat with their social and fund-raising activities as well as taking the message to the voters during election campaigns. They are also a proud lot, jealously guarding their local bastions, the constituency associations, from what they perceive to be an overbearing Central Office. For all the machinations and divisions that have afflicted the parliamentary party and its professional organisation over the years, the grass roots have been a traditional source of strength and continuity. They have not always, however, been a vibrant force.

THE FIRST SHOOTS

Apart from the emergence of some Tory-sympathising clubs in large towns and cities across the country in the late eighteenth century, there was little in the way of an organised party on the ground until the 1830s. The Great Reform Act of 1832 provided the stimulus for the emergence of several hundred Conservative and Constitutional Associations. Yet this upsurge of local activism, which was encouraged by Tory aristocrats, proved a false dawn. Many associations refused to have anything to do with the infant party headquarters in London, beginning a long tradition of suspicion of central interference in constituency affairs, while most became defunct after the party returned to power in 1841. The schism over the Corn Laws in 1846 revived local activism in the shires, with many local Tories joining county protection societies. The split had damaged the party's chances of developing an active following across the country. As Martin Pugh notes in his book *The Tories and the People*, 'the key to the

modern revival of Conservatism' was not to be found in the rural shires but in Britain's sprawling towns and cities in the 1850s and 1860s. It was here that the party laid down its strongest roots. Forced to compete with an increasingly active Liberal Party on the ground, the party soon recognised the value of amassing support in industrial areas like Lancashire and Glasgow. A new generation of working men's clubs and their complement of friendly and benefit societies rapidly became the mainstay of Conservative support.

The passage of the Second Reform Act in 1867 and the burgeoning number of Conservative associations and working men's clubs prompted Disraeli to establish the National

Lord Randolph Churchill in 1880 *(Hulton/Getty)*

Union to coordinate the sprawling grass-roots activity. As Conservative fortunes improved in the 1870s, the rank and file grew in confidence, eager to assert their views on the parliamentary party and leadership. Defeat in the 1880 general election unsettled the nerve of many middle-class activists and supporters. They were demoralised, venting their frustration with the new leadership of Stafford Northcote, whom they considered ineffectual and unsympathetic to requests to strengthen the National Union. Many local associations, especially those representing urban constituencies, wanted to see a real devolution of authority to the National Union. Their grievances were quickly seized upon by Lord Randolph Churchill's 'Fourth Party' and his campaign for 'Tory Democracy'. He was successful in getting himself elected to the National Union's Central Council in 1883, but failed in his mission to transfer powers from the official party machine in Westminster to its grass-roots rival in the country. The power struggle reaffirmed the concentration of organisational resources in the hands of the professional party. Some rank and file began to lose faith altogether in the party hierarchy, having to settle for a position of subservience with little or no influence in the direction of the party.

VICTORIAN FLOWERING

At this moment of danger arose a new grass-roots organisation in 1883 which would become one of the most popular Conservative political movements ever. The Primrose League was formed by members of Lord Randolph Churchill's Fourth Party to rectify 'the failure of Conservative and Constitutional Associations to suit the popular taste [and] to succeed in joining all classes together for political objects'. In the same year, Gladstone's Liberal government passed the Corrupt Practices Act, which limited campaign expenditure and restricted the numbers of paid activists political parties could employ. The Primrose League circumvented the Act by mobilising a whole new

Primrose League badge c.1889. The motto is *Imperium et Libertas* ('Empire and Liberty'). The badges, often enamelled and with the appearance of pieces of jewellery, were particularly appealing to women *(TopFoto)*

The Oxford branch of the Women's Unionist and Tariff Reform Association at Blenheim Palace in July 1908 (*Oxfordshire County Council Photographic Archive*)

army of *volunteers* for the party. By appealing to the 'maintenance of Religion, of the Estates of the Realm, and of the unity of the British Empire under our new Sovereign', it reached out to a wide cross-section of support, particularly among the newly enfranchised working class. Emulating the hierarchical structure of the Freemasons and the Orange Order, the League comprised 'habitations' with knights and dames who could rise through the ranks to become grand masters, mistresses and chancellors. Colourful badges, medals and elaborate costumes were all part of the Primrose League's attraction. The League excelled in laying on activities, from tea parties and garden fêtes to magic lantern shows and summer balls. Initially sceptical, Salisbury and senior party figures soon came to appreciate the League's worth as both a deferential and a politically benign organisation. The League increasingly helped with electioneering and also served an important educational purpose, publishing numerous pamphlets which sought to 'instruct working men and women how to answer the argument of the Radicals and the Socialists and the Atheists in the workshops and in the public houses and at the street corners . . .' With a membership exceeding well over a million by the early 1890s, it enjoyed a larger following than the trade union movement. As Pugh has noted, the habitation in Bolton, Lancashire, alone boasted 6,000 members in 1900,

A group of 'pilgrims' from the Primrose League pay homage to Disraeli's home, Hughenden, in Buckinghamshire in 1928 (Popperfoto)

which was as large as the entire national membership of the Independent Labour Party in that year.

Despite its medieval facade, the Primrose League was progressive in its approach to women. For many upper-class women, the League was a natural extension of volunteering in charity and education. It rapidly established itself also as a platform for middle-class (and some working-class) women, making the Conservative Party a more receptive vehicle for women than any other party in the late Victorian era. By 1885 several thousand women were involved in canvassing, the preparation of electoral registers and the distribution of campaign literature. Within ten years the Primrose League had established itself as the political home of hundreds of thousands of women – a huge boon to the Conservative Party in the country. Few Conservative men dared quarrel with Lady Jersey, a prominent Primrose Dame, who asserted that 'no political contest can be fought thoroughly and properly without the help of ladies'. Barred from taking leading positions in the League's governing body, the Grand Council, the Primrose Dames formed the Ladies' Grand Council in 1885, which gave them a collective voice within the League. By the time women received the vote in 1918, the party was able to draw on the loyalties of women who, for at least two generations, had been the backbone of a socially popular and upwardly mobile bastion of grass-roots Conservatism.

EDWARDIAN BLUES

The dual existence of the Primrose League and the National Union with its affiliated associations and clubs had built a healthy base of grass-roots support for the party as it entered the twentieth century. All this was to be severely rocked by the schism over Tarrif Reform. The gloss from the Primrose League's appeal was also damaged by its popular attachment to the Empire, which had suffered as a result of the controversies surrounding the Boer War. By 1912 the League's membership had fallen to just over 650,000. Many of its political activities and functions had begun to lapse, leaving it dangerously adrift while new groupings, such as the Tariff Reform League, began to amass a popular following among the grass roots. The Budget Protest League, the Middle-Class Defence League, the Union League and the Anti-Socialist Union were some of the other groups and leagues all jostling for position and competing for support from the voluntary party. The annual conferences of the National Union became battlegrounds between rival factions, prompting Balfour to remark that he would rather consult his valet than listen to the disparate views of conference delegates. Meanwhile, local associations up and down the country were locked into the intense struggle between Tarrif Reformers and free-traders. Unlike the Liberal Party, which fell apart during the First World War, the Conservatives rallied behind the flag and Bonar Law restored some order, putting behind them a prolonged period of crisis.

MATURING INTO A MASS PARTY: 1920s–50s

The advent of mass suffrage in 1918 provided an opportunity for the voluntary party to adapt to the needs of an electorate that had trebled in size to twenty-one million. Local associations would now become home to all grass-roots activists, displacing the dwindling number of Primrose League habitations in the early 1920s. Local organisation developed in sophistication: the sheer scale of raising funds and delivering party propaganda required a much larger and more active membership than ever before. Key to the success of these initiatives was the quality of local leadership. As Stuart Ball points out, more than any in other party, the upper and upper-middle classes swelled the ranks of local association chairmen across the country in the interwar period. They provided the party with social prestige and a sense of public service, as well as

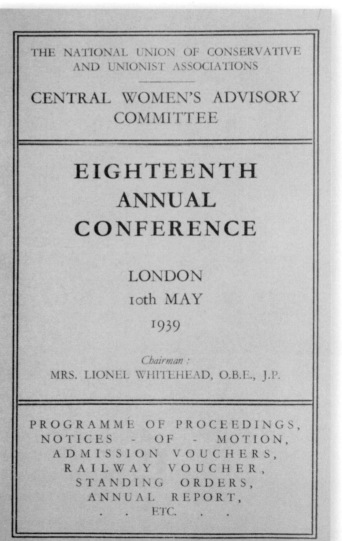

THE NATIONAL UNION OF CONSERVATIVE AND UNIONIST ASSOCIATIONS

CENTRAL WOMEN'S ADVISORY COMMITTEE

EIGHTEENTH ANNUAL CONFERENCE

LONDON
10th MAY
1939

Chairman :
MRS. LIONEL WHITEHEAD, O.B.E., J.P.

PROGRAMME OF PROCEEDINGS, NOTICES - OF - MOTION, ADMISSION VOUCHERS, RAILWAY VOUCHER, STANDING ORDERS, ANNUAL REPORT, . . ETC. . .

Programme of the Central Women's Advisory Committee annual conference in 1939 *(Bodleian Library)*

Eden, with his film-star good looks, was hugely popular with women members, as shown here at a mass meeting of Women Conservatives at the Royal Albert Hall, London, in 1956 *(Bodleian Library)*

'the munitions of political warfare: influence, financial backing, support of the local press and a large supply of prospective candidates who were educated, socially respectable and could pay their own way'. The success of associations in mobilising support and ensuring electoral dominance in the 1920s and '30s was in no small measure achieved by the influx of huge numbers of lower middle classes into the party's grass-roots organisation. They were to prove the foot soldiers who delivered pamphlets through the letter boxes of suburban Britain, where so much of the party's electoral strength was forged.

With women enfranchised in 1918 and 1928 (when their voting age was reduced from 30 to equality with men at 21), the party went out of its way to encourage their active participation on the ground. As the League had paved the way, most women were from middle- to upper-class backgrounds with the time and resources to engage in rounds of social and fund-raising activities. The party encouraged the semi-autonomous women's branches by arranging meetings and events at convenient times (usually during the day and not in the evenings). In 1919 Central Office changed the rules of the party so that women were allocated a minimum of one-third of the places on representative bodies both at the centre and in the constituencies. Although women members in fact outnumbered men, the association chairmen and other leading figures would still almost invariably be men, as would the parliamentary candidates. The National Women's Advisory Committee became a chief exponent of greater integration between women's branches and their affiliate associations. Women marched on apace in the grass-roots organisation of the party: by 1928 they constituted a membership of nearly a million, with 2,000 to 3,000 women members on average per constituency. By comparison, the Labour Party – although starting from a much lower base could claim only 200,000 individual members (male and female) by the time MacDonald formed its second government in 1929.

As the century progressed, women gradually infiltrated the ranks of constituency organisers, chairmen and professional agents. Spurred on by the mass recruitment drive under Woolton in the postwar period, women accounted for slightly over half of the 2,805,032 members in 1952. But progress on the ground was still not matched by increased representation in the parliamentary party. The 1960s and 1970s saw a decline in female participation on the ground because of changes in lifestyle and the labour market, but many women, especially those in retirement, continued to make a significant contribution.

FINDING A VOICE: 1950s–80s

Thanks to Woolton's ambitious membership drives and the instant success of the Young Conservatives, the grass roots of the Conservative Party of the 1950s and '60s went from strength to strength. With a mass membership of nearly three million at its peak, the amplified opinions of the rank and file began to make an impact on the leadership of the party. Local associations retained much of their control over candidate selection and fund-raising even after the Maxwell-Fyfe reforms of 1948–9, while the party's annual

YOUTH APPEAL

The Junior Imperial League, the party's first youth organisation, was founded in 1906 to reach out to a younger generation of supporters in the wake of heavy defeat. Initially membership was open only to young men between 16 and 25 years of age, but after women were admitted in 1919, the League became an active and integrated part of the party. Under the encouragement of party chairman, J.C.C. Davidson, the Junior Imperial League organised a plethora of activities in the 1920s such as weekend schools, model parliaments and public-speaking competitions. Another body, the Young Britons,

also came into existence in the mid-1920s to promote good citizenship, patriotism and 'the realisation of simple Conservative principles' for children between the ages of 6 and 16. Not seeking to be overtly partisan in its approach, the party believed the Young Britons would 'counteract the blasphemous and seditious doctrine of the Communists' as represented by the socialist Sunday Schools. Widely popular in the 1920s and 1930s, the Young Britons' membership peaked at half a million.

The advent of war in 1939 spelt the end for the Junior Imperial League, but the creation of a new body in 1946 heralded an era of popular

The Young Conservatives' stall at the Bolton Conservative Association fair in 1950 *(from the collection of Dr Stuart Ball)*

Conservatism among young people in postwar Britain. Within three years, over 2,500 Young Conservative (YC) branches had been formed with a membership of well over 150,000. The rapid growth of the YCs was largely due to the success in providing a venue for young people to meet at dinners, dances, sporting events and other social gatherings in an austere postwar country. The YC social scene became legendary in the 1950s and '60s; it even became one the most popular informal dating agencies in the country. They also proved valuable canvassers during election campaigns, with a generation of future Tory MPs receiving their first taste of politics in the organisation. Despite a gradual fall in membership in the 1960s and 1970s, the YCs continued to broaden their appeal beyond the middle classes and infused otherwise ageing Conservative associations with youthful energy and enthusiasm.

In the 1980s, the YCs became more politically motivated, inspired by Margaret Thatcher's radical crusade. An affiliated body, the Federation of Conservative Students, had to be disbanded by Norman Tebbit in 1986 after espousing views that were deemed too extreme, as well as embarrassing the party during conferences featuring drunken brawls and ransacking of university halls of residence. Young Conservative membership fell dramatically in the 1990s, with some constituency branches in cities like Bristol claiming only a handful of members. The Young Conservatives were rebranded as 'Conservative Future' in

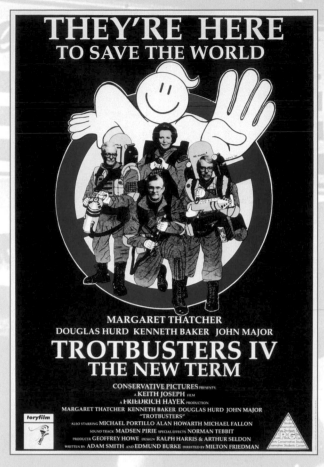

A Federation of Conservative Students poster from the late 1980s (Bodleian Library)

1998 by one of its most famous former members, William Hague. After a tentative beginning, the new body has overseen something of a revival of the party's youth wing. From the historic low in 1998 of only 4,000 members, Conservative Future has more than doubled its following to well over 10,000. Although a far cry from the heyday of the 1950s, the party will have to call on the services of a rejuvenated youth movement in the years to come.

Conservative Association representatives at the annual conference in Westminster Central Hall in 1945 *(Hulton/Getty)*

conference became an increasingly important sounding board for Cabinet and shadow Cabinet Ministers to fly kites, build reputations and make policy announcements. The 1950 conference is traditionally seen as a high point in its influence over the leadership (see chapter six). Six years later Anthony Eden was stung by accusations of dithering over what do about the Suez Canal, and became even more determined to act when the crisis came to a head a month later.

In the latter part of the last century, the rank and file tended to support the incumbent leader when in trouble, even when the parliamentary party pressed for a change in leadership. Heath thus received the overwhelming support of the grass roots in 1975, despite the two defeats in 1974. Few positively welcomed a change in leadership, particularly in favour of someone who had yet to make a significant mark on the party. Party activists thus remained fiercely loyal to Heath's successor fifteen years later, refusing to believe – as a majority of backbench Tory MPs did believe – that Mrs Thatcher had become an electoral liability. Thatcher had great respect for the rank and file, who she believed were the party's true conscience, with instincts much closer to her own than most of the members of her last Cabinet. When her Environment Secretary, Nicholas Ridley, announced plans for phasing in the poll tax over a three- to five-year period to the party conference in 1987, the assembled delegates, buoyed by their party's third successive election victory, called for a much swifter introduction. As the debate progressed, Mrs Thatcher turned to Ridley to remark, 'We've got to think again on this, Nick'. The pace was duly quickened, with fateful consequences for her premiership three years later.

A SHRINKING FORCE: 1980S–2004

Since the early 1960s, changes in society have led to a decline in membership and activism for all political parties. By the early 1970s, membership had fallen to below one and a half million, and by the mid-1980s it had fallen to less than three-quarters of a million. The ready availability of more exciting recreational pursuits, an erosion of class lines and an explosion of single-interest politics all made their impact. Technological advances, from the use of computers to direct mailing, also meant local associations no longer required as many helpers as before. During the eighteen years in office after 1979, the voluntary party succumbed to a mixture of complacency and disillusion. The loss of many Conservative councillors during successive local elections in the 1980s and 1990s, when voters chose to protest against the government, further damaged local strength. The haemorrhaging of such an important constituency of the party was to have disastrous consequences when it tried to regroup after the 1997 defeat: only in the last few years has the party managed to recover some of its strength in local government. The grass-roots membership shrunk to around 300,000 members in the late 1990s, and studies showed that less than half of that total could be described as 'active', while the average age of members had risen to a worrying 62. This shrinking and ageing band of party activists did their best to keep local associations alive in the dark years of the mid- to late 1990s, but were not able to compete successfully with the dynamism of New Labour nor with the Liberal Democrats. Local Conservative associations meanwhile struggled to raise sufficient funds for the national party, making it even more reliant on large donations.

In opposition after 1997, the party made concerted efforts to revive the grass roots by giving it a formal voice in leadership elections and through reforms designed to give it enhanced participation in policy development and direction. Perhaps Hague's most important legacy as leader was to increase internal party democracy. A new voting system gave ordinary members a vote in the key run-off stage of a leadership election, while Hague held ballots over several organisational and policy initiatives. Policy forums were also established to encourage debate and consultation between the leadership and the rank and file. Under Duncan Smith, the party conference was shortened and debates on the floor were curtailed as officials attempted to make it a more disciplined event. The combined effect of these reforms was to stimulate a modest recovery in membership numbers, at the cost of tensions within the party, particularly over the outcome of the 2001 leadership contest, where the parliamentary party's preference for Kenneth Clarke was overruled by the mass membership's preference for Duncan Smith. The creation of a new party Board to replace the National Union also courted controversy with activists, who complained that they were under-represented and that associations were losing some of their independence. The dust has yet to settle on the welter of organisational changes made since 1997, but spirits were lifted by the new sense of purpose imported by Michael Howard. It remains to be seen how far the grass roots, which for so long underpinned Conservative strength in the country, can recover their former vitality.

BONDS OF SOCIETY

Fundamental to the electoral success of the Conservative Party has been the forging of strong bonds with the various powerful interests of British society. For much of the last 150 years, the party has managed to adapt to significant changes in society, sensing the changing social and political pulse of the nation. Religion, class, gender and other interests have provided the party with hugely important reserves of support. The declining importance of some of these has, however, done much to undermine the identity of the party in the early twenty-first century.

THE PARTY AT PRAYER

Conservatives have traditionally valued Christianity as essential for the bonding and moral well-being of society. For much of the nineteenth century, disputes over civil rights, conformity and nonconformity and the establishment of the Church of England were intricately bound up with political debate. After major disagreements over Catholic Emancipation in the first three decades of the century, the party of Disraeli and Salisbury developed strong bonds with Anglican clergy and congregations. It became the staunchest

An election poster from the 1951 general election appeals to mothers (*Bodleian Library*)

Mrs Thatcher meets the Chief Rabbi for Great Britain and the Commonwealth, Immanuel Jacobovits, in 10 Downing Street *(PA)*

ally of the Church of England, defending its role in the provision of education in the 1890s and 1900s. Conservatives were to benefit from their consistent opposition to disestablishment of the Church in Wales, with many in the Welsh hierarchy identifying with the party in the first two decades of the twentieth century. The battles over Irish Home Rule during these years also aligned the party closely with the Protestant cause not only in Northern Ireland but also in Liverpool, Manchester, Lancashire and the West of Scotland. Its seems remarkable now that working-class areas like Toxteth in Merseyside and almost all the constituencies in Glasgow returned Conservative MPs until the 1960s.

Conservatism became increasingly respectable among Nonconformists in the interwar years, when many switched their allegiance to the party from the Liberals. The Anglo-Jewish elite also identified with the party in this period, only to be limited by a climate of anti-Semitism in some right-wing quarters (which had almost thwarted the rise of Disraeli). Nevertheless, support for Mrs Thatcher's Conservative Party in the 1980s among the Jewish community was particularly strong, many of whom shared her emphasis on individual responsibility and self-reliance. She had a particular liking for Chief Rabbi, Immanuel Jacobovits, who she viewed as much sounder than most Christian leaders. Among the most prominent Jewish Conservatives to rise through the ranks under her reign were Keith Joseph, Lord Young, Leon Brittan, Nigel Lawson, Malcolm Rifkind and Michael Howard. The last three decades of the twentieth century saw a loosening of religious ties and allegiances as society became more secular, and the traditional model of the family also began to break down. The party has found not found it easy to come to terms with these changes. In the 1980s some Church of England leaders and leading Tory politicians began to blame each other for failing to provide leadership on issues of personal morality and the defence of the family. The party's bond with the Church of England loosened, and it never forged links with the Christian Right as the Republicans did in America. Although many Conservatives continue to share the values and beliefs of the Anglican tradition, the party has sought to forge links with other religious denominations, particularly the Muslim and Sikh communities, as in Bradford and parts of London.

CLASS APPEAL

Ever since the Second Reform Act in 1867, the party has striven to appeal to a broad cross-section of the population. In the 1880s and 1890s, the expanding middle class swung firmly behind the Conservative banner, remaining loyal to the cause for much of the century that followed. Only in 1945 and 1997 did middle-class voters desert the party in droves. In the case of 1945, many returned to the fold within six years to become the bedrock of the party's support during the 1950s and early 1960s. However, the party could not have won any general election in the last 130 years without a substantial degree of support from the working class. Research has shown that they constituted the majority of the electorate until the mid-1980s. Remarkably, the party of the landed and commercial elites and of the established Church managed to win 50 per cent of the working-class vote in the two decades that followed the extension of the mass franchise in 1918. Deference, aspiration and loyalty to the Empire were instrumental in this groundswell of working-class support. The party of Baldwin deliberately sought to broaden the Conservative appeal by pursuing an ambitious programme of social reform as well as emphasising the dangers to social harmony and stability for socialism and the rise of the Labour Party.

Once the economy began to recover in the 1950s, with the rise in living standards and spread of home ownership, the party reconnected with the hopes and aspirations of the lower-middle and working classes. New towns across the country like Harlow, Stevenage and Basildon now became fertile territory for the party to amass support. As the proportion of middle-class non-manual workers and owner-occupiers rose steadily in the 1950s and 1960s, the party invested in more-sophisticated polling techniques and targeted campaigns to lure voters who were ambitious and socially mobile. The gradual erosion of class barriers paved the way for a sustained period of electoral success in the 1980s and early 1990s. Mrs Thatcher's three successive election wins were underpinned by healthy levels of support from the professional (AB) classes to the skilled working class

A poster from the 1931 general election, appealing to the working classes *(Bodleian Library)*

STOP THIS
FROM U.S.A.
FROM JAPAN
FROM BELGIUM
FROM CZECHO-SLOVAKIA
GRAIN FROM RUSSIA
MADE IN GERMANY
BY VOTING CONSERVATIVE

THE GENDER GAP

Women have been not only the stalwarts of the party's grass roots but also a key component of Conservative electoral success between the 1920s and the 1980s. Recognising the valuable contribution of women volunteers, the hierarchy was not unsympathetic to women's suffrage from the end of the nineteenth century. The Conservative and Unionist Women's Franchise Review steadily made the Conservative case for the enfranchisement of women (with property qualifications) in the Edwardian period. A generally sympathetic leader, Balfour, regularly corresponded with Christabel Pankhurst, the prominent campaigner for women's votes. Due to a combination of internal dissent then and a latent fear of the risks involved in extending the franchise, the party retreated from making what could have been a bold declaration in favour of women's suffrage. Despite reluctance

in some quarters to embrace the move when it eventually came in 1918, Conservative leaders made a concerted effort to attract the millions of new voters. 'Women will have, with us, the fullest rights. The grounds for the old agitation is gone, and gone forever', Stanley Baldwin declared when he introduced a Bill in the House of Commons in 1928 to extend the franchise to all women over 21. Although there were doubts whether the 'new flapper' vote would fall into the Conservative fold (with some justification after the party's surprise defeat in 1929), more women than men would vote for the party in almost every general election since then. The gender gap reached its postwar peak in the 1955 election, when there was an 8 per cent difference in Conservative support between men and women. Research in the 1990s suggests that, had there been no women's suffrage, the Labour Party would have held office continuously until 1979. During the 1980s, the Tory party lost its traditional advantage with women voters, largely because women's lifestyles had changed. What was once a source of electoral strength for the party had become a weakness in the late 1990s and early 2000s, with women deserting the party in greater numbers than men. The party will have to regain the trust of women voters if it is to stage a convincing electoral recovery.

Conservative women boast historic 'firsts' in British politics, such as Nancy Astor becoming the first woman MP to take up her seat in the

Nancy Astor rejoices after being elected as the Member of Parliament for Plymouth Sutton in a by-election in 1919 (Hulton/Getty)

The new intake of Tory women MPs in 1931 stroll along the terrace outside the House of Commons (*Bodleian Library*)

House of Commons, and the election of Margaret Thatcher as Britain's first woman party leader and Prime Minister. But they have been the exception rather than the rule. The Labour Party has fielded more women candidates than the Conservatives in every single general election since 1918. It looked as if women would gain a foothold in terms of the party's parliamentary representation in 1931, especially when thirteen female Tory MPs were elected. In 1945 however, only one of those was returned to Parliament, while the total number of Conservative women MPs since has never exceeded twenty, of whom only a handful have risen through the ministerial ranks to reach the Cabinet. It is paradoxical that a party that has enjoyed such a healthy following among women activists and voters has not chosen more women to serve in Parliament. Many were surprised and disappointed that Mrs Thatcher did so little to encourage more

Tory women to stand for Parliament, let alone promote those within the parliamentary party beyond junior ministerial level. Despite several attempts by the official party machine to boost participation, and occasional overhauls of selection procedures, local associations have been reluctant to select more women candidates. Only once the last vestiges of prejudice are swept away will the party be able to reflect more fully the society it seeks to represent.

Virginia Bottomley, one of two women MPs to serve in Major's Cabinet, addressing the 1996 annual conference (*TopFoto*)

(C2s). Only from among the unskilled and unemployed (DEs) did the party receive consistently low levels of support. One of the ironies of the Tories' success in this period was that the party could no longer depend on clearly defined reservoirs of class-based support. Class was no longer a reliable determinant of party loyalty, as New Labour's success at polls has showed in recent years. In an age of electoral volatility and disillusion with mainstream parties and politics in general, twenty-first century Conservatives have yet to carve out a new agenda to suit the needs and concerns of an increasingly 'classless' society.

CONSERVATIVE-SUPPORTING INTERESTS

The bond between the party and the powerful interests and institutions in British society has been a consistent theme of the last century and a half. In the early and mid-nineteenth century the party was influenced heavily by the agricultural interest, which was dominant in the British economy. As industry and commerce developed and continued to expand during the century, Conservatives forged new alliances. In the 1870s the brewing industry switched its allegiance from the Liberal Party, which had become a champion for the temperance movement, to the party of Disraeli and Salisbury. It is no coincidence that so many public houses were named after leading Tories. Indeed, Middleton, the party chairman at the time, once declared that every pub in England should become a small bastion of Conservatism. Labelled the 'brewers' friend', the Tory party maintained its long and financially rewarding association with brewing throughout the twentieth century.

The armed forces also established strong links with the party, mainly on the back of Disraeli's reclaiming of the Tories as the party of empire. From the late nineteenth century, the party was seen to be much more of a champion of the armed forces than its rivals. By 1929, some 17 per cent of Tory MPs had a military background in the regular army. Although this proportion was to shrink after the Second World War, the Tories remained the party that the Services looked to as their principal champion.

The financial interests represented at their apex by the City of London have remained the most loyal supporters of the party throughout much of its history. Traditionally trusted as the most competent guardians of the economy, the party has received strong support from merchant bankers, financiers and entrepreneurs. This bond became even more entrenched when the Thatcher government deregulated the financial sector in the 1980s. British industrialists also bonded more to the Tories, the more threatening

Labour become towards free enterprise. The postwar Labour government's programme of nationalisation thus proved a most valuable boom to the Tories: there was no mistaking now who was the friend of business. Organisations such as Aims of Industry and British United Industrialists were later to channel huge amounts of money into the party's coffers. One of the most damaging aspects of New Labour for the Tories has been Blair's ability to convince the City and industry, as well as another bastion of Tory support in the past, the press, that a Labour government would be more in their interest than a Tory administration.

THE PARTY OF THE NATION

'The Tory Party, unless it is a national party, is nothing', Disraeli proclaimed in 1872. In the 100 years that followed that speech, the party was able to draw on support from all corners of the United Kingdom. From the shire counties to the market towns, provincial cities and sprawling metropolitan areas, the party was the predominant electoral force in England – outnumbering Liberal and Labour rivals in parliamentary representation in most regions for much of the last century. As for the rest of Britain, a strong defence of the Union also helped ensure that the party's appeal resonated elsewhere, particularly in Scotland and in Northern Ireland during the first half of the twentieth century. Yet fifty years on, huge swathes of metropolitan England and almost all of Scotland and Wales had become barren wastelands for Conservatives while the Ulster Unionist parties have been deeply antagonised by government policy toward the province. The challenge for the party in the early twenty-first century will be to reclaim its mantle as the party of the whole nation.

TORY ENGLAND

The ascendancy of Liberal and Whig politics in the 1850s and 1860s confined the Tory party to the largely non-industrial areas of England, particularly in the South. Under Disraeli and Salisbury, Conservatism put down firm roots in the great metropolitan cities, boroughs and districts of the Midlands and the North. Lancashire in particular, with its industry and strong Protestant following, was lured into the Tory fold in the 1860s, remaining there for years to come. By the turn of the century, many of England's largest cities, including London, which had been a radical stronghold for much of the 1800s, returned a large number of Conservative MPs to Parliament. England's second largest city, Birmingham, and its surrounding area, which had been the 'Grand Duchy' of Joseph Chamberlain's Liberal Unionists, became a beacon of Conservatism. In the general elections of the early 1920s, all twelve Birmingham seats were won by the Conservatives. The party truly represented the length and breadth of England during the interwar years. In 1931, a staggering 402 out of 492 English constituencies elected Conservatives to Parliament.

Only on a few occasions have the party's heartlands been penetrated by rival parties, most notably in the landslide defeats of 1906, 1945, 1997 and 2001. However, it is only in the last few decades that the Tory sweep of England's electoral geography has begun to unravel. The Thatcher years hastened the retreat of Tory representation in the large cities and urban areas, which dated back to the early 1960s, as industrial decline and high levels of unemployment seriously damaged the party's standing and compromised the One Nation ideal of Disraeli and Baldwin. As the political scientist, Ivor Crewe, notes, the landslide victories of 1983 and 1987 were '"two nations" elections: the Conservatives advanced where there was prosperity and growth but retreated where there was deprivation and decline'. In the late 1990s, the Conservatives could not rival New Labour's appeal, which seemed to chime much better with the socially progressive attitudes and cosmopolitan lifestyles in the last decade of the twentieth century. Not one single inner-city constituency (outside London) elected a Conservative MP in 1997 and 2001, with the Liberal Democrats displacing the party as the second largest electoral force in many northern metropolitan areas. The Conservatives had become the party of rural and suburban South-East England, and little else. Despite signs of a modest, and patchy, recovery in urban areas of the Midlands and the North-West in the 2004 local council elections, the Conservatives still have a long way to go before they restore their fortunes in metropolitan England.

DEFENDING THE UNION

The Union of England with Scotland, Wales and Northern Ireland (as well as the whole of Ireland before 1922) has occupied a central position in the politics of the Conservative Party. For most of the nineteenth century, the party sought to maintain the Union with Ireland, often having to make concessions in the form of greater self-government and property rights. Conservatives feared an independent Ireland would undermine the empire and pose a threat to the rest of the Union. The battle at the end of the century over Irish Home Rule emboldened the Conservatives' defence of the Union, fortified by their

The defence of the Union was a hallmark of the party's 1959 election campaign *(Bodleian Library)*

alliance with the Liberal Unionists (with whom the party eventually merged in 1912). The party soon came to terms with the loss of Ireland in the 1920s, and maintained strong links with the Unionists until late in the century.

Unionism in Scotland had become an important force during the 1880s and 1890s, when the split in the Liberal Party over Irish Home Rule heralded the end of a thirty-year period of Liberal dominance north of the border. Disraeli's and Salisbury's patriotic appeal to the Empire helped to lure Scottish voters into the Tory fold. The Conservative-Liberal Unionist alliance won over half of the Scottish seats in the 1900 general election. Unionism prospered from a combination of religious allegiance and imperial sentiment in the decades that followed. The Conservatism of Churchill and Macmillan, which was characterised by rising living standards and social cohesion, proved just as popular with Scots as it did with the English. In the general election of 1955, the zenith of Tory fortunes in Scotland, the party won 50 per cent of the popular vote on both sides of the border.

Tory support began to slide as Labour established itself as the dominant political force in Scotland, taking votes in the 1960s and 1970s from those who bore the brunt of industrial decline in the country. The rise of the Scottish National Party (SNP) also mounted a further challenge to the party in the late 1960s and 1970s. Mrs Thatcher's forthright opposition to devolution in the late 1970s stimulated a minor revival of Tory fortunes north of the border; but it was short-lived. Many Scots resented the fact that they had been left behind by the Thatcher revolution – both socially and economically. Despite John Major's strong defence of the Union, in which he warned that devolution would be a 'Trojan horse' for independence, the party was wiped from the political map altogether in the landslide of 1997. Having suffered such a humiliating defeat at that election and from the 'settled will' of the Scottish people expressed in the referendum of Blair's government on devolution, the party agreed to support the Scottish Parliament. Despite regaining some lost ground since the nadir of 1997, Conservatism in Scotland remains a shadow of its former self. Ironically, if Scotland were even to follow Ireland to independence, it could damage Labour hugely, to the great benefit of the Conservative Party.

T E N

THE ELECTION MACHINE

The Conservative Party has won fourteen of the twenty-three general elections since the introduction of the mass franchise in 1918, either with an overall majority or as the largest party in the House of Commons. Its perennial quest for power has produced an election machine that has been the source of curiosity, admiration and envy for political parties across the Western world. From persuading the retainers to go out to vote to projecting a nationwide media campaign, the Conservatives have often been in the vanguard of political campaigning. In this final chapter, we look at the world of the Tory election campaign, tracing the rise and fall of a formidable electoral machine through all its many parts.

THE MAKING OF A MACHINE

FORGING AHEAD

Tory candidates were left very much to their own devices during general election campaigns after 1832. They were personally responsible for the costs of holding an election, from the salaries of the returning officers to the transportation of electors to and from the polling station; they even had to pay for the polling booths. Although the first Reform Act had swept away rotten boroughs and the most overt forms of corruption, candidates would still have to lavish huge sums of money on their campaigns in an effort

An election address to the electors of Maidstone
from Wyndham Lewis and Benjamin Disraeli in 1837
(Bodleian Library)

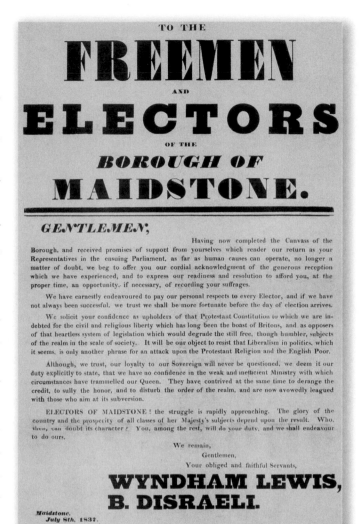

to win over the independent voter. In the 1830s and 1840s, an individual candidate's election expenses could run to thousands of pounds. Disraeli's successful campaign in Maidstone in 1837, for example, cost over £40,000, an enormous sum and one which was loyally met by his wife, Mary Ann. Hustings and public meetings in the mid-nineteenth century were often a major spectacle, as rival candidates accompanied their speeches with bands, parades, buntings and lavish refreshments. Election leaflets and posters, on the other hand, were often plain and uninspiring. Newspapers like *The Times* and the *Morning Chronicle* would publish speeches often in full by party leaders, but there was no other outlet in which to publicise a coordinated national campaign. Peel's Tamworth Manifesto in 1835 was, however, a new departure in electioneering. It was not only the first attempt of any party leader to print and distribute a manifesto to his electors; it was also widely used by Conservative candidates across the country as providing a uniform Tory message for their own campaigns.

Voter registration was another area in which the party led the field in its search for votes. Local Conservative candidates and agents were much quicker off the mark than their Whig and Liberal counterparts in setting up Registration Societies to encourage eligible voters to add their names to the electoral register, which had been introduced by the 1832 Reform Act. Until 1918 much of the responsibility of registration was left to local parties and candidates. As we saw in Chapter 6, Peel and the party's first chief agent, Francis Bonham, were pioneers in fostering the development of local Conservative

Registration Societies from the party's first headquarters in the Carlton Club. By the 1841 general election, the party had succeeded in registering thousands of electors and managed to field nearly 500 candidates. It was a triumph for a party which only nine years earlier rejected any attempt to enlarge the electorate and reform the old system of patronage and corruption.

LOSING THE INITIATIVE

After the party split over the repeal of the Corn Laws in 1846, Bonham deserted the party along with his leader, taking with him the party's central funds and files, while local registration societies bore the brunt of the split, many of them ceasing to exist altogether. The Whigs and Liberals, strengthened by their new alliance with the Peelites, began to make the running in election campaigns in the 1850s, mobilising a more united and purposeful body of candidates, agents and party workers than anything the Conservative Party could muster under Derby's lacklustre leadership. In 1859, Whigs, Peelites and radical Liberals joined forces under Lord Palmerston to form the Liberal Party, producing two successive general election victories in which they polled 65 per cent of the vote. The Liberals made impressive advances in their campaigning, as well as inspiring making innovative use of party caucuses in towns and cities across the country. Not until after the Second Reform Act in 1867 were the Tories able to match the sophistication of the Liberal election machine.

The party leadership, particularly under Derby, showed little interest in cultivating what was to become a major element of political life and campaigning in mid-Victorian Britain – the press. The split of 1845–6 led many metropolitan papers, including *The Times*, *Morning Chronicle* and *Morning Post*, to align with the Liberal–Peelite coalition. Edward Stanley, son of Lord Derby, lamented in 1851 that 'the party in general seemed to regard the newspaper interest as their natural enemy, and any attempt to turn it into a friend as a mere waste of time'. Disraeli founded *The Press* in 1853 to counter the loss of support within the 'fourth estate', but its circulation of 3,000 scarcely dented the Liberal–Peelite dominance of the national newspaper press which, as Bruce Coleman points out, was divided two to one against the Conservatives by the early 1850s. The party thus missed the opportunity fully to connect with the largely urban and bourgeois readership of the mid-nineteenth century. The party moreover compounded its error by neglecting to forge good relations with the burgeoning number of provincial newspapers, many of which had fallen into the Liberal fold by the early 1860s.

REGAINING THE INITIATIVE

The Second Reform Act of 1867 created the opportunity for the party to construct a powerful election machine to rival the Liberals. Under the direction of Disraeli and his new Principal Agent, John Gorst, the party began to revive. Gorst purchased a press agency to circulate copies of speeches, reports of meetings and favourable parliamentary sketches to supportive papers in the provinces. Strenuous efforts were also made to win back the national press, successfully with the *Morning Post* and also the *London Evening Standard*, which became one of the most reliable Tory papers for decades to come. The Conservative victory of 1874 was facilitated by the party's new friends in the press and through the adoption of simple but highly effective national campaign themes – patriotism, national unity and social reform.

Following the redistribution of constituencies and a third extension of the franchise in 1884–5, the party strove hard to take full advantage of the changing electoral scene. The Corrupt Practices Act transformed electioneering by severely restricting the amount of money any single candidate could spend on his campaign – including the bribery of voters. Before 1883, agents were personally employed by the candidate to assist with registration, but the party now realised their potential as efficient campaign organisers, and encouraged local associations themselves to employ agents on a professional basis. A special magazine, *The Tory*, was published specifically for agents, offering advice on how to watch out for electoral pitfalls and corrupt practices among their opponents. By the turn of the century, agents were an indispensable feature of the Tory election machine, taking their lead from the indefatigable Captain Middleton, the Principal Agent in Central Office.

National campaigning developed apace in the later nineteenth century. Both Disraeli and Salisbury recognised the benefits of addressing large audiences during general elections. Party leaders and senior

Disraeli making a speech at the market ordinary in Aylesbury during the 1874 general election campaign. *Illustrated London News*, 1874 (Hulton/Getty)

politicians increasingly began to travel up and down the country utilising the ever-expanding and ever-speedier Victorian railway system. Local hustings between rival candidates were complemented by large public meetings, both indoors and outdoors, where the party's top brass could seek to inspire the voters, many recently enfranchised, with their rhetoric. Thousands and sometimes tens of thousands of people flocked to see and hear politicians, about whom they knew little until the growth of the cheap popular press in the 1880s and 1890s. Lord Salisbury, although as a member of the Lords never standing as a candidate himself, relished the opportunity to address the masses, often for several hours. The landslide victories of 1895 and 1900 were testament to the advances the party had made in the realm of local and national campaigning.

A CALL TO ARMS

Radical threats have always galvanised Conservatives to mobilise support through the best means available at the time. The great reforming Liberal administrations of Asquith

Joseph Chamberlain addresses a crowd of supporters from his car during the 1906 general election *(Hulton/Getty)*

A Budget Protest League poster from 1909 *(Bodleian Library)*

and Lloyd George after 1906, provided one such challenge, with the defeated Conservative Party entering one of its most fratricidal periods in opposition, the new 'legion of leagues' spared no time in spreading their message to the electorate through a concerted campaign of leafleting and billboard posters. The Budget Protest League thus waged a fierce war of words against Lloyd George's far-reaching 1909 budget, as well as launching a series of often witty cartoon posters.

During the 1910 general election campaigns, the party began to emulate the pioneering publicity of the leagues, distributing some forty million leaflets in both elections. Central Office worked hard to cultivate relations with the national newspapers, appointing Sir Malcolm Fraser as its first press adviser, while gramophone records with election messages were produced and sold across the country. The party in 1910 regained some 116 of the seats lost in the landslide of 1906, an achievement that had much to do with the effectiveness of its nationwide propaganda campaign. Arthur Steel-Maitland's reorganisation of the party placed an even greater emphasis on good press relations, including the setting up of an effective press bureau in Central Office in 1911. Much of the money raised in the years preceding the First World War was channelled towards the employment of district agents who could intervene to bolster campaigns in marginal seats.

The First World War and the Reform Act of 1918 ushered in yet another electioneering strategy. The task of registration was transferred from election agents to the state, removing from the local campaign machine an important means of communication and influence with the electorate. Many Conservatives were convinced of the necessity for 'political education' to combat what they perceived as the overwhelming threat of 'Bolshevism' in Europe and the rising tide of socialism at home – both of which might seduce an ill-educated electorate. In the years that followed the First World War, a pioneering publicity operation was assembled within Conservative Central Office, which drew on the expertise of men who had been at the forefront of the country's wartime propaganda campaign. J.C.C. Davidson, who had served in the Colonial Office during the war, recalled in his memoirs that his first task as Party Chairman was 'to apply the lessons of the Great War to the organisation of political warfare'. He was joined by a group of individuals who had made their name as propagandists and intelligence officers

SIR JOSEPH BALL: THE MASTER OF SPIN

One of J.C.C. Davidson's most successful appointments as chairman was Joseph Ball. After rising through the ranks of MI5 during the First World War, Ball was recruited by Davidson to become the party's first full-time Director of Publicity in 1927. Davidson recalled in his memoirs that Ball possessed an impressive combination of 'firmness of character, highly trained mind and infinite industry' as well as 'experience . . . in the seamy side of life and the handling of crooks'. It was the latter skills Davidson encouraged Ball to deploy, utilising the same techniques to penetrate the Labour Party as he had as an intelligence officer for MI5 in infiltrating the British Communist Party. Ball's clandestine efforts involved sending agents into the Labour Party's headquarters as well as into its printing firm, Odham's Press. Ball thus managed to secure both confidential Labour reports on the political mood in the country but also advance 'pulls' of their leaflets and pamphlets. This enabled the Publicity Department in Central Office to respond instant-

aneously to their opponent's propaganda (an early forms of 'instant rebuttal' championed by Labour as its own in the 1990s). Although Ball's intelligence-gathering activities could often verge on the unscrupulous, his skills gave the party a significant campaigning advantage. He loyally advised both Baldwin and Neville Chamberlain on matters of political intelligence both inside and outside the party, and in the latter's case he even tapped the telephones of Tory MPs who opposed the Prime Minister's appeasement policy.

Ball's presence was felt in the three main areas of political communication – advertising, the press and film. He made the most of his press contacts throughout his time at Central Office, along with Davidson, who was particularly adept in cultivating friendships with influential proprietors, such as the Berry Brothers who owned the Daily Telegraph *and* The Sunday Times. *Some of Ball's attempts to influence the newspaper industry crossed a hidden frontier. He took the step of secretly purchasing a paper called Truth, hoping that*

in Whitehall during the war. Driven by an unbending determination to defeat 'Bolshevist subversion', their aim was to equip the Conservative Party of the 1920s with the propaganda weapons that would outwit socialism and ensure its own electoral hegemony for the good of the nation.

the acquisition would act as a bulwark of support for Neville Chamberlain. Instead, it became a source of embarrassment, with its columnists regularly espousing extremist views that could be pro-German and anti-Semitic in tone. Ball soon severed his links with Truth, but he continued to manage the press on behalf of Chamberlain after May 1937 when he entered Downing Street. Rather like Alastair Campbell some sixty years later, Ball was an unusually adroit operator of the Lobby and a master of spin. He often gave very partisan briefings in Number 10 on behalf of Chamberlain and the government as a whole. Ball was knighted in 1936 for his services to the Conservative Party. As Robert Blake has written, Ball was the 'quintessential eminence grise' of the interwar period, tirelessly working behind the scenes to project a modern image for the party using all the weapons at his disposal. One of his lasting achievements, however, was not in the area of spin and propaganda, but in policy work as the first director of the Conservative Research Department, where he laid some of the foundations for the party's future success.

The influential Sir Joseph Ball, who stopped at nothing to raise the profile of the party in the interwar years (*Eleanor Mason Brown*)

PIONEERING PUBLICISTS

Davidson and Ball invested much time in improving the party's relationship with the press. By the late 1920s the Central Office Press Bureau was expanded to offer several services for correspondents who were increasingly thirsty for political news. The Lobby Press Service, run from the bureau, supplied the 'party press' (230 weekly and daily provincial papers) with a wide range of leading articles and accompanying notes for editors – all free of charge. On the back of this activity, Baldwin encouraged the setting up of a General Press Service to meet the demands of the national newspapers. Eager to ensure that the party received the best possible coverage beyond the loyal Tory press, it was also decided that a front organisation, known as the Industrial Press Service (IPS), would circulate paragraphs and articles to non-Conservative papers. The IPS was ostensibly independent, but was used by the party with great effect to plant anti-socialist stories. Special articles regularly appeared under the byline of 'Christopher Straight', the *nom de plume* of two sympathetic journalists, G.W. Gough and E.T. Good. In addition to such covert forms of news dissemination, the Central Office Press Bureau published a selection of popular magazines, such as *Man in The Street*, *Home and Politics* and *The Elector*, all of which sold surprisingly well.

One of the areas in which the party led the way in the interwar years was in political advertising. Its success was built on employing advertising agencies on a professional basis to design and formulate slogans, leaflets and posters. The most successful relationship the party forged in this period was with the agency J.H. Benson's, who were renowned for their Guinness advertisements in the 1920s and 1930s. Although Benson's was responsible for devising the uninspiring 'Safety First' slogan in the 1929 general election campaign, the majority of its posters were extremely striking and imaginative in their use of colour and imagery. Positive campaign posters such as 'The

Left: Conservative Mobile Bookshop in Bexley in 1948 distributing party magazines and publications *(Popperfoto)*

Right: 'The Conservative Sun-Ray Treatment' poster from the 1929 general election campaign *(Bodleian Library)*

PEACE ABROAD
REDUCED COST OF LIVING
WIDOWS PENSIONS
IMPROVED EDUCATION
EQUAL FRANCHISE
OLD AGE PENSIONS
ORPHANS PENSIONS
RATING REFORM
800,000 HOUSES
PURE FOOD & MILK
The CONSERVATIVE SUN-RAY TREATMENT

Conservative Sun-Ray Treatment' and 'The Escalator to Prosperity' proved particularly effective, while Benson's idea to place a picture of Baldwin on cigarette cards became an instant marketing success. The party invested over half of its budget for the 1929 campaign in publicity, which went towards the distribution of 500,000 posters across the country. Despite losing the 1929 election, the party continued its contract with Benson's, whose posters and leaflets were an important feature in both the 1931 and 1935 election campaigns.

The party was also innovative in using the new medium of film. No other party utilised it so effectively in the interwar years. Many in Central Office were wary of using the BBC (founded in 1926) to present positive propaganda, believing it to be biased against the party – a view that has echoed down the years. One Central Office official was so alarmed by the BBC's radio broadcasts that he asked party workers to 'listen in every night and take down in shorthand anything that savours of tendentious socialist propaganda'. Complaints were regularly sent from Central Office to the BBC's Director-General and Chairman.

Davidson and Ball also set their sights on the private film industry. By the late 1920s, cinemas were enormously popular, reaching an audience of over 20 million a week. Newsreels, which preceded the main film, became the perfect medium with which to present the party in a favourable light. Davidson recruited Patrick Gower, another career civil servant who had served several prime ministers, in 1929 to succeed Ball as the party's Chief Publicity Officer. He established the Conservative and Unionist Films Association as a separate department within Central Office. Together with Albert Clavering, the department's 'Honorary Organising Director', he was as well the owner of a cinema chain. Gower forged close contacts with leading figures in the film business, who were

The Daylight Cinema Van in 1925 *(Bodleian Library)*

instrumental in preparing Baldwin for his performances before the cameras, as he did with radio listeners. By the 1935 election, Baldwin was fully at home with the most modern broadcasting techniques, becoming the first premier to make use of the 'sound bite'.

Gower and his team set about developing mobile cinema vans which would bring party propaganda films even closer to the electorate – especially in the rural areas where film was still a novelty. Purpose-built with a hooded viewing screen and projector, the vans became an instant success after their introduction in 1925. By the time of the 1929 election, the party had ten cinema vans touring the country, as well as thirteen vans equipped with indoor projection equipment for village and town halls. They proved spectacularly popular: during the 1935 election campaign an estimated 1.5 million people saw the party's films, which were both entertaining and educational, and produced to a high technical standard. By the mid-1930s, the Conservative election machine was several steps ahead of both the Labour Party and the diminishing Liberal Party. Under the direction of the National Publicity Bureau, formed specifically to fight the 1935 election, the party unleashed a barrage of propaganda on the electorate, who responded by electing an impressive tally of 387 Conservatives to lead the National Government.

SPEARHEADING THE PROFESSIONAL CAMPAIGN

The Second World War took its toll on all aspects of party life, not least in its capacity to fight an election. Within a decade, however, the party had rediscovered its campaigning zeal, exploiting the new medium of television to particular effect. A new generation of talented advisers, publicists and advertising consultants came to the service of a revived and forward-looking Conservative Party. The likes of Geoffrey Tucker, Gordon Reece and the Saatchi brothers brought the highest levels of profession-alism to the party's election campaigns, exceeding anything the Labour Party could afford to produce. This advantage would again be lost in the last decade of the century.

Women party workers in Central Office prepare for the 1959 general election campaign (Hulton/Getty)

EMBRACING THE TELEVISION AGE

In the aftermath of defeat in 1945, Lord Woolton acted swiftly to ensure that new forms of communication with the electorate were fully explored by the party. Woolton and his new Chief Publicity Officer, Mark Chapman-Walker, were convinced very early on that television opened 'an enormous new field of political activity'. Although Churchill did not share their enthusiasm for the new medium, shunning the cameras as much as he could, party officials in Central Office meticulously groomed other leading Tory politicians for their first televised appearances. Under the guidance of Chapman-Walker and John Profumo, who was appointed the party's first Head of Broadcasting, Eden and Macmillan became the party's first accomplished performers. Eden recorded the party's first election broadcast in the 1951 campaign, while Macmillan took part in the first broadcast

outside an election in 1953 – ably assisted by a sympathetic Bill Deedes, from the interviewer's chair. The broadcasts took the form of formalised question-and-answer sessions, which had been carefully rehearsed, but they were at least an advance on the newsreels in the 1930s, when politicians simply read a script to camera. Macmillan in particular would go on to master the art of television. No other Labour leader until Harold Wilson could match Macmillan's polished, beguilingly relaxed performances in front of the camera.

Woolton would not settle for only the leading lights to equip themselves with the skills for the small screen; he actively encouraged local associations and aspiring parliamentary candidates to 'excel in broadcasting technique'. In 1952, the Publicity Department installed a mock television studio at Central Office for this

The contribution of the advertising industry to the party's publicity campaigns grew enormously during the 1950s and 1960s. The party hired Colman, Prentis and Varley in 1950 to bring its image up to date; so successful were they in achieving this that they worked for the party in every general election until 1964. Their posters displayed pictures of 'ordinary' people and used uncomplicated language, in contrast to the traditional portrait of the party leader and an old-fashioned slogan. The 1959 poster 'Life's Better with the Conservatives . . . Don't let Labour Ruin it' was one of the most effective campaigns launched

The famous 1959 election poster *(Bodleian Library)*

express purpose. *Winifred Crum-Ewing ran the studio throughout the 1950s, writing many of the scripts and arranging one-day courses in broadcast technique. One of the candidates to receive training from Crum-Ewing in February 1956 was a young Margaret Thatcher. As television audiences continued to grow in the late 1950s and early 1960s, new formats for presenting politicians were explored. The party invited independent broadcasters, such as Kenneth Harris and Robin Day, to conduct unrehearsed interviews with senior party figures. Meanwhile, the party made use of its army of cinema vans* until the 1955 general election. *The party chairman, Lord Hailsham, dissolved the Conservative and Unionist Film Association in 1959.*

From the late 1960s, the party concentrated on television as the most effective medium to reach a mass audience. Under the supervision of Geoffrey Tucker, the publicity supremo who devised the party's election-winning 1970 campaign, party political broadcasts (PPBs) enjoyed a new lease of life. As we shall see in Chapter 10, Tucker employed the best TV producers and directors in the business – outside the confines of the BBC – to film a string of innovative PPBs. Although their attempts to present the warm and convivial side of Edward Heath never fully succeeded, Tucker's team rammed home the 1970 campaign theme of 'rising prices'. One broadcast interspersed an interview with an 'ordinary housewife' with short clips showing a pound note being cut in two.

Macmillan recording a party political broadcast in front of a television camera at 10 Downing Street *(Hulton/Getty)*

by the party in the postwar period. Colman, Prentis and Varley also employed the latest marketing and research techniques to identify target groups in the electorate, such as skilled manual workers (the group that later became known as the C2s).

THE TUCKER ERA

Following a stagnant period in the mid-1960s, the party embarked on a new phase of professional campaigning. Geoffrey Tucker had been the brains behind the famous 1959 campaign at Colman, Prentis and Varley. He had struck up an excellent professional relationship with the party's key lieutenants in Central Office, notably Lord Hailsham, the chairman, and Michael Fraser, the influential *éminence grise* and also Director of the Conservative Research Department. In 1968 Tucker was brought directly into the party's

Geoffrey Tucker in 1968 *(PA)*

1970 election poster *(Bodleian Library)*

Remember Labour's
broken promises

For a better tomorrow
vote Conservative

employment to plan the attack against Harold Wilson's Labour government for the coming general election. Before he took up the reins as the Chief Publicity Officer, Tucker had worked on the successful launch of Ariel, the biological soap powder, in Italy. Transferring the market research techniques pioneered in such advertising campaigns to the Publicity Department in Central Office, he revolutionised the party's approach to campaigning. He was influenced in particular by Richard Nixon's successful 1968 Republican presidential campaign, which had used the 'high road, low road' strategy. This involved projecting an optimistic Tory vision to the electorate (the high road) as well as pressing home the more immediate concerns about the high cost of living (the low road under Labour). The overall vision was crystallised in the 1970 campaign slogan 'a better tomorrow', while the message on the doorstep focused on the decreasing value of the pound.

Tucker was instrumental in introducing the brightest and most creative talent to the party ahead of the 1970 campaign. He chose the firm Davidson Pearce to conduct the party's advertising, and re-cruited Gordon Reece, a young television producer, and Ronald Millar, an up-and-coming playwright, to assist with the broadcasting and speech-writing. Both continued to serve successive party leaders into the 1990s. Known as the 'Communications Group', or more simply 'the team' by Heath, Tucker's admen and television producers fought one of the most professional publicity campaigns the party had yet seen. As Richard Cockett has com-mented, the 1970 campaign 'broke important new ground for the Conservatives, as it was the first time that the party had put all its faith in "publicity" professionals from outside Central Office'.

THE SAATCHI ERA

Following the 1974 election defeats and Heath's removal as leader the following year, Margaret Thatcher set to work reinvigorating the Tory election machine. Her decision to appoint Gordon Reece as the new Director of Publicity heralded a new era of professional campaigning for the party. In 1978 Reece hired Saatchi and Saatchi, the largest advertising agency in Britain with a turnover of £71 million a year, to undertake all aspects of the party's publicity. The partnership, which lasted almost twenty years, was built on the close working relationship between the party's chairmen (Lord Thorneycroft and Cecil Parkinson) and Tim Bell, the agency's managing director. Bell was a true believer in Mrs Thatcher's mission to change the party and country and he struck up an instant rapport with her, which continued even after he left Saatchi and Saatchi in 1985. The Saatchi brothers, Charles and Maurice, and their lieutenant Jeremy Sinclair, were the creative brains behind a series of eye-catching poster designs and PPBs. The Saatchi and Saatchi campaign leading up to the 1979 election, including the famous 'Labour Isn't Working' poster, which showed a long dole queue snaking out of sight, made a tremendous impact to the company's advantage as much as to the party's.

Throughout the elections of the 1980s and the closely fought contest in 1992, Saatchi and

Maurice Saatchi, the party's advertising supremo during the 1980s *(Hulton/Getty)*

One of the most memorable Saatchi and Saatchi adverts *(Bodleian Library)*

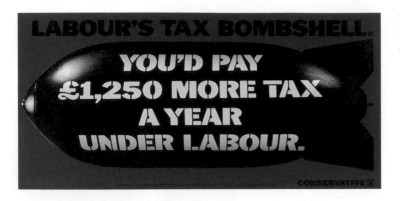

The 1992 election posters played heavily on negative campaigning against Labour (*Bodleian Library*)

Saatchi continued to produce memorable campaigns. Mrs Thatcher took a detailed interest in the agency's work, inspecting every press advert and poster before expressing a preference. Working to the party's campaign and policy brief, Saatchi and Saatchi would meticulously prepare a strategy months, or even years, in advance of the start of a campaign. The adverts were simple and hard-hitting. 'Labour's Policy on Arms' (in 1987), 'Labour's Tax Bombshell' and 'Labour's Double Whammy' (in 1992) were among the most successful negative campaign adverts used by the agency. Jeremy Sinclair, the agency's creative director, who worked on the Tory account for four elections, reflected: 'We just brought our aggressive advertising style to politics . . . We did do some positive ads, but who remembers them now? It is not peace and tranquillity which attracts people's attention.' Innovative techniques were applied to other areas too. Public relations specialists, like Christopher Lawson (the former marketing director of Mars, the confectionary manufacturers) and Harvey Thomas, were brought into Central Office in the early 1980s to give the party a new corporate identity. Lawson designed the blazing-torch logo in 1982, which was printed on all the party's paperwork and advertising and promotional material. Ahead of the 1987 election it was updated as the 'Torch of Freedom' and remains the party's official logo to this day. Direct mail and telephone canvassing were also exploited fully during the 1980s, while the party invested considerable amounts of money in opinion poll research. Communications became increasingly orientated around television news coverage: the publicity team in Central Office began to schedule 'photo opportunities', such as poster unveilings and press conferences, to suit the demands of the television news bulletins. Harvey Thomas was instrumental in turning party conferences and campaign rallies into televisual events, equipped with autocues and striking backdrops. Large corporate donations flooded into the party's war chest during this period, enabling it comfortably to out-spend the Labour Party, the Social Democratic Party and its successor, the Liberal Democrats, both locally and nationally. Following the success of the 1992 campaign, when the party spent £5.8 million on advertising alone, it looked as if the Conservatives would enter the twenty-first century as an unassailable electoral force. It was not to be.

CAMPAIGN BLUES AND THE RISE OF NEW LABOUR

The Conservatives had defined the modern age of election campaigning and communications. Their advantage over Labour's own efforts had only been lost on a few occasions since 1918. By the mid-1990s, however, the tables had turned more decisively in Labour's direction. On the morning after Mrs Thatcher's landslide victory in 1983, Labour's General Secretary, Jim Mortimer, decried the premium placed by the Conservatives on slick advertising. He adamantly declared that the Labour Party would never resort to such tactics: 'We are not presenting politicians as if they were breakfast food or baked beans.' Mortimer, like the rest of Labour's 1983 election team, was consigned to the dustbin of history when the party commenced its own electoral revolution. Within four years, Labour had jettisoned the red flag in favour of the red rose, emulating the most successful features of the Tory election machine. Under the direction of Peter Mandelson, Labour's Director of Campaigns and Communications, and Philip Gould, the opinion pollster and strategist, the Labour Party went from strength to strength in mounting an effective challenge to the Conservatives in the late 1980s and into the 1990s. While Labour advanced, the Conservatives began to falter after their surprise win in 1992. Exhausted and financially overstretched, the machine soldiered on towards the 1997 election, but it soon became clear that even Saatchis could not rescue the party from a series of problems. 'New Labour, New Danger' failed as a slogan because Blair and his team worked so hard to remove any

NEW LABOUR NEW DANGER

One of Labour's leaders, Clare Short, says dark forces behind Tony Blair manipulate policy in a sinister way. "I sometimes call them the people who live in the dark." She says about New Labour: "It's a lie. And it's dangerous."

'New Labour, New Danger', although eye-catching, failed to deter millions of voters switching from Conservative to Labour in 1997 (Bodleian Library)

William Hague's 'Save the Pound' campaign in 2001 (PA)

'danger' from a New Labour government. New Labour, in contrast, projected an optimistic advertising campaign and assembled a formidable machine, tightly controlled by Mandelson and Gordon Brown at its headquarters in Millbank. Crucially, the Conservatives lost their local campaign advantage in many of the key marginal seats which decided the election.

Between 1997 and 2001, New Labour reigned supreme in the battle to win the hearts and minds of the electorate. The Conservatives under Hague ended their long-standing contract with the Saatchi brothers, employing a smaller Edinburgh-based firm, Yellow M, in 2000 to run their advertising campaign. The party simply could not compete with New Labour's strength of numbers on the ground, nor could it rival a series of potent negative poster adverts. The first few years of the twenty-first century have seen the Conservative Party attempting to learn from the election-winning techniques employed by Tony Blair's Labour Party. Central Office was remodelled along the lines of New Labour's Millbank machine, to include a war room, 'Geneva' call centre and a rapid-response computer data base. Michael Howard's surprise appointment of Maurice Saatchi as party co-chairman in 2003 was further intended to restore a campaigning zeal, not only in Central Office but throughout the party.

As the party strives to mount a successful challenge in the forthcoming general election, eyes have turned to the human face of the Tory election machine: the candidate. One of the reasons why the party struggled in the last decade is the narrow profile of its candidates. Despite efforts at the top of the party to encourage local associations to select candidates from a variety of backgrounds, the overwhelming majority of candidates in

John Taylor, who was unsuccessful in his bid to become the party's first black MP in 1992 *(Bodleian Library)*

winnable seats have been white, male, middle-class and middle-aged. There have only ever been two ethnic minority Conservative MPs elected in the party's history: Sir M.M. Bhownagree in 1895 and, almost a century later, Nirj Deva in 1992. In the 1992 general election John Taylor's candidature in Cheltenham, the first black Conservative to be selected for a safe seat, ended in controversy following infighting and abuse from parts of the constituency party. Some party members even urged people to vote against Taylor, allowing the Liberal Democrats to win the seat. Although progress has made in the last few years in selecting a wider range of candidates, particularly those from ethnic minorities, the party has a long way to go before it can reflect the racial, as well as social and gender mix of twenty-first century Britain.

ELECTION HIGHLIGHTS

GREAT VICTORIES

It is not only the scale of an election win that qualifies it to be considered a truly 'great' victory, but also its significance in closing and opening chapters in the life of the party and the nation. The greatest victories of the nineteenth century were 1841, 1874 and 1886, ushering in the Peel, Disraeli and Salisbury governments. By 1841 the party had been rebuilt from scratch after the electoral nemesis of 1832, while the general election of 1874 marked a turning point in British political history, ending thirty years of Liberal ascendancy and opening the door to a new era of Conservative governance. On both occasions, the party demonstrated that its electoral fortunes could be restored following years of frustration and division in opposition.

In the age of the mass franchise, the Conservatives have secured large mandates to continue their work in government. In 1935 the party won 47.8 per cent of the popular vote with a huge total of 387 MPs under the leadership of Stanley Baldwin, who returned to Downing Street as Prime Minister of the National Government. The 1930s represented the high point of the Conservatives' electoral fortunes in terms of the share of the vote, reflecting the electorate's trust in the party as the protectors of the national interest

A jubilant Margaret Thatcher waves to crowds in Central Office on 4 May 1979. Her husband, Denis, stands on her right, with son, Mark, on her left. Lord Thorneycroft, party chairman, stands to the right of Denis Thatcher *(Hulton/Getty)*

in uncertain times. Both the 1959 and 1983 general elections were two of the most emphatic Conservative wins in the postwar era. In each case, the party had convinced the electorate that it could competently manage the economy and provide the conditions for further prosperity. Harold Macmillan's boast in 1957 that 'most of our people have never had it so good' certainly struck a chord with the voters two years later, when they re-elected his government with an overall majority of 100 (44 fewer seats than Mrs Thatcher's majority in 1983). Perhaps the two most important Conservative victories of the twentieth century were in 1924 and 1979. In less than ten months after the first Labour government took the seals of office, Stanley Baldwin had regrouped his party to present a strikingly ambitious programme for government. Winning with a staggering majority of 199 (the largest overall majority any party has won since the introduction of the mass franchise in 1918), Baldwin had transformed the electoral fortunes of the Conservative Party in one of the shortest periods of time in British political history. Thatcher's 1979 victory, achieved with the largest postwar swing to the Conservatives from Labour since 1945, heralded a new era in British politics. Like the results in 1924, the party did well across the country and not just in its heartlands, and middle-class base.

TALES OF THE UNEXPECTED

The party has had its fair share of unexpected election results in modern times. In July 1945 it marched unsuspectingly into its greatest defeat since 1906. Winston Churchill and many around him were convinced that his wartime leadership would produce a postwar victory for the party. Most Labour MPs and independent commentators expected him to sweep back to power. However, his stewardship of the party and the state of its organisation were both defective by the end of the war. Central Office and local associations simply lacked the manpower and the facilities to deliver a well-run campaign. Despite this, senior party officials and Tory agents continued to predict a Conservative victory after polls had closed on 5 July. They were in for a shock: Labour had won its first landslide victory with a majority of 146 seats. Some twenty-five years later, many observers believed that Harold Wilson's Labour government was on course to win a record third term. Under Edward Heath, the party had recovered well after its crushing defeat in 1966, investing much time in developing new policies and a highly professional campaign strategy. Opinion polls and pundits continued to predict a Labour victory even after the release of gloomy trade figures during the course of the campaign, which had further dented Wilson's reputation on the economy. The surprise came when Heath led the party to victory in June 1970, overturning a Labour majority of nearly a hundred. Perhaps the most startling result for the party in recent times was that of the 1992 general election. As in 1970, opinion polls predicted a narrow Labour victory for Neil Kinnock – even the BBC's and ITN's exit polls predicted a hung parliament. The night of 9 April 1992 was one of intense excitement for the party following the declaration at 11.23 p.m. of the result in Basildon, Essex. That was the moment when John Major turned to his wife, Norma, saying, 'You may not know it, but that's it, we

Major out on his soapbox in Luton during the 1992 campaign (PA)

THE LAST HOURS OF TORY RULE, 1–2 MAY 1997

The last hours of the party's eighteen years in power, for all their inevitability, were not short on drama. At the eye of the storm lay the composed figure of the outgoing Prime Minister, John Major. Halfway through the 1997 general election campaign, Major had reconciled himself to defeat. The question now was how badly the party would lose. Two days before polling day, Central Office number-crunchers predicted that the party would win 240 seats. At 5 p.m. on 1 May, election day, Major received a phone call that would confirm his gravest fears. Smith Square informed him that they had seriously overestimated the size of the Tory vote and the party was heading for a catastrophic defeat. Up to that point he had been in buoyant mood, spending the day touring the committee rooms in Huntingdon with his wife, Norma. His demeanour changed dramatically. Close aides who travelled with him back to his home in the constituency. The Finings, described him as being 'shell-shocked'.

Despite their best efforts, the Prime Minister's advisers could do little to lighten Major's spirits. A handful of personal staff from Number 10 and Central Office arrived at the house with several portions of fish and chips, one of his favourite dishes. They were greeted by a deadly silence; Major himself ate without muttering a word. It was as if he had just witnessed a terrible car crash. After the meal, Major repaired to his study to discuss arrangements for the following day with his

Principal Private Secretary in London, Alex Allan. He also spoke on the phone with Brian Mawhinney, who as party chairman had managed the day-to-day running of the campaign. Major resolved to phone Tony Blair to concede defeat before he went to his Huntingdon count.

When the polls closed at 10 p.m. and the exit polls were broadcast, predicting a Labour landslide, Major watched the television alone and began to write his acceptance speech. At 1.30 a.m., he telephoned Blair who was already at his count in Sedgefield. During their five-minute conversation, Major conceded defeat and congratulated him. 'It is a testing job, unique and sometimes enjoyable', ajor said, adding, 'You have a big majority, you should enjoy it.' Relations between the two men had deteriorated during the campaign, particularly after Blair predicted that the Conservatives would scrap the state pension if re-elected for a fifth term. But their conversation was honest and amicable. Major returned to the living room to watch the first results being declared. The extent of the defeat became clear when Labour gained the safe Birmingham seat of Edgbaston. According to one present, Major was transfixed in front of the television, whispering to himself, 'I just don't believe it, I don't believe it.' Ironically, in his constituency home 200 miles north, Blair was uttering the same words to the same results. One by one, Tory strongholds were swept away – from Hove to Wimbledon, Harrogate to Worcester. There was genuine regret when Michael Portillo lost his seat to the New Labour juggernaut and muffled cheers when others, like David Evans, the populist right-wing MP who had been a constant thorn in Major's side, lost their seats. At 2.30 a.m., Major and his team were driven to the count and to hear the declaration of the result. His own majority, 18,140, was the largest Tory majority in the land, but it was still well below the figure he achieved five years before.

Major had decided a few days before that he would stand down as party leader in the event of a heavy defeat, but was in two minds about when to make the announcement. When he arrived at Central Office at 5 a.m., he was greeted by Michael Portillo. Major clasped his hands warmly and was patted on the back by exhausted party workers as he walked up the stairs in the front hall. 'Okay we lost', Major declared stoically in a cheery speech to the assembled crowd in Central Office, but he predicted the party would come back to fight another day. Having consulted with Mawhinney and Cranborne, he decided to postpone his announcement to stand down as leader until later that morning. Back at Number 10, Major repaired upstairs to the flat for a breakfast with his family and close aides, before he made his way around the staff to bid them farewell. During a short speech thanking them for their service after six and a half years, some began to cry, while others did their best to hold back the tears. His last request was to ask that they refrained from clapping him out – as was the tradition for departing prime ministers – for fear that he would lose his composure.

With Norma and his children by his side, Major left the front door of Number 10 at 11.25 to make his last speech as Prime Minister. He congratulated the incoming government, saying that they would inherit an economy much stronger than that bequeathed to the party eighteen years before. 'When the curtain falls it is time to get off the stage and that is what I propose to do', Major said, making way for his surviving parliamentary colleagues to choose a new leader. After tendering his resignation to the Queen at Buckingham Palace, Major headed south of the river to watch cricket at the Oval, only a few miles away from where he had started out in life.

'When the curtain falls, it is time to get off the stage', John Major leaves Downing Street on 2 May 1997 (Corbis)

have won.' His joy was mixed with sorrow a short while later as he watched the pictures of his party chairman and loyal lieutenant, Chris Patten, losing his seat in Bath. Major's victory in 1992 was a moment of real drama. It was a new peak in the party's electoral fortunes, winning over 14 million votes – the highest total any party has received in any general election before or since.

CRUSHING DEFEATS

The defeats of 1832, 1906 and 1945 must rank as three of the heaviest in the party's long history. Although the party underwent periods of soul-searching and difficulty in their wake, the defeats, bar that of 1906 perhaps, did not actually crush the party so badly that it found electoral recovery an almost impossible task. The defeat of 1997 was the most crushing defeat of the twentieth century, coming only five years after John Major's personal triumph at the polls. The Conservative Parliamentary Party was cut to half its former size; and its share of the vote, 30.7 per cent, was the lowest since 1832. It was a truly awful night for the Conservative Party. Never before had the party failed to win a single seat in Scotland. Seven Cabinet ministers lost their seats, including the Foreign Secretary, Malcolm Rifkind and, perhaps most famously of all, Michael Portillo, who lost the 'safe' north London suburban seat of Enfield Southgate on a swing of 17 per cent to Labour. If 1992 had been a night of relief and jubilation for the party, then

1997 surpassed it as one of despair and disbelief.

The result of the 2001 general election was in many ways even more harrowing for the party. Managing to win only one additional seat and improving its share of the vote by a mere percentage point, the party had found itself singularly incapable of regaining any lost ground after the rout of 1997. Rarely has the party lost two successive elections in such dramatic style.

It will take all the reserves of energy, strategic and tactical brilliance to transform the party's electoral fortunes once again. However, if the last 150 years or so are anything to go by, there is every chance that the Conservative Party will savour victory in the not too distant future.

William Hague bows out after the party's catastrophic defeat in June 2001 (PA)

ACKNOWLEDGEMENTS

First we would like to thank John Hales, who assisted with the research during the spring and early summer of 2004. Julia Harris was utterly efficient in typing the text, as was Sue Martin in compiling the index. Elizabeth Jones again proved herself an invaluable organiser *sans pareil*. We are extremely grateful to John Barnes, Stuart Ball, Robert Taylor and Daniel Collings for reading over drafts of the book. At the Bodleian, we would like to express our gratitude to Helen Langley, Colin Harris and particularly Emily Tarrant, of the Conservative Party Archive, for her advice and help during the course of our research.

We interviewed a number of historians, biographers, journalists and politicians for the book, including Stuart Ball, John Barnes, Lord Baker of Dorking, David Butler, John Campbell, Bruce Coleman, Nicholas Crowson, Lord Deedes, Norman Gash, William Hague, Anthony Howard, Richard Kelly, Charles Moore, Lord Norton, Martin Pugh, Lord Rees-Mogg, Andrew Roberts, Richard Shannon, Richard Thorpe, Robert Waller and Philip Williamson. We would also like to thank Michael Howard for writing the foreword, Daniel Ritterband, from Mr Howard's Private Office, and the staff of Conservative Central Office for their cooperation.

At Sutton Publishing, we have been blessed with a superb editorial team. Christopher Feeney, Elizabeth Stone and Jane Entrican were extraordinarily patient and professional in seeing the project through to the end. Helen Holness and Gina Rozner also ensured the publicity side of the book ran smoothly.

We are also indebted to Eleanor Mason Brown for the caricature of Sir Joseph Ball in Chapter 10.

Anthony Seldon would like to thank his governors, colleagues and pupils at Brighton College for stimulating conversations about the party, the Dibb family and Mrs Jean Pappworth for their understanding in Sark, and the James family and Miss Sarah Jackson for their understanding in Essouaria, Morrocco, and above all his own wonderful wife and children as always.

Peter Snowdon would particularly like to thank Daniel Collings, friend and collaborator, for both his research and assistance in reading over and indeed drafting various parts of the book. He was a constant source of encouragement throughout the project. Last but not least, he would like to acknowledge David Farley, Andrew Trinick and his parents for their friendship and support.

SELECT BIBLIOGRAPHY

The most detailed account can be found in the six volumes of the Longman 'History of the Conservative Party' series:

Stewart, Robert, *The Foundation of the Conservative Party, 1830–1867* (London: Longman, 1978)

Shannon, Richard, *The Age of Disraeli 1868–1881: The Rise of Tory Democracy* (London: Longman, 1992)

——, *The Age of Salisbury 1881–1902: Unionism and Empire* (London: Longman, 1996)

Ramsden, John, *The Age of Balfour and Baldwin 1902–1940* (London: Longman, 1978)

——, *The Age of Churchill and Eden, 1940–1957* (London: Longman, 1995)

——, *The Winds of Change: Macmillan and Heath 1957–1975* (London, Longman, 1996)

OTHER HISTORIES OF THE CONSERVATIVE PARTY INCLUDE:

Ball, Stuart, *The Conservative Party and British Politics 1902–1951* (London: Longman, 1995)

—— and Seldon, Anthony (eds) *Recovering Power: The Tory Party in Opposition since 1867* (London: Macmillan, forthcoming)

Blake, Robert, *The Conservative Party from Peel to Major* (London: Heinemann, 1997)

Clark, Alan, *The Tories: Conservatives and the Nation State 1922–1997* (London: Weidenfeld & Nicolson, 1998)

Coleman, Bruce, *Conservatism and the Conservative Party in Nineteenth-Century Britain* (London: Edward Arnold, 1988)

Colley, Linda, *In Defiance of Oligarchy: The Tory Party 1714–1760* (Cambridge: Cambridge University Press, 1982)

Evans, Brendan and Taylor, Andrew, *From Salisbury to Major: Continuity and Change in Conservative Politics* (Manchester: Manchester University Press, 1996)

Feiling, Keith, *A History of the Tory Party 1640–1714* (London: Oxford University Press, 1924)

——, *The Second Tory Party 1714–1832* (London: Macmillan, 1938)

Green, E.H.H., *Ideologies of Conservatism* (Oxford: Oxford University Press, 2002)

Jupp, Peter, *The Emergence of the Conservative Party, 1680–1830* (London: CPC, 1996)

Moore, Sheila, *The Conservative Party: The First 150 Years* (London: Country Life, 1980)

Ramsden, John, *An Appetite for Power* (London: HarperCollins, 1998)

Seldon, Anthony and Ball, Stuart (eds), *Conservative Century: The Conservative Party since 1900* (Oxford: Oxford University Press, 1994)

FOR BIOGRAPHIES OF IMPORTANT LEADERS OF THE PARTY, SEE:

Duffy, Michael, *The Younger Pitt* (London: Longman, 2000)

Gash, Norman, *Lord Liverpool* (London: Weidenfeld & Nicolson, 1984)

——, *Peel* (London: Longman, 1976)

Blake, Robert, *Disraeli* (London: Eyre & Spottiswoode, 1966)

Roberts, Andrew, *Salisbury: Victorian Titan* (London, Weidenfeld & Nicolson, 1999)

Adams, R.J.Q., *Bonar Law* (London: John Murray, 1999)

Middlemas, Keith and Barnes, John, *Baldwin* (London, Macmillan, 1969)

Jenkins, Roy, *Churchill* (London: Macmillan, 2001)

Turner, John, *Macmillan* (London: Longman, 1994)

Campbell, John, *Edward Heath* (London: Jonathan Cape, 1993)

Young, Hugo, *One of Us: A Biography of Margaret Thatcher* (London: Macmillan, 1991)

Seldon, Anthony, *Major: A Political Life* (London: Weidenfeld & Nicolson, 1997)

OTHER USEFUL WORKS ARE:

Baker, Kenneth, *The Prime Ministers: An Irreverent Political History in Cartoons* (London: Thames & Hudson, 1995)

Campbell, Beatrix, *The Iron Ladies: Why do Women Vote Tory?* (London: Virago, 1987)

Clark, Alan, *Diaries* (London: Weidenfeld & Nicolson, 1993)

Crowson, N.J., *The Longman Companion to the Conservative Party since 1830* (London: Longman, 2001)

Dale, Iain (ed.), *Dictionary of Conservative Quotations* (London: Politicos, 1999)

Dorey, Peter, *The Conservative Party and the Trade Unions* (London: Routledge, 1995)

Garnett, Mark and Lynch, Philip (eds), *The Conservatives in Crisis* (Manchester: Manchester University Press, 2003)

Green, E.H.H., *The Crisis of Edwardian Conservatism* (London: Routledge, 1995)

Goodhart, Philip and Branston, Ursula, *The 1922: The Story of the Conservative Backbenchers Parliamentary Committee* (London, Macmillan, 1973)

Kavanagh, Dennis, *Thatcherism and British Politics: the End of Consensus?* (Oxford: Oxford University Press, 1990)

Langley, Helen (ed.), *Benjamin Disraeli: Scenes from an Extraordinary Life* (Oxford: Bodleian Library, University of Oxford, 2003)

Major, Norma, *Chequers* (London: HarperCollins, 1996)

Maguire, G.E., *Conservative Women: A History of Women and the Conservative Party 1874–1997* (London: Macmillan, 1998)

Marsh, Peter, *The Discipline of Popular Government: Lord Salisbury's Domestic Statecraft 1881–1902* (Brighton: Harvester Press, 1978)

O'Gorman, Frank, *British Conservatism: Conservative Thought from Burke to Thatcher* (London: Longman, 1986)

Parris, Matthew, *Great Parliamentary Scandals* (London: Robson Books, 1997)

Phelps, Barry, *Power and the Party: A History of the Carlton Club, 1832–1982* (London: 1982)

Pugh, Martin, *The Tories and the People 1880–1935* (Oxford: Blackwell, 1985)

Rose, Norman, *The Cliveden Set* (London: Jonathan Cape, 2000)

Seldon, Anthony (ed.), *How Tory Governments Fall* (London: Fontana, 1996)

——, *Number 10: An Illustrated History* (London: HarperCollins, 1999)

——, *The Foreign Office: An Illustrated History* (London: HarperCollins, 2000)

Shepherd, Robert, *The Power Brokers: The Tory Party and its Leaders* (London: Hutchinson, 1991)

Smith, Jeremy, *The Tories and Ireland 1910–1914: Conservative Party Politics and the Home Rule Crisis* (Dublin: Irish Academic Press, 2000)

Stewart, Graham, *Burying Caesar: Churchill, Chamberlain and the Battle for the Tory Party* (London: Weidenfeld & Nicolson, 1999)

Sykes, Alan, *Tariff Reform in British Politics 1903–1913* (Oxford: Oxford University Press, 1979)

Whiteley, Paul, Seyd, Patrick and Richardson, Jeremy, *True Blues: The Politics of Conservative Party Membership* (Oxford: Oxford University Press, 1994)

Williamson, Philip, *Stanley Baldwin: Conservative Leadership and National Values* (Cambridge: Cambridge University Press, 1999)

INDEX

Pictures are shown in **bold**